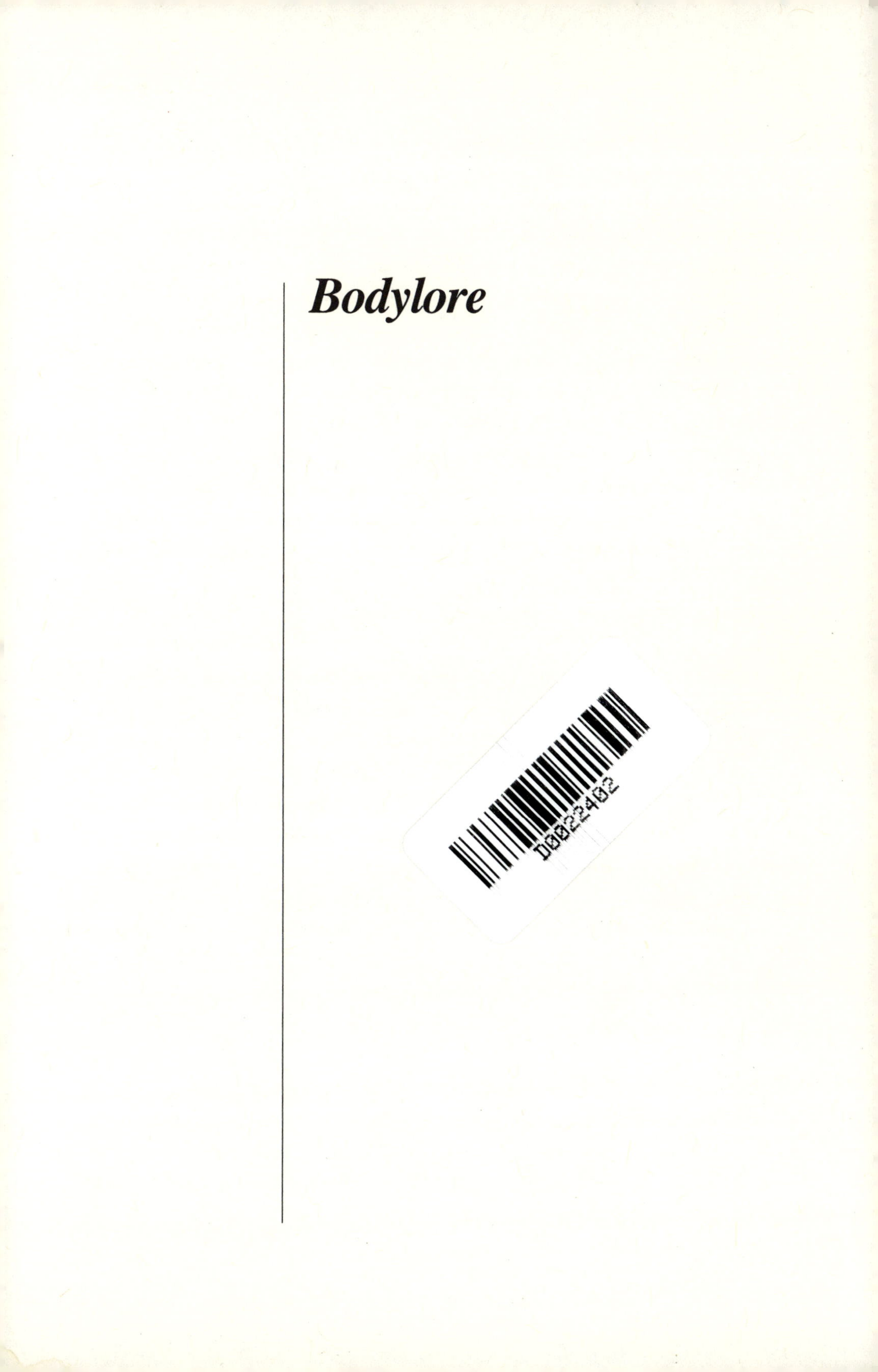

Bodylore

Bodylore

Publications of the
American Folklore Society, New Series
General Editor, Patrick B. Mullen

Edited by
Katharine Young

THE UNIVERSITY OF TENNESSEE PRESS • KNOXVILLE

Cloth: 1st printing, 1993.
Paper: 1st printing, 1995.

The paper in this book meets the minimum requirements of the American National Standard for Permanence of Paper for Printed Library Materials. ♾ The binding materials have been chosen for strength and durability.

Library of Congress Cataloging in Publication Data

Bodylore / edited by Katharine Young.—1st ed.
p. cm.—(Publications of the American Folklore Society. New series)
Includes bibliographical references and index.
ISBN 0-87049-799-5 (cloth: alk. paper)
ISBN 0-87049-890-8 (pbk.: alk. paper)
1. Body, Human—Social aspects. 2. Body, Human—Symbolic aspects.
3. Body, Human—Folklore. I. Young, Katharine Galloway. II. Series: Publications of the American Folklore Society. New series (unnumbered)
GN298.B63 1993
306.4—dc20 93—15390
CIP

Contents

Illustrations

Preface

This book presents an array of discourses whose nexus is the body. Each paper investigates one constellation of symbolic properties. Their cumulative effect is to display the body's social construction: a different body is being invented in each discourse. The term I coined for these inventions is *bodylore.*

The notion of the body as invented, not given, is one of the founding premises of bodylore. The body is among our cultural artifacts rather than our natural objects. The term *inscription* describes this gesture of invention. Bodily inscriptions, both literal and figurative, attest to the incorporation, the corporealization, of culture. Lore about the body makes evident what sort of object, or subject, the body is supposed, in various circumstances, to be.

The body, its surface structures and accouterments, its internal processes, its interiorized essences, its seals and openings, bears the insignia of culture. Investigating bodily practices, rituals, taboos, and myths delineates a metaphysics in terms of which we conceive and experience ourselves and others. Language about the body, metaphors and sayings, turns of phrase, forms of talk, construct the body, shape our apprehensions of it, and delimit its uses. Representations of the body, in words as well as objects, can be inspected to reveal notions of embodiment. It is these perspectives that folklore contributes to the investigations of the body emerging in anthropology and history, literature and psychoanalysis, philosophy and communication, semiology and psychology, performance theory and cultural studies, feminism and sociology, aesthetics and critical theory.

Bodylore not only locates a subject matter for folklore in the body, it also explores theoretical issues with respect to embodiment and how the body, bodily phenomena, and bodily discourses are being constituted and reconstituted in cultural lore. Some of these theories consider the materiality of the body and its carnivalization in a Bakhtinian vein; some, following Mary Douglas, focus on body boundaries and ritual contamination; others hold a Marxist or feminist view of materializing the body; and still others adhere to a social constructionist notion of the body as a symbolic object. In all of them, the body fails simply to condense itself into the given. It is at issue. Bodylore explores the way discourses navigate the body and the way the body anchors discourses.

Bodylore materialized as a field of inquiry at the 1989 American Folklore Society meetings in Philadelphia. A series of encounters with Susan Slyomovics provided the impetus for this materialization. At the 1985 American Folklore Society meetings in Cincinnati, I presented a paper on narrating the body in medicine. The next year in Baltimore, Susan presented a paper on the *zar,* a Middle Eastern ceremony of spirit possession and exorcism; I gave one on ghosts as cultural representations of the notion of the self separate from the body. We formed the habit of hearing each others' presentations. In Cambridge in 1988, Susan presented her paper on the body in water and I did one on surgical inscriptions.

We decided we ought to be able to put together a panel we could both be on. She wanted to do a paper on Muslim women's body-painting rituals and I wanted to do a piece on the corpse. What could these disparate inquiries possibly be supposed to have in common? The body, I thought. They, and our previous papers, were about the ontological conditions of the body: the body-as-object and narrative embodiments (medicine); possession of other bodies by spirits (the *zar*); dispossession by spirits of their own bodies (ghosts); rituals of purification (spas); the boundaries of the self (surgery); and now, the painted body (the henna ceremony) and the dead body (the corpse). We figured we were onto something. I wrote up a notice and sent it off to the American Folklore Society Newsletter, inviting submissions on the folklore of the body. Susan left to me the conceptualization and organization of these panels.

As submissions for the panels came in, the lineaments of the discourse began to come through. Sorting through them, the term *bodylore* occurred to me, at once to name and to materialize a new field of inquiry. I decided to so entitle our corpus of presentations. A flush of abstracts on blood appeared: blood rituals, menstrual lore, taboos, and transgressions. It seemed to me that menstruation itself could be conceived as a breach of bodily boundaries and that menstrual taboos reinscribed boundaries. To address this issue, I composed a panel called "Boundaries and Transgressions." A paper by Jane Przybysz on quilted clothing also addressed the problem of body boundaries so I put it in here.

A polarization began to appear between presentations of the physical body and representations of the metaphysical body, the one understood as the brute, literal, natural, or material body; the other understood as the pure, symbolic, conceptual, or ethereal body. This polarity lies at the root of Mikhail Bakhtin's carnivalesque contrast between the proper body and the grotesque one. I put together a second panel called "The Carnivalesque." There Phyllis Gorfain presented the Renaissance body of Hamlet as a site of representation for discourses of the grotesque and the ethereal. My own paper on the corpse as the locus of grotesque imagery in medicine also appeared here.

The ephemeral aspects of the body were concentrated in a third panel called "Metaphysical Bodies." Its focus was how the self is supposed to be inserted into or separated out of the body, its constituent substances and incidental attributes. Here Elizabeth Wickett presented her paper on Muslim holy men who split, levitate, disembody, or dematerialize.

Two papers on the painted body, Susan Slyomovics's and Deborah Kapchan's, suggested a key to bodylore: the notion that culture is inscribed on the body. That winter I came across a film on tattoo by a group of ethnographic filmmakers, Barbara Attie, Nora Monroe, and Maureen Wellner. "Skin and Ink" became the visual focus for a fourth panel called "Surface Inscriptions."

Thus a discourse was invented at the 1989 American Folklore Society meetings in Cincinnati: bodylore. I would like to acknowledge the audibility in the discourse of voices heard there that are not seen here: Ilana Abramovitch, Paddy Bowman, Charles Briggs, Esther Newman, Marilynn Phillips, Ruth Psofar, Carrie Stern, and Susan Stewart. I would also like to acknowledge the visibility here of inaudible voices: Barbara Attie, Nora Monroe, and Maureen Wellner, who presented the film "Skin and Ink," have provided the cover photograph of the tattooed woman.

In the wake of the Cincinnati panels, bodylore began to substantiate itself as a field of inquiry. I organized a second series of panels for the 1990 American Folklore Society meetings in Oakland; the term *bodylore* appeared in other panels; papers turned up from scholars not connected with any bodylore panels. In an arabesque on "Surface Inscriptions," the first panel in Oakland considered "Inscribed Surfaces: On Bodies on film." A second cluster of papers directed to the physiological, sexual, and scatological properties of the body formed a panel called "Engendered Transgressions: Exaggerations, Denigrations, and Deformations of the Flesh." A third batch of papers contrasted the closed body within which emotions are contained, behind which thoughts are concealed, with the open body, on whose surfaces emotions condense, through whose apertures thoughts materialize. These constituted a panel called "Embodied Emotions: Imagining the Body; Materializing the Mind." Here Dorothy Noyes's paper on gigantic representations of aristocratic, archaic, animalistic, mythic, and demonic bodies appeared.

Barbara Babcock and I put together a third pair of panels for the 1992 American Folklore Society meetings in Jacksonville. There we contrasted the inscription of the world on the body with the fabrication of the world out of the body. Papers on "Corporeal Representations and the Making of the Body" investigated how representations invent the bodies in which they are invested. Papers on "Modalities of Perception and the Making of the World" investigated how the body invests itself in the world it invents.

In the meantime, a colleague of mine, Max Miska, sent in a paper on the blood bowl ceremony, a Hakka Chinese ritual of mourning. More blood. Roger Abrahams persuaded Barbie Zelizer to send along a paper on the assassination of President Kennedy. More corpses. Amy Shuman induced her associate, Susan Ritchie, to send in a paper on medical discourse and its positioning of the subject. Blood, death, and rhetoric. A collection of ten papers by Phyllis Gorfain, Deborah Kapchan, Maxine Miska, Dorothy Noyes, Jane Przybysz, Susan Ritchie, Susan Slyomovics, Elizabeth Wickett, Katharine Young, and Barbie Zelizer was sent off to Carol Orr, then director of the University of Tennessee Press, and, at his invitation, to Pat Mullen of the Publications of the American Folklore Society. They decided to publish the book jointly. In the meantime, Burt Feintuch at the *Journal of American Folklore* agreed to do a special issue on bodylore, coedited by Barbara Babcock and me. A number of other papers from the panels, and elsewhere, appear there.

The papers for the book, intricately interconnected, fell into numerous arrangements. Deciding how to fit them together was a puzzle. I did not want to focus on gender as an issue, not because it didn't occur but because I wanted to regard it, under the aegis of bodylore, as one of several possible symbolic constructions of the body. The women's body painting Deborah Kapchan studied is a profoundly gendered form of bodily inscription. Susan Slyomovics's study of spas focuses on antithetical conceptions of women's bodies. The mother's body is a source of imagery and taboo in Maxine Miska's study of Hakka Chinese mourning rituals. Jane Przybysz takes up Hélène Cixous's notion of *écriture feminine* to examine quilts as artifacts that elaborate an experience of gender off the body. Contradictory discourses of gender are mounted up on the body in Phyllis Gorfain's study of *Hamlet*. A vein of effeminacy even runs through the body of a male saint in Elizabeth Wickett's study.

Another temptation I resisted was to separate the exotics, as if Miska's Hakka Chinese or Wickett's Egyptian sheikhs or Kapchan's Moroccan brides fabricated extraordinary bodies, supernatural bodies, in contrast to the ordinary, natural bodies of the domestic Euro-American discourses. The difficulty with the implicit contrast between exotic and domestic is not just intermediate cases. Is the antithesis between grotesque bodies and proper bodies, apparent among the Catalans in Dorothy Noyes's study, at the root of European culture? Or do traces of the archaic render it exotic? Are the French women in Susan Slyomovics's spa study exotic in contrast to the familiar American women? The difficulty turns out to be that there are no domestic bodies. All constructions, once they are disclosed as inventions, defamiliarize the body. Each of them makes us see the extraordinariness of our corporeal conceptions.

Indeed, I decided not to sort the papers by subject matter at all. I could have put together a macabre pair of papers by Barbie Zelizer and me on corpses, or, adding Miska's, on death, or, alternatively, adding Susan Ritchie's, on medicine. But these affinities were incidental to my purposes. Instead, I decided to arrange papers in terms of their phenomenology of the body. My central concern became what sort of thing the body is conceived to be and how that conception is articulated. A clear point of insertion was surface inscriptions: the appropriation of the surface of the body as a site of representation for cultural discourses. And in this respect, Deborah Kapchan's chapter, "Moroccan Women's Body Signs," instantly became emblematic for me of the opening discourse. The minutely filigreed arabesques inscribed on the hands and feet of Moroccan brides impart to them and impress upon them conceptions of embodiment. Body painting provides a concrete metaphor for the inscription of culture on the body. With this in mind, I inveigled Barbara Attie and her associates into providing images of the tattooed body for the cover of the book, images that invoke an assault on the body in order to aestheticize it. But another imagery haunted me, an imagery of erasure, absence, exscription. The body is not a tabula rasa but a palimpsest. Every discourse overwrites other prior discourses. Susan Slyomovics's study, "The Body in Water: Women in American Spa Culture," addressed absence as well as presence, the dissolution of the boundaries of the body as well as their articulation, disembodiment as well embodiment. Juxtaposed, these two chapters set out the terms of a discourse of surfaces. I paired them under the heading *Inscription/Exscription.* The other chapters I decided to arrange in terms of other antithetical categories that brought out both affinities and differences. None of them is neatly pigeon-holed under these categories. Rather, their juxtaposition brings out a line of thought about the body.

Examining the surface of the body, as Kapchan's paper does, draws attention to the skin as the boundary between inside and outside, subject and object, self and world. Slyomovics's chapter introduces the question of whether the skin renders the body permeable to outside influences or protects it from them. So the issue of the boundaries of the body was at hand. And with it came its antithetical category: transgressions. Hence the second section, *Boundaries/Transgressions.* Phyllis Gorfain's study, "When Nothing Really Matters: Body Puns in *Hamlet,*" explores an analogy between the hierarchically ordered domains of the kingdom, the theater, and the body, whose boundaries are blurred, transgressed, infringed, breached, subverted, and overrun by a carnivalesque discourse. Hence the play's preoccupation with body boundaries, body parts, and body puns signifies a cosmic disruption. In one of the later sections, the specific analogy between the body of the king and the body of the state reappears, eerily, in Barbie Zelizer's study of the death of President Kennedy. And the body as cosmos appears again in the transmutation of the four elements of the cosmos into the four humors of the Renaissance body in my study of the body in medicine. In this section, Gorfain's chapter also sets out the terms of the investigation of the category of the grotesque as opposed to the category of the ethereal.

Also in this section, Maxine Miska's chapter, "Drinking the Blood of Childbirth: The Reincorporation of the Dead in Hakka Funeral Ritual," on the shifting relationship of the living to the dead in seance and ritual, focuses on women's bodies as unbounded, transgressive. The transgressive character of women's bodies also materializes later, as it were, in the quilts Jane Przybysz studies. And in Wickett's study, the essence, the spirit, the metaphysical body of the person might be said to transgress its own boundaries. In Miska's chapter, the mother's body is not only the site on which symbolic imagery is mounted up—the blood in the blood bowl ritual is the blood of childbirth—but also the source of symbolic imagery—the ancestor tablets are the body of the mother. This paper turns attention explicitly to body symbols as well as the symbolic body.

The third set of papers inspects antithetical discourses of the body under a third pair of categories: *Grotesque/Ethereal.* The dismembered body, the body of parts in grotesque realism, appears as the dissected body of the corpse in my chapter on pathological examinations, "Still Life with Corpse: Management of the Grotesque Body in Medicine." This body is overwritten by the etherealized discourse of orthodox medicine. In another section, medical rewritings of the body are elaborated in Susan Ritchie's paper on humanism in medicine. Here Dorothy Noyes considers representations of the grotesque and the ethereal in the giant figures mounted up in a Catalan festival in "Contesting the Body Politic: Spectacle and Participation in the Patum of Berga." The festival plays out in a schematic, concentrated, aestheticized form, tensions recurrent in Catalan provincial society. Elsewhere the ambiguities of the carnivalesque reappear in Attie's tattoos and Kapchan's body painting, whose aesthetic claims are disturbingly set against refigurations that can be seen as disfigurations, dissolutions, and deformations of the flesh. The rarefications of the spa experience in Slyomovics's study are directed toward the solidity, the materiality, the substance of the body. In another section, aestheticism and materiality are played out in Przybysz's study of quilts as fabrications of women's bodies. At its extreme, ethereality becomes spirituality and the self becomes separable from the body.

Jane Przybysz and Elizabeth Wickett pursue disparate senses of embodiment in *Embodiment/Disembodiment.* In "Quilts and Women's Bodies: Dis-eased and Desiring," Przybysz explores an *écriture feminine* in which a material representation of the self is fabricated off the body. Positioning the subject elsewhere reorganizes the kinesthetic and affective experience of body and self in time and space. Her inquiry challenges mind/body dualism by at once dismantling assumptions of bodiliness, corporeality, especially the body's objectlike properties, and at the same time reconstituting some of the properties of mentality as materiality. In "The Spirit in the Body," Wickett investigates a discourse in which body and spirit can be disconnected so that the spirit persists in the absence of the body. The spirit of a Muslim sheikh is infused into places he has been, structures he has inhabited, objects he has handled. But the mind/body dualism constituted here is transmogrified: the bodily substance of the saint is itself attenuated into pale, light, foamy, or vaporous substances, and at the same time his spiritual manifestations take on materiality. Wickett's study discovers both the insubstantiality of the body and the bodiliness of the spirit.

In the last section, *Body/Text,* both chapters examine the textualization of the body, one through the inscription of the body as a text, the other through the reconstitution of the body in texts. In "A Body of Texts: The Fiction of Humanization in Medical Discourse," Susan Ritchie argues that the power of medicine over the body issues from its textualization, a textualization both sustained and assaulted by the medical humanities. In an earlier section, textualization appears in my chapter on the dissected corpse in which the grotesque body is overwritten by the etherealized discourse of medicine. In this section, Barbie Zelizer's study of the Kennedy assassination, "From the Body as Evidence to the Body of Evidence," witnesses the transmutation of body into text till the corpse becomes the corpus delicti. At issue is which is the privileged hold on the body: presence in the flesh or representation, interpretation, codification in the text.

Each speaker, writer, or reader shifted, intensified, clarified, extended, or redirected the notion of bodylore. In the course of our ongoing explorations and presentations, bodylore has become incorporated within folklore as a discourse. Forthcoming presentations in papers, panels, conferences, and books continue to open it up. It also extends beyond folklore to other discourses of the body. The introduction indicates the range of issues now at hand with respect to bodylore. Having been invented, bodylore, in its various incarnations, now lives a life of its own.

Katharine Young
The Avocado Grove
Escondido, California

Acknowledgments

This book has got into print on account of the staunch interest of Carol Orr, former director of the University of Tennessee Press, from the first appearance of bodylore at the 1989 American Folklore Society meetings in Philadelphia. A salutary reading by her outside reader enabled us to re-see and re-write our work with brio. I should also like to acknowledge an insightful and appreciative reading of the book by Pat Mullen, Editor of the Publications of the American Folklore Society, and an acute but skeptical one by his outside reader. Both of these provided suggestions we took up in our rewritings. A bracing critique by Janet Langlois not only minutely influenced certain passages of writing but also substantially reshaped the framework of the book. The preface was a response to some of her suggestions. The current staff of the University of Tennessee Press, including Kim Scarbrough, Jennifer Siler, and Meredith Morgan, have been responsible for seeing the manuscript through to completion. I would especially like to thank Barbara Attie and her colleague Maureen Wellner for the, to me, seductive and disturbing image of the tattooed woman on the jacket. Their film on tattoo, "Skin and Ink," produced with Nora Monroe, is available from Women Make Movies, 225 Lafayette Street, New York City 10012. The photograph incarnates a central concern of the book with the inscription of culture on the body.

Introduction

Culture is inscribed on the body. Our beliefs about the body, our perceptions of it and the properties we attribute to it, both symbolic and literal, are socially constructed. The body is being invented. The way we hold our bodies, the way we move them, the way we accouter them, display our membership in a culture. Surface inscriptions cut off the body, mount up on the body, or pierce into the body its symbolic properties.

Incisions: scars, tattoos, subincisions; excisions: circumcisions, reductions, extractions, amputations, and also shaving, plucking, manicuring, barbering; implantations: face, breast, penis implants, ear inserts, eyelid, nose, nipple, navel, or genital inserts, leg and arm prostheses, nose, breast, buttock, and testicle prostheses, false nails, teeth, and hair; deformations of the flesh: face, chin, breast, bottom lifts and tucks, foot-binding, bottom, penis, waist, breast, head and tooth-binding, hair curling and straightening; discolorations: painting, bleaching, dying, tinting; adumbrations: masks, eye masks (monocles, spectacles, goggles), nose and mouth masks (bandits and surgeons), face masks, head masks (executioners, Greek actors), body masks (Muslim women's robes), veils (brides and mourners), swaddling and shrouding (masking the newly living and the newly dead); accouterments: clothing, head gear, hand gear, foot gear, finger bands, wrist, arm, and neck bands, head bands, waist bands, ankle bands; exposures: cut-outs, cut-aways, low-cuts, high-cuts—these inscriptions that are condensed or materialized on the surface of the body are extensions, literalizations, of the sense in which on us all, on all our bodies, culture is inscribed.

Culture is at the same time fabricated out of the body. The way the body is bounded, its orifices and cinctures, its bilateral symmetry, its hierarchical organization, its solidity, its mobility, the hold it has on things, the way it is lodged in the world, are adumbrated into mutually constituted and mutually substantiated structures of the realm of the ordinary. The body, extended into space, elaborated into cosmology, inscribed into the social

---

Some acute suggestions of Amy Shuman's and Marie-Laure Ryan's have perceptibly affected the text. For those, I thank them.

order, is exteriorized, turned inside out, to form the objective structures of the social world. Culture consists of aspects of the self seen, as it were, from the outside. The body yields "natural symbols," in Mary Douglas's phrase (1973: 81), ways of conceiving and arranging phenomena that have their root in the phenomenology of the body.

The body, in turn, takes in aspects of culture in the form of dispositions, made up, as Pierre Bourdieu contends, of "the internalization of these same objective structures" (1987: 81). Dispositions are habits of thought or feeling that dispose a person to act or think in characteristic ways. The formation of these dispositions in the body is the device by which culture forms members. The body becomes a *habitus,* a locus for what Bourdieu, following Jean-Paul Sartre, describes as "the *dialectic of the internalization of externality and the externalization of internality,* or, more simply, of incorporation and objectification" (1989: 720; emphasis in original). The body both expresses and takes the impression of culture.

Surface inscriptions render the skin a site of representation. Instead of just registering natural impulses, which are supposed to originate in the body and to be expressed out of it onto the surface, skin is appropriated by a cultural discourse to display, enact, and embody its assumptions. Such surface condensation concentrates meaning along the contours of space where it touches the body, along the contours of the body where it touches space. Thus an epistemology is displaced and relocated: interiors simplify, exteriors empty, skin materializes as the boundary between self and world, the point of articulation of difference between bodies and between body and world.

This ontological shift in the status of skin reifies the body as a representational object. Christopher Crocker argues that because social identities are "seldom mirrored by bodily differences, they must be represented by symbolic additions either worn or graven in some way into human flesh" (Crocker 1982: 80). Without the proper inscriptions, as Claude Levi-Strauss notes, bodies fail to appear as social persons (1967: 256). But the reverse is also the case: bodily differences are appropriated to represent social identities. Folds, hollows, and protrusions of the body, its hue and height and girth, are taken to evidence other differences. Hence the temptation of women's bodies for inscribing culture differentially. Gender is a cultural inscription. The juts and furrows, apertures and protuberances, of the body are appropriated as the lodgement for a social discourse of gender, a lodgement that takes its legitimation from the representation it has appropriated.

Corporeal artifacts and mentafacts, as Victor Turner suggests (1967: 28), tend to preserve a disparity, a polarization, an estrangement between the physical and what might be called the metaphysical properties of the body. The literal, material, biological, natural body, conceived as solid, substantial, material—the body as it is perceived—is set against the symbolic, spiritual, conceptual, ideological body, conceived as rarefied, insubstantial, ethereal—the body as it is thought. The body object is opposed to the body image.

The bodies of women have been opposed to the bodies of men and associated with what Mikhail Bakhtin calls "the material lower bodily stratum" (1984: 368), with sex, death, birth, life, filth. But in the course of their histories, the bodies of women, still opposed to the bodies of men, have undergone a transmutation from the grotesque to the ethereal, or from the demonic to the romantic, the low to the high. In presenting themselves, therefore, women can be concerned, on the one hand, to suppress evidences of the grotesque and, on the other, to concoct evidences of the ethereal. An aestheticized discourse of the sort Hélène Cixous calls *écriture feminine* is constructed (1986), a discourse peripheralized, transient, miniature, domestic, decorative, and corporeal, the signatures of women on their bodies. *Women's writings* embody signs of the self separate from the body. Other discourses articulated on the body and elaborated off it likewise constitute an *écriture feminine:* quilting, lacework, cookery, clothing, pottery, knitting, embroidery, bodily accouterments, practical arts, decorative crafts, aestheticized necessities. So it is that such disembodied discourses come already gendered.

Écriture feminine domesticates, marginalizes, trivializes, conventionalizes, and dogmatizes culture. At the same time, it assaults, loosens, and transforms the boundaries of the body. The production of an orthodox discourse provides the structure for insurrection, for smuggling in the heterodox, the alienated, the iconoclastic in the guise of the conventional. Discourses designed to represent the proper, the domesticated, the aestheticized, the feminized, are also positioned to sabotage it, to overthrow what they underpin. Such inscriptions are subversive and subverted texts of a self secreted and celebrated off the body.

Surface inscriptions relocate presentations of self, in Erving Goffman's phrase (1959), on the surface of the body. Instead of molding the lineaments of the body it encloses, skin is taken as a contoured surface on which signs of the self are inscribed. Surface inscriptions reformulate the way we attend to the surface of the body for clues to its inhabitant. Impressions of that person are now controlled, intended, displayed, rather than tucked inside the body and secreted out of it. They are set pieces, not spontaneous evolutions. Surfacing flouts our notion of the self as interiorized, privatized, concealed within the body. Presentations of self in surface inscriptions become formalized, stylized, aestheticized. They fix what might be understood as ephemeral, surface that might be considered internal, display that might be thought private, conventionalize what might be regarded as natural. By inversion, the expressive properties of the body are impressed upon it. We read self-image off the skin.

The reconstitution of skin as a representational surface entails its dissolution as a container of the self. The person is no longer held inside the skin but somehow dismantled and remounted on the outside. The skin, marked, exscribed, retextured by another discourse, becomes ambiguous. These appropriated surfaces of the body deflect as well as invite inspection of the person. They are opaque, turned out toward us, the perceivers, rather than transparent, oriented inward to the self. This opacity, this closure, this resistance of the inscribed surface of the Other creates the fissure we suppose to separate and alienate us. Across the fissure, the inscribed body comes to be the romanticized or demonized Other.

Fiddling with the boundaries of the body is both disturbing and seductive. It loosens us from our conventions, the constraints of what Paul Schilder calls our body image (1950: 206), and so unmoors us. We are exposed to the fear and excitement of transgressions. Altering the skin, like all deformations of the flesh, smacks of what Bakhtin calls the carnivalesque (1984: 7). The inscription is incorporated, taken into, made into, the body. The body becomes a discourse of apertures: punctures, cuts, slices, not made to enter an interior, but to proliferate surface. The grotesque body is an open body, a body of parts, of slits and bumps: rude, improper, coarse, vulgar, profane. From this perspective, the tattooed body is a grotesque body. Tattoos rearticulate its surface, multiplying its inscriptions, reinscribing its parts. They constitute the appropriation of the surface of the body at once by the self and by the culture: both are inscribed on the skin. On account of this grotesquery, tattoos are associated with the improper, the dark side, the underworld, the demonic. Of course this dark world has its romance, the tang of the taboo, the quest of the forbidden. The interplay between the romantic and the demonic appears in tattoo in its conjugation of aestheticism with violence:[1] tattoo assaults the body in order to enhance it.

Art inscribed on the skin is suspect. The artistic surface becomes indistinguishable from the corporeal one. Nothing separates itself off as a work of art. Instead, the boundary of the self is re-articulated. Tattoo is at once a dissolution of the symbolic boundaries of the body and a reconstitution of the body as an aesthetic object. The inextricability of art from the body persists in permanent inscriptions. But ephemerality also impugns the claims of bodily inscriptions as art: not only do inscriptions adhere on the body but also they vanish off it.

Inscription condenses the surface of the body, solidifies its substance. The body presents itself as if to be observed, handled, manipulated, even by its subject. It seems to take on materiality, substantiality, objectivity. Elaborating its representational properties bolsters the misrepresentation of the body as object. In the course of the body's history, the self is dislodged from the object and reconstituted as a different order of event: immaterial, insubstantial, subjective. The self can then be reinserted into a body with which it remains incommensurable. It becomes an essence mysteriously linked to a substance. This incommensurability sets in motion a drift of the discarnate body from the incarnate, a polarization of substances, a rift between subject and object. Mind is split from body and we are precipitated into the Cartesian ontology: inside the solidified body is concealed, sealed, a dematerialized self.

The exorcised body-object can be reappropriated as a representation of the disembodied self. In this gesture, an attenuation of the body is undertaken to match the etherealization of self. The bodily substance can be literally reduced: pared, thinned, muted by diets, asceticism, anorexia, athletics, spas. In these discourses of rarefication, the body becomes the material analogue of mentality. Appeals to the rarefied self accompany assaults on the solidified body. The physical body is coerced to fit the metaphysical. But the attenuation of substances is not necessarily literal. Etiquette, for instance, exscribes the brute, material, physiological processes of the body from its presentation. Ideally, as Mary Douglas puts it, "social intercourse pretends to take place between disembodied spirits" (1973: 101). Saints may inscribe discourses of rarefication on the body in two ways. Either they may purify the body, often by washing, or they may exscribe the body from the discourse, abandoning it, neglected and unkempt, to the realm of corrupt substances. At its extreme, the corrupt body may be scourged in order to release the pure self. The sacred or aristocratic language of discourses of rarefication inscribe purity or perfection on the body.

Alternatively, the body may be eschewed as a representation of the self. In this gesture, surface readings are denied. Persons claim a separate status for the self which may find its representation elsewhere, off the body. Such disjunctions of the self with the body can be expressed by persons who hold themselves or are held to bear negative inscriptions of the sort Goffman describes as stigmas (1963): the fat, the thin, the scarred, the crooked, the dismembered, the deformed: dwarves, giants, the fat lady, the tattooed man, the two-headed baby; but also women, transsexuals, people with dark skins, slanted eyes, long noses, protuberant ears, or conversely, by people with pale skins, round eyes, stub noses, short earlobes, by heterosexuals, and even by men. The negative valence given these inscriptions is culturally specific. Such bodies are invoked as counters against which to define the orthodox, the proper, the conventional, the acceptable. As Maurice Natanson writes: "The alien, the strange, the pathological, the demonic, the freakish, and the hellish may be analogical possibilities we come to by way of the outskirts of the familiar" (1970: 37). Counter bodies incarnate the carnivalesque periphery of the realm of the ordinary.

Rejection of the grotesque for the inhabitants of counter bodies entails either repudiation or romanticization of the body. The austerities of some religious orders, the abstinence of practitioners of the new chastity, the fasting of visionaries, are all gestures of repudiation. The attribution of heightened sensibilities to blind people, communion with the supernatural to the mentally retarded, spirituality to the physically disabled, intuition to women, are gestures of romanticization. At their extreme, abrogations of the body take the form of disembodiment: trances, psychotic fugues, altered states of consciousness, spirit possession, dream walking, astral projection, out-of-body experiences, souls, spirits, ghosts. In these instances, the metaphysical body is conjured up out of the realm of the physical. Though conceived as ephemeral, insubstantial, evanescent, these manifestations can retain a residue of materiality in the form of light, thin, diaphanous, translucent, cloudy, foamy, or vaporous emanations.

By extension, persons who fail to locate themselves in their bodies, or who dislocate themselves from their bodies, can find loci of self off the body in texts, artifacts, practices, phenomena, ideologies, or discourses. We move from body as text to texts of the self. When these disembodied inscriptions are utterances or writings, they can continue to incorporate gender marking and other signs of the self off the body. At the same time, the bodily loci of discourses inform the structure of texts. A hierarchy of perceptual modalities in the body informs the discursive conventions of the texts. Characteristically, in texts, as in perceptions, vision is given priority. Visuality implies remoteness, alienation, estrangement, the separation of bodies and their reconstitution as objects. This modality produces the discourse of objectivism. Other modes of apprehension, taste, touch, smell, and hearing, are held in disrepute. Tactility, at the opposite end of the sensory spectrum, implies proximity, relationship, intimacy, the dissolution of boundaries between bodies and their reconstitution as subjects. This modality produces the discourse of subjectivism. Modalities of perception come to inform metaphors of knowledge.

Disembodied inscriptions can take bodily form. Representations of the body: descriptions, imitations, impersonations, materializations, schematizations; configure assumptions about embodiment. Bodily phenomena that are discorporated and reincorporated in representations render these assumptions available to inspection. They make apparent what it is about the body that is being mentioned, elaborated, denied, intensified, surfaced, interiorized, displayed, or concealed. What Edward T. Hall calls "extensions" or "extension systems" are elaborations of the properties of the body into external phenomena (1977: 29). Tools, for instance, are extensions of hands. But further, the environment shaped by the tools is the spoor of the body on the world. Corporeal attributes can be objectified and hence expressed, suppressed, and impressed on a body double: puppets, masks, actors, mimes, dancers, drawings, diagrams, sculptures, dummies, dolls, idols, effigies, scarecrows, or relicts. Representations of the body focalize what we take to be represented bodily: expression, mood, emotion, temperament, character, and intelligence, as well as the culturally specified indications of their status.

"States of embodiment," to adopt Nancy Scheper-Hughes's phrase (1989: 221), become a central focus of inquiry. Scheper-Hughes and Margaret Lock attempt to fuse together the categories of Cartesian dualism in terms such as *bio-social, psycho-social, somato-social,* and the *mindful body* to express the "ways in which the mind speaks through the body, and the ways in which society is inscribed on the expectant canvas of human flesh" (1987: 10). How we are inserted in our own bodies, the hold we have on them, the sort of thing we suppose the body to be, its metaphysics, are both in flux and at issue. A spectrum of possibilities from the absolute indissolubility of the physical and metaphysical bodies to their absolute immiscibility presents itself. To perceive objectivity as a condensate of subjectivity, subjectivity as an evaporate of objectivity, is to hold out against the contingent history of mind and body and thereby to recover a sense of the body as neither self nor object, but both. The self is materialized, the body inspirited. Bodylore attends to the embodied self.

Katharine Young
Berberrie House
Merion, Pennsylvania

Note

1. The relationship between aestheticism and violence was suggested to me by Maxine Miska.

References

Bakhtin, Mikhail. 1984. *Rabelais and his world.* Trans. Hélène Iswolsky. Bloomington: Indiana Univ. Press.

Bourdieu, Pierre. 1987. *Outline of a theory of practice.* Trans. Richard Nice. Cambridge: Cambridge Univ. Press.

Cixous, Hélène, and Catherine Clément. 1986. *The newly born woman.* Trans. Betsy Wing. Minneapolis: Univ. of Minnesota Press.

Crocker, J. C. 1982. Ceremonial masks. In *Celebration: Studies on festivity and ritual,* edited by Victor Turner. Washington, DC: Smithsonian.

Douglas, Mary. 1973. *Natural symbols: Explorations in cosmology.* New York: Vintage Books.

Goffman, Erving. 1959. *The presentation of self in everyday life.* New York: Anchor, 1963.

———. *Stigma: Notes on the management of spoiled identity.* Englewood Cliffs, NJ: Prentice-Hall.

Hall, Edward T. 1977. *Beyond culture.* New York: Anchor.

Levi-Strauss, Claude. 1967. *Structural anthropology.* Trans. Claire Jacobson and Brooke Grundfest Schoepf. New York: Anchor.

Natanson, Maurice. 1970. *The journeying self: A study in philosophy and social role.* Reading, Mass: Addison-Wesley.

Scheper-Hughes, Nancy. The state, bodies and pauper funerals in northwest Brazil: A political economy of the self. Abstracts for the 88th Annual Meeting. Washington, DC: American Anthropological Association.

Schilder, Paul. 1950. *The image and appearance of the human body: Studies in the constructive energies of the psyche.* New York: International Universities Press.

Turner, Victor. 1967. *The forest of symbols: Aspects of Ndembu ritual.* Ithaca: Cornell Univ. Press.

Inscription/Exscription

The body exhibits surface inscriptions: cultural discourses condensed and materialized on the skin. In body painting, culture is literally inscribed on the body. Thus an intentional, exteriorized, corporealized discourse is open for inspection. The minute, delicate, intricate designs traced on the hands and feet of the Moroccan bride elaborate a visible aesthetic that encodes an implicit ideology. At the same time, the practice of body painting stands as a metaphorical representation of the inscription of culture on the body. The particular practice exemplifies the general custom by which the body is inscribed into culture.

The inscription of culture on the body necessarily entails the exscription of what is already written there. It is a rewriting, an overwriting, an erasure. The imagery of washing away prior discourses is condensed in the immersion of the body in water. In spas, the skin is treated by turns as a transpicuous membrane through which influences pass into the body and as an impervious integument that seals off the body from foreign substances. A discourse of absence is opposed to a discourse of presence.

The materialization, condensation, and evaporation of cultures on the skin produce a discourse of surfaces.

1. Moroccan Women's Body Signs

Deborah Kapchan

> Meanings and values are embodied in material things and actions . . . The meaning of art is completely inseparable from all the details of its material body. The work of art is meaningful in its entirety. The very construction of the body-sign . . . has primary importance in this instance.
>
> —Medvedev and Bakhtin (1985: 7, 12)

Ḥenna is an elaborate form of body marking that accompanies rites of passage (particularly marriage) or festive occasions among women in Morocco. Marking the body is a way of inscribing it into a system of cultural discourse that can be read by members of society. On *nhar an-nqash,* "day of engraving (or inscription)," a Moroccan bride is quite literally the designated carrier of social symbols. These symbols take the form of geometric and floral patterns applied ritually, over the span of six to eight hours, on her hands and feet. The act of inscription itself entails a reading of the social values and codes that have engendered the doing, the defining of the body, whose definition is brought into relief by a social fabric of shared beliefs. The design of the ritual act becomes clear only after close and patient observation of its lines and cross-lines.

Contextual analysis reveals that henna art is the locus of a complex of social structures that play themselves out in gender-specific body ornamentation. As such, henna art is a genre that can tell us much about gender coding and renewal of the Moroccan female community. The juxtaposition of ritual henna occasions with secular ones in the Moroc-

---

My thanks to Roger Abrahams, Elizabeth Warnock Fernea, Henry Glassie, Susan G. Miller, Margaret Mills, Robert Blair St. George, and Katharine Young for their astute and helpful readings of this paper in all of its stages.

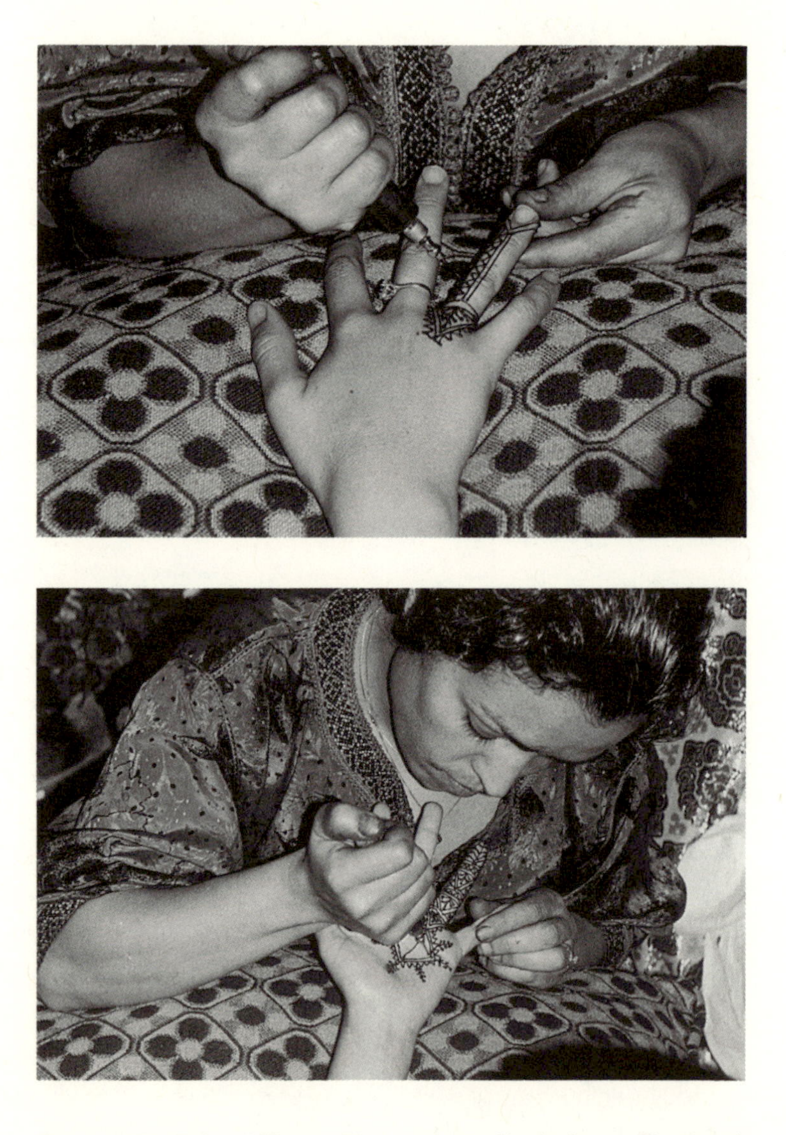

Fig. 1.1. The Painted Finger: The *nqasha* applies the henna. Photograph by Deborah Kapchan.

can calendar allows Moroccan women the reflexive capacity to distance themselves from the meanings ritually mapped onto them during the wedding ceremony; in mocking the seriousness of ritual, they reinterpret and reevaluate the initiation rites of marriage. Also at issue are Moroccan concepts of the body and the reexamination of ideas of public and private space and time with regard to gender. This chapter, based on my acquaintance with Zohra Kaddori, a henna artist (*nqasha*) in Beni Mellal, Morocco,[1] will thread out several readings of the art and ritual application of henna with the intention of establishing the symbolic depth and importance of this feminine art in the Moroccan context.

What does the art of henna tell us about Moroccan concepts of the female body and what does that body (physical, social, symbolic) bring to the art and ritual application of henna? As will be seen, transformation of the physical body effects changes at all levels of Moroccan society. The painting of the bride acts to beautify her; it is auspicious and marks her as an initiate into the most paradigmatic of all Moroccan institutions: marriage. The richness of the significance of marriage in Moroccan culture surfaces in the henna ceremony, and, by transference, in the designs themselves. The implications of voluntary inscription in the secular henna ceremony are different. As a self-initiated event, meaning is more open and more openly manipulated. That the female body itself has become a canvas of sorts for the display of feminine artistry is of particular importance in a culture that has traditionally kept the female body covered and out of public view.

Henna art displays feminine celebration to the general public, and its medium employs a particularly feminine aesthetic. As a folk art, it has significance as both a vehicle for feminine expression and an artifact that finds its place among other Moroccan so-called plastic arts. The term *plastic* is not wholly inappropriate here, as the hennaed body, too, is malleable, symbolically as well as physically. It is the nature of this art to fade away—usually within three weeks—making its documentation difficult. Yet its very transience lends it much of its potency. As it must always be reapplied, henna art has the potential to express a multiplicity of meanings and forms, one of which is the renewal of the feminine community itself.

There is a surprising dearth of information regarding body marking and decoration in North Africa, despite its obvious artistry and social importance. Little attention has been paid to tattoo (for exceptions, see Field 1958; Herber 1950; Sijelmassi 1986; and Searight 1984) and even less to the ephemeral art and artifact of henna design. In the case of henna, the reasons for this neglect may be attributed to a historical undervaluation of both ephemeral and feminine arts. Scholars can remedy this by incorporating the art of henna design and its ritual application into the history of art in Morocco. As a thorough understanding of henna's significance in Moroccan society cannot be had without understanding its relation to tattoo, this examination casts a net around body-marking practices in Morocco generally in order to focus more clearly on the art of henna design.

Marks on the skin, whether ephemeral or permanent, evoke an explicit and quite visceral response. A woman whose swollen neck is tattooed in the hope of cure for a goiter, for example, displays not only the social belief in the healing powers of tattoo but also a permanent testimony to the efficacy or nonefficacy of those beliefs. Her history is portrayed on her flesh; her mere presence summons inquiry from the viewer. A narrative is promised.

Moroccan women are tattooed for diverse reasons (Searight 1984), but tattoos generally fall into two categories: adornment and expressions of prophylactic, supernatural belief. Women are tattooed either for beauty or to prevent or cure conditions such as sterility, goiter, and premature infant mortality. Tattoos are also thought to effectively ward off the evil eye and to guard against the potential devastations of evil spirits (*jnun*). Although Sijelmassi (1986) posits that tattooing was originally part of the initiation rites marking entry into female adult life, this kind of tattooing is not customarily practiced today. A tattooed woman joins a subset of shared experience with other "marked" women, yet, as tattooing is no longer a part of the ritual canon in Morocco, each woman has her own narrative to tell regarding the where, why, and when of her particular mark (*washm*). In a very real sense, the tattoo acts as a visual memory for its wearer—an encapsulated, incorporated account of personal history.

Surface painting of the skin as exemplified in the decorative art of Moroccan henna design is equally communicative, but it expresses an expanded repertoire of meanings within a somewhat different aesthetic. Unlike tattoo, henna forms a part of the social canon of ritual and festivity in Morocco, and its ephemeral and revisable nature make it a more able carrier of multiple symbols than the indelible tattoo. The ephemerality of henna design dictates a changing relationship as the designs and the circumstances of application change and as the woman herself changes with the passage of time. The important difference between tattoo and henna is that henna art is not only visible but is *revisable;* its coherence, symbolic and physical, is only temporary. It does not establish a woman in a particular narrative but provides the possibility of multiple interpretations on multiple occasions. A hennaed woman may signify a recently initiated bride, but she may also signify the recent festive gathering of a community of her peers, a gathering initiated by women in which women take possession of their own bodies and responsibility for their own aesthetic. In a society in which gender roles are highly polarized and socially prescribed, this sort of self-conscious act is particularly salient.

Baraka

Body marking codes the social body with significance just as it marks the physical body with design and change. Just how the social and physical bodies are transformed corresponds, in part, to the nature of the substance used, as well as to the social beliefs surrounding it. Historically, the henna substance has been a matrix for abundant prophylactic and apotropaic folklore, which has contributed to its decorative significance. As the henna plant is still the nexus of a rich folklore and a carrier of *baraka,* "divine blessing," its power to evoke both historical and dynamic meaning is indelible. In fact, by virtue of its baraka, henna possesses many of the curative and prophylactic qualities that were formerly (and sometimes still are) attributed to tattoo, whose capacity to change the appearance empowered it to affect the physical and mental body as well. Like tattoo, baraka works through the physical body to affect the metaphysical one. These two bodies are not antithetic (as in the Cartesian dichotomy) but sympathetic; they represent two parts of an even larger whole whose state they both partake of and contribute to—namely, the social body.

When something has baraka, it is blessed or holy. Baraka as a noun might correspond to the Christian notion of grace; it is a state of being, possessed by people of virtue. In the Moroccan idiom, baraka exists in degrees. The baraka of holy women and men, for example, is of sufficient magnitude to heal and bless others, and it is this baraka that is solicited at their shrines. The baraka of saints survives the body in that it is an effective power for healing and blessing even after death, but it is inextricably linked to the body in that its power "resides" (in popular belief and practice) in the place of entombment. In both life and death, baraka may be said to inhabit the body. It is both material and ethereal, able to permeate the skin. Henna's status as a bearer of baraka reinforces its connection to the body. Henna paste is an earthy substance that penetrates and stains the top layers of skin. It is a botanical agent that acts, in popular belief, to purify the body from the outside in. The skin is porous and not a seal to the self; it allows baraka to pass through and infuse the less directly biological—that is, the psychological, social, and spiritual bodies.

Although henna coloration is temporary, its status is somewhere between the indelibility of tattoo and the superficiality of commercial cosmetics that may be removed with water. Even substantially, henna is ambiguous: when applied, it is a viscous paste, somewhere between liquid and solid.[2] Henna, like baraka, transforms the body in subtle ways; because of its baraka, henna has the potential to change the *nafs,* the "earthly soul" or "carnal spirit." In more practical language, using henna produces feelings of well-being. Douglas (1984: 112) refers to baraka as a "success power":

> Another characteristic of success power is that it is often contagious. It is transmitted materially. Anything that has been in contact with *baraka* may get *baraka.* Luck was also transmitted partly in heirlooms and treasures. If these changed hands, Luck changed hands too. In this respect these powers are like pollution, which transmits danger by contact.

As Douglas has shown, concepts such as baraka are necessary to balance social conceptions of pollution, which are particularly salient in ritual moments and circumstances of transformation such as marriage. If baraka can permeate via the skin, so can polluting substances. It is noteworthy that henna is often applied during times when female blood, which is impure, is at issue; namely, during wedding celebrations (before consummation) and shortly before delivery of a child. Both of these transitionary events involve a dynamic engagement of self with other at the borders of the skin, and both encounters change the status and, effectively, the identity of the woman. In the case of birth, what is inner becomes outer; from one skin, another emerges, bringing prestige to the mother (especially if she mothers a son) as a fecund and useful member of society. In the case of marriage, the blood of the broken hymen externalizes what the bride has internalized—the social acceptance of responsibility for a sexual life that must be controlled and hidden. No longer an *ʿzba,* "virgin," a married woman presents a threat to social order should her sexuality go unchecked (Mernissi 1975). She is a potential pollutant to society and must come to terms with the power ascribed to her.

It is the blood of menstruation that first makes a girl eligible for marriage. The blood that consequently ensues from her first intercourse with her husband marks both her previous purity and the end of that purity, the beginning of her sexual life. Henna designs accompany the bride through this passage into womanhood—the loss of innocence—just as they accompany the laboring woman through her travails, also signaled by a profusion of blood. Baraka fortifies the initiate against the pollution and the *stigma* of pollution that is ultimately linked to these rites of passage. Through henna, baraka enters the skin from without, purifying what is within while what is polluting is discharged.

Baraka also means "enough." When a woman has baraka, she is blessed with sufficiency; she has all that she needs. In corporeal terms, the woman's body is in balance with her surroundings and her society. Henna possesses baraka by virtue of its being a favored flower and cosmetic of the Prophet Mohamed, who used it to dye his beard. A synonym for the henna plant in Arabic is *nor-Nbi,* "light of the Prophet" (Westermarck 1928).

The ramifications of henna's baraka-bearing status are great. When applied to the skin in the form of paste, the henna plant is thought to rejuvenate; it is attributed with a cooling, refreshing quality and has been used in a healing capacity to counter fever, hair loss, ringworm, chapped feet and hands, and itching sores (Westermarck 1928). Some women apply it to their entire body, leaving it on for just a while, then washing it off. This is thought to give the skin vitality as well as a subtle, desirable hue. Baraka, then, transforms a simple cosmetic into a rejuvenating one, a medicinal poultice into a healing salve, a festive decoration into an auspicious symbol. Although henna is not seen to effect physical changes—reversing sterility, for example—the baraka that henna effuses is thought to have a positive influence on such matters; thus its association with ritual moments when fertility is at issue, such as weddings, births, and circumcisions (Lacoste-Dujardin 1985).

Nhar an-Nqash: Henna and the Bride

Henna is applied at changes of life states, but it is most particularly linked with the henna ceremony that forms a part of a girl's passage to womanhood. Henna designs thus lead associatively to the passive liminality that is the common experience of all brides. Yet the silence and fasting that accompany the bride's inscription into the role of wife are in inverse proportion to the merriment of the women around her. For the bride, the henna ritual is the overture to a marriage ceremony that, for her, will be more solemn than festive.

The transformative power of the ritual process is that it entails an internalization, consciously or not, of the core values of the society in which it is performed. This may be a subsociety—as is a women's society—or it may be the dominant society.

> Ritual works by sending messages through symbols to those who perform and those who receive and observe it. The message contained in a symbol will be felt holistically through the body and emotions, not [necessarily] decoded analytically by the intellect . . . Thus the ultimate effect of the repetitive series of symbolic message sent through ritual can be extremely powerful, acting to map the model of reality presented by ritual onto the individual belief and value system of the recipient . . . (Davis-Floyd 1987, crediting Munn 1973)

Although it is not clear that the bride is completely unable to establish a conceptual distance from the social meanings traced onto her during the henna ritual, a "model of reality" is clearly being mapped onto her, and it is important to examine just what messages are being sent, in what contexts, from and to whom.

For most weddings, a professional nqasha is engaged. The henna leaves have already been sent by the groom to the bride, along with other gifts of food and clothing. The henna has been carefully sorted, ground with mortar and pestle and then sifted, perhaps by the bride's mother. When the nqasha arrives, she is presented with the henna powder, which she then kneads with warm water until it is a viscous green paste. It is then placed in a bowl with an egg, symbolizing "white luck" and, perhaps, fertility. Other ingredients, such as lemon juice, rose water, and even diesel fuel (said to darken the color, but inauspicious for brides) are sometimes added. Before the nqasha is ready to begin her designs, she must prepare the fixative that is dabbed with cotton on the henna after its application. This mixture also varies with the nqasha, but is usually a combination of water, sugar, ground cloves (or rose water or perfume), lemon juice, and mashed garlic. The air is, needless to say, full of fragrance. Henna itself has a subtle but very distinct scent—rather "planty," like chlorophyll—that, I am told, "men don't like." The smell undoubtedly carries associations of nonmale occasions and feminine exclusivity. It is not only applied decoratively on women's skin but also used to dye their hair; its smell permeates the women's *ḥammam,* or "public bath." It thus engenders no fondness on the part of men, though women, in general, have no aversion at all to its smell, and some like it. The smell of henna not only invokes a feminine domain but also may be experienced as actually constituting a temporary boundary of the painted subject herself.

The most modern method of henna application is with a syringe. Zohra has been using one for three years and says that it originated in Marrakech—though she doesn't know with whom. Before the syringe, a thin silver rod, wooden stick, or sometimes an empty Bic pen cartridge was used to drag a thin line of henna across the skin. The syringe cuts the time of the traditional methods in half. It takes Zohra about one and a half hours to complete one hand, and a little longer to do a foot.

The *nhar al-ḥenna,* "day of henna" (also called *nhar an-nqash,* "day of engraving"), usually takes place the day before the official wedding party begins and the day after *nhar al-ḥammam,* "day of the bath." Purified by many hours at the public bath, the bride is ready to receive the designs that will accompany her transition from girl to woman. At her wedding she will soon become a self-conscious object, literally displaying herself in several ornate costumes, seated on a pedestal-like chair, her hair and face made up, her hands and feet hennaed.

At the bridal henna ceremony, the bride is about to be "born" into womanhood and wifely duties, and her behavior reflects an embryonic state. It is not insignificant that henna stain is reddish in color; the bride is heralded into her new life in a wash of red, much as a newborn arrives in such a wash. In actual fact, the blood of the bride's broken hymen will be displayed publicly immediately after the consummation. The power ascribed to this blood is a focal point of the wedding ceremony; the honor of the family and the purity of the bride are therein. In this sense blood may be considered "symbolic capital"—a social currency that maintains that not only has the groom received goods that now belong to him (are his private property) but that these goods have been untouched, except by him (Bourdieu 1977). The henna designs are the insignia of this exchange (blood for dowry). Whether henna can be definitively linked with blood symbolism is unclear. Underscoring this interpretation is a custom (practiced in Algeria, however) that takes place in the male henna ceremony: after the groom's palms are dabbed with henna, the bowl containing the henna is passed among the male guests; the last male to hold the bowl lets it drop and smash on the floor that the bride's hymen might break just as easily on the wedding night (Lacoste-Dujardin 1985).

Feminine blood has an ambiguous status in Moroccan society. It is both powerful, the source of family honor, and polluting—a menstruating woman is in a state of impurity. Henna also is an ambiguous substance. Although it possesses baraka and purificatory status, it also acts to beautify the feminine subject, thereby contributing to vanity. Henna's association with blood becomes clearer upon analysis of one conversation with Zohra in which she describes a bloodletting ritual. She says that natives of Marrakech not only *neqsh,* decorate or "engrave," with henna but also used to naqsh with the *sizwar,* "scissor":

> It is the Marrokshis that naqsh a lot. They used to naqsh even with incisions (*sharat*) . . . I'm a *nqasha.* They call that a *sharaṭa.* He comes and he incises the women. There's dancing and women entertainers (*shikhat*) and crowds . . . And when they incise them, they put in the place of those incisions, henna and saffron . . . because that incision (*sharṭ* is like henna design (*naqash*). It's just done for fat women . . . They take out the bad blood . . . It's like tattoos, yes, it's like tattoo.

This association of Zohra's indicates several things. First, fat women were believed to have excessive, polluting blood, which had to be siphoned for health (traditionally men have also had their blood let, often by barbers at the marketplace). This remedy was celebrated much like henna application is celebrated today, with dancing and general festivity. Zohra further equates *sharṭ* with *naqash,* asserting that they are similar functions; incision and henna design, via baraka, both act to purify the body. After the blood is let, henna is even applied directly to the wounds. Henna is not equated with blood, but it is ritually related to it. Apart from the secular henna ceremonies, all others involve a certain amount of bloodshed (marriage consummation, birth, circumcision). If blood is polluting, henna may be seen as a countervailing force. And just as henna application sparks remembrance of these ritual incision events (which, Zohra mentions, have not been practiced with any frequency since the 1970s), so do they, in turn, refer Zohra to the practice of tattooing. This relation of genre is a native recognition.

It is interesting that Zohra refers to the *sharṭa as* "he." There are certain categories of men that can act as go-betweens in the polarized world of gender relations in Morocco.

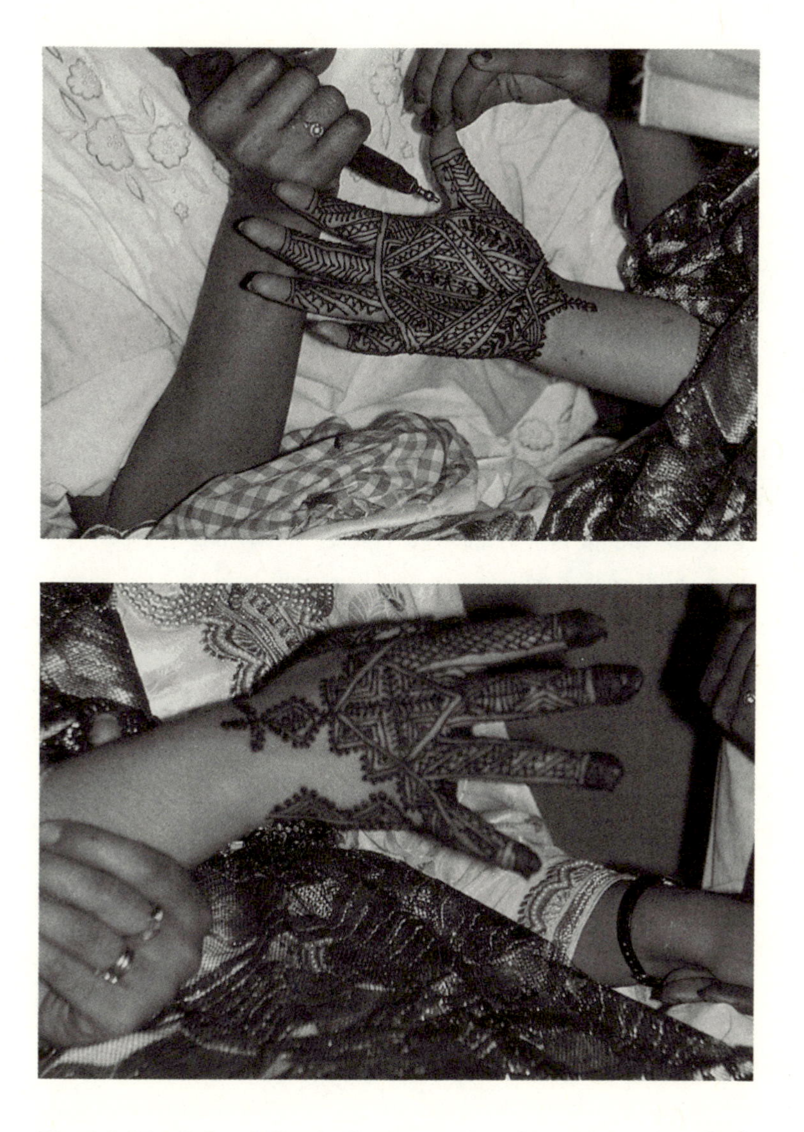

Fig. 1.2. The Painted Hand: The boundaries of the skin are inscribed. Photograph by Deborah Kapchan.

As Abu-Lughod has shown (1986), women do not defer to all men, but *kat-hashamu,* or "are modest," only in front of men of equal or greater status. The sharaṭa, as someone who works with a polluted substance, is no doubt considered unworthy of deference.[3]

It is usually during the henna ceremony that the bride begins a vigil of silence and fasting, a signal of her imminent change of status. Maher remarks on the special behavior of the bride in her description of a Moroccan wedding: "The bride, who has neither spoken nor eaten for the previous three days, is led to a room where she is later joined by the groom and the marriage is consummated" (1974: 169). And while the bride turns inward, she is marked outwardly. The designs put upon her by the nqasha are the center of her visual attention (fig. 1.1). And attention it is, as she must be sure to hold her hands perfectly still and extended in order not to smudge the thin threads of henna with a wrinkling of the skin. The henna is applied meticulously to both the palms and the top of the hands and is extended up the arm to about two inches above the wrist (fig. 1.2). The soles of the feet are solidly caked with henna (no decorations here), but the designs begin immediately at the edges of the soles and travel up sometimes well past the ankles (fig. 1.3). The nails on both the hands and the feet are dipped in henna so as to cover them completely (henna stains the nails permanently with an orange color that lasts until the nail grows out).

Because all her limbs will eventually be decorated, the bride is forced into a hyper-sensitive cognizance of inhabiting her skin. She turns inward to better realize her body; the threshold of her virginity is also the threshold of a new life of social expectations. The application of henna plays on these themes of inner and outer, drawing attention to the boundaries of self and other, but also to the boundaries between an old and a new self, and to the significance of the hymen, the skin, the red stain. Henna is applied to the surface, but it possesses baraka, which inhabits the body. Henna is visible to the public, conveying public messages, but it also pivots the bride into the private realm of her own thoughts and sensibilities.

The henna may take anywhere from four to eight hours to apply, depending on method. As it is usually kept on for eight hours or overnight, the bride is without the use of her hands for at least this long. By the time the feet have been done (they are always done after the hands) the bride has virtually lost the use of all her limbs. She cannot handle food or tend to her bodily needs without assistance until the henna has dried. It would seem, then, that she fasts more by regulation than by discretion. Yet the fasting continues beyond the henna ceremony. This is not a religious fasting, as in the holy month of

Ramadan, but is more like a self-imposed test. Hunger also reveals boundaries and insists on corporeal acknowledgment. The bride practices control not only in consumption but also in speech and facial expression. In mastering her body, she affirms the self.

When the henna is ceremoniously scraped off with a silver bangle, the "girl" may be said to embody the "bride." The designs are intricate, calling attention to their lines rather than the spaces they entwine. The eye is led to follow them like a path until the patterns and their regularity become clear. The patterned designs usually travel up the arm and foot and culminate in a triangular filigree above the wrist and ankle, an arrow that directs the eye to the rest of the body.

This is a rite of passage, and the bride exhibits the passivity that Van Gennep attributes to the liminal phase in such rites (1960). To say, however, that the bride is a tabula rasa, a blank slate, is to deny the import of previous experiences that have prepared her for this ritual (Turner 1969: 103).[4] It is conceivable, of course, that internal dialogue is completely suspended during the henna ritual, but it is presumptuous to assume this simply because of outward manifestations of submission. Indeed, the bride displays (and the verb here is key) some characteristics that are *counter* to those that Turner regards as belonging to a "liminal entity" (102); she is an ostentatious display object that is highly marked as a sexual being with elaborate adornment.[5] For her husband's family, she is attractive property acquired. Her expressionless face may be read as submissive; she is quiet and shy; she is the ideal woman, beautiful yet demure. Indeed, the bride wears a mask that receives and reflects the meanings of feminine definition that predominate in the larger Moroccan society. But the mask is apparent to all, and its reasons for being are even more telling than its expression.

Secular Henna Ceremonies

If henna is visible to all who gaze upon it, what then are the socially constructed meanings assigned to it? This depends on the context of the doing and its viewing. And for this discussion it is useful to separate henna ceremonies in marriage rites from what I call *secular* henna ceremonies. These two categories are in many ways antithetical. Although henna art in Morocco is most paradigmatically associated with the former (the ritual inscription of the bride), women use decorative henna on many other social occasions as well. In fact, the function of renewal in the henna ceremony is most clearly seen in the more secular forms of the henna occasion; namely, those ceremonies that are initiated by women for the express purpose of creating festivity for themselves and their peers. According to Zohra, secular henna ceremonies are most popular in Marrakech, though practiced in other regions of Morocco.[6] Of them, she says,

> *Marrokshi* [those living in Marrakech] can be sitting around. One woman says [to the others], "get up, I want to make myself happy" [*bghit n'-ferḥa bi ras-i*]. She gets up. She brings the nqasha . . . There's chicken, there's meat, and all of that. What is happening with this woman? [lit., "what does she have?"] She's doing henna [*and-ha al-ḥenna*] She's happy with herself. She gets up. She brings women entertainers [*shikhat*],[7] she brings the nqasha, she invites her girlfriends and loved ones. And there's henna-ing and laughing and playing, cooking, *shikhat* and crowds. And that's it. That's the occasion of henna. You don't have any reason, no wedding or anything, just happiness . . .

It is in this kind of ceremony that the degree to which women have appropriated the genre of henna art and ritual becomes evident. It is their art and their festival. It is, in a sense, art for art's sake, given that renewal is a consequence and correlate of art. This is a *ḥefla,* "party," and not an *ʿrs,* "wedding." The verb from which ḥefla derives is *ḥefala,* "to gather, assemble . . . to pay attention, attend, give one's mind [to]." The second form of this same verb (*ḥeffala*) means "to adorn" and "to decorate"(*Hans Wehr Dictionary of Modern Written Arabic*). The conscious attention given to adornment in the secular henna ceremony contrasts to the bride's self-conscious adornment.

Apart from the passivity of the bride during henna application, all others participate in an air of jocularity and festivity. This is true of all henna occasions. There is sometimes singing and dancing, but there is always laughter and levity, albeit mixed with moments of sober reflection on life and its circumstances. If young girls are present, their celebration is a vicarious one, unfettered with themes of confrontation and boundary definition. Married women, on the other hand, have their own reasons for festivity. As a married woman is more socially secure, she is also more free to discover and express her own will and desires in the company of her peers. A henna ceremony postmarriage is thus qualitatively different from a bridal henna ceremony as experienced by the bride, who is closely surveyed by her future husband's female kin. Secular henna occasions provide a time and space for self-expression rather than inhibition, and the designs come to signify sexual self-possession rather than initiation. Although the designs remain the same, the meanings ascribed to their application are not. Secular henna ceremonies are, in effect, an inversion of the henna ceremony as experienced by brides. They are no longer prescribed events but have become subscribed, self-authored. The marks applied in the "private" domain of a small group of women later serve as public attestation to the reality of feminine community; that is, in the public presentation of the hennaed limb, gender boundaries are revealed, domains circumscribed, and a feminine art and presence is affirmed. Women thus embroider their "privacies" into the public fabric.

The secular henna ceremony is clearly a feminine festive occasion. Although the henna ceremony involves only a small segment of the female community at any given time, all women participate in the festival of henna application at regular intervals throughout their lives. The etymological link between the henna ceremony and festival is present in Arabic itself: the word that is used to describe a secular henna occasion, *ḥeflat al-ḥenna,* is the same word that is used to mean both "festival" and "performance." The saying goes, ḥ*enna ᶜliya i- ḥen ᶜlik Allah,* "wear henna and God will have compassion on you." The verb ḥena, "to feel sympathy . . .compassion . . . pity . . . [or] tenderness [for]" (*Hans Wehr*), is homologous with the word *ḥenna,* forming part of the same semantic family.[8]

The process of henna application is both an honoring of God (by employing a baraka-endowed substance) and an honoring of the women present at the festivities. Although forms of exaggeration usually associated with festive behavior are not highly salient, the fact that this is a monosexual occasion does serve to reverse the usual symbolic order of domination; if only temporarily, women have charge over their language and their bodies. The henna occasion also provides a rich forum for the study of feminine humor.

Visibility, Revisability, Ambiguity

The high visibility of body marking in Morocco is an important factor in its definition. In the case of henna, the lacelike designs that cover hands and feet serve to both disguise and elaborate the feminine form. The designs draw and repel the gaze of the observer at the same time by establishing a decorative boundary, a reflector, between gazer and gazed upon. The designs also permit the subject to see herself, and in this sense they are reflective, they mirror the subject. A relationship exists between the art work—the henna design—and the subject of the work, the woman herself. Why is the woman being marked? Is it a voluntary event or a culturally prescribed one? Who does the woman hope to please thereby? The answers to these questions vary with the particular henna occasion. The fact that they are posed—consciously and unconsciously—evidences the importance of the henna event as a ritual that puts values and beliefs into question anew with each enactment, thus engendering renewal of the women present at the festivities.

The hennaed woman becomes a double subject, forming the essential substance of the publicly visible art work and constituting its very theme (subject). She is both form and content. Although the reflection that results from the process of henna application is not consciously acknowledged in the native discourse, the talk around the henna ceremony—talk that is concerned with major life issues such as marriage, divorce, and widowhood—reveals what is at stake. In the henna ceremony, women not only confront the marking of superficial boundaries but also are involved in the recognition and renegotiation of personal and social boundaries.

The role of physical adornment—whether it be henna design, tattoo, or other—is an ambiguous one in Moroccan society. Moroccan art has traditionally avoided the recreation of the physical form in the public realm as this is thought to be reserved for Allah alone. Yet body marking draws attention to and aestheticizes the human form, making it a living icon. The designs themselves are floral and geometric, but the total depiction is of the body, highlighted and elaborated. Although henna has prophylactic and curative qualities, contains baraka, and has purificatory potential, it also acts to beautify the feminine subject, thereby objectifying and eroticizing her. Henna application is forbidden during the holy month of Ramadan, for example, as it conveys vanity and self-conscious sexuality. It is the self-consciously sexual aspect of body design that imputes ambiguity to its symbolism, for a sexually alluring woman and the promiscuity she can incite are of a highly polluting nature according to Islam (Mernissi 1975) and can pose threats to social concepts of patriarchal honor (Abu-Lughod 1986).

Ambiguity is echoed in the designs themselves, which act to both reveal feminine sexuality and hide that sexuality in layers of other socially significant meanings. On the most superficial level, body marking can be seen as an elaboration of the human form and as a covering or disguise. This reversible quality is especially evident in henna design, whose lacelike patterns cover the hands and feet like gloves and stockings, serving to highlight as well as hide. But highlight what and hide from whom? In applying henna designs, are women deferring to a male desire, or even a dominant ideology, that would have them objectified yet rendered impotent under cover (Roach 1979: 416)? Although this is one interpretation of a practice that clearly fits within the genre of adornment (a genre whose forms often arise as a response to the desires of those for whom one is adorned), it is the least explanatory. A bride is hennaed with marks that bear her into a new life with a man and into a new system of hierarchy in her husband's family. She is most certainly painted for them in a visual acknowledgment of her new status in their order. But secular henna ceremonies, being initiated by the women themselves, are of a different order. A husband may or may not appreciate the designs on his wife's limbs, but before he even glimpses them, they are admired and appraised by the women present at the henna party. Henna application, in this case, is voluntary and self-initiated. This clear appropriation and transformation of the marriage ritual effectively reestablishes women's claims to their own bodies.

It is not necessary to elaborate too much on the ambiguous status of the feminine body in the Islamic context. As the bearer of children (particularly sons) the female body is held in esteem. Yet the desire inspired by it is viewed as a threat to social and religious order (Mernissi 1975); consequently, the socialization of a girl's body in terms of gesture and position is rigidly structured compared to a boy's bodily education. These restraints on her movements limit her physical expressions. In festive situations (especially in dance) these limits are sometimes broken (Chebel 1984: 23). The valorization of the female body by means of ritual adornment among female peers acts to counter the negativity and tension inbred in women since childhood.

Feminine Gatherings

In all the different kinds of henna gatherings, the henna artist plays a special role. Although she is occasionally a woman who is down on her luck, so to speak, and must work outside the home to provide for herself and her children (see Messina 1988), she is sometimes, especially in marriage applications, a woman of honor—someone who has been to the *ḥajj* (pilgrimage to Mecca), for example, or even (as is often the case in Algeria) the bride's mother-in-law. More often, however, the nqasha is a woman (or girl) of neutral status (that is, neither prostitute nor holy woman), a woman who, as Zohra describes herself, has a *ras khafīf,* a "light head," meaning an aptitude for learning things quickly. *Driya kan hezz al-ḥaja,* says Zohra of herself, "I pick things up quickly."

More important than who the nqasha is, is the function she plays in the female community. The nqasha not only serves to break the monotony of the inner routine (inside the house and inside the head) but also acts as a news bringer, a messenger, a gossip. As the nqasha spends hours upon hours with a bride and her family or with a woman and her friends, she becomes an immediate confidante. She is a receptor and transmitter of personal experience stories (Stahl 1983). Even if (as in a large town or city) the families talked about are not known by those present at the henna party, the stories related add to the narrative repertoire that forms so much of the social fabric between women. The nqasha, whether she be a divorcée like Zohra, living in her deceased father's house with her three children and her mother, or a high school student earning some supplementary income for her family, is always treated as an honored guest, evoking a high register of hospitality.

Although women are usually very busy cleaning, cooking, washing, and so forth, they still find time to socialize. This is especially true of women whose daughters or daughters-in-law have taken over some of the household responsibilities, or for women whose class status allows them a maid. (In Morocco, maids are paid a pittance, and even middle-class families may have one.) The visits invariably take place in the afternoon and are occasioned by sweets and tea. During these visits, the nature of time changes. For the guest, it is a time free from chores, a chance to relax, to be served, and to offer interesting conversation and news. For the hostess, the reception of guests provides an opportunity to demonstrate her knowledge of the codes of hospitality; if she is successful, she will create an ambiance that evokes adjectives such as *zwin,* "beauty," or *fenn,* "art." Kanafani, in her examination of women's gatherings in the United Arab Emirates, portrays them as rites unto themselves: "Visits are rites of passage in the sense that the guest and the host are in a marginal transitional state as they both undergo tests that will eventually either increase or decrease their prestige in the community, or reinforce their original status . . . In this context aesthetic rites are incorporation rites . . . aimed at reducing the danger created by rivalry and antagonism (1983: 92, 98). Although the Moroccan visiting "rites" are somewhat less elaborate than those in the U.A.E. (perfuming as a social activity is not practiced in Morocco), the concept of the aesthetic performing an incorporative function that plays on the distribution and acquisition of symbolic power does apply.

These times of feminine gathering are important for reasons other than diversion from chores. It is during these times that women exchange both gossip and personal "memorates," true stories that are often emotionally charged (see Stahl 1983). Although the degree of women's seclusion from the male world is dependent on factors of class and region (Maher 1974; Harway and Liss 1988), the need for women's alliances is felt throughout the female society. Because women are semicloistered from experiences in the larger, male world (one woman referred to it as being "divorced from life"), they are even more reliant on gleaning the richness of others' experiences (second-hand) to add to their own. The stories they relate one to another provide essential elements in their construction of self and world. This is especially true on the subject of gender politics, for whereas men seldom mention their life with women (or wives) when talking among themselves, women talk freely with each other about the intimacies of their lives with men (Lacoste-Dujardin 1985: 13).

Of course, women's times are more or less formal, depending on the occasion and the funds available to fete it. A naming ceremony (a ceremony held seven days after the birth of a child in which the child officially receives a name) may be more festive than a wedding. Henna events can range from a quiet gathering of several women to an all-out party, complete with professional musicians and dancing. The more formal the fete, the more it is marked by music, dancing, and elaborate costume. The powers discovered by the collective in these instances are those already alluded to: women experience a naturalness not possible in the company of men, a bond of community in the sharing of experience and an affirmation of their importance to one another, even if that importance is sometimes played out in an antagonistic or competitive way.

Placing henna in the context of women's gatherings helps elucidate the cultural and personal importance of the henna ceremony in the development of female power structures. Women's own valuation system, their codes of feminine hierarchy established by factors of personality and skill, their verbal genres and life stories, their beliefs, and all that is changed and exchanged at women's social gatherings is transcribed, symbolically, onto the body in a latticework of design. At the secular henna ceremony a woman is her own property. This, perhaps, is the only context in which we can talk sensibly about privacy. But in the case of henna, it is a privacy inseparable from and in dialogue with its public presentation. The public, in this case, is dual: it is both the feminine public of the folkloric event and the more general public that, although not bodily present at the festivities, is ultimately the audience when the art work is displayed. As the henna bleeds into the epidermis and takes hold, so do these categories bleed into each other and become one body. As Clark and Holquist remind us, "I need the authority of others to define, or author, my self. The other is in the deepest sense my friend, because it is only from the other that I can get myself" (1984: 65). The self, in this context, is not a private matter, nor can it be circumscribed beneath the skin. The process of henna application, in fact, attests to the permeability of the skin. Paradoxically, however, the designs are almost always geometric and closed, as if providing a map to the territory of the subject, as if the feminine could be boxed, held under seal, as if boundaries were not subject to flux. Appropriately, this "map" disappears by itself; it cannot be made to stay.

The pertinence of the high visibility of henna is again evidenced, for the designs are visible not only to family and peers but also to the public on the street. The hands hang clearly visible below the sleeves and sandaled feet (along with shorter and shorter *jellaba* styles), allowing the henna designs to be fully appreciated by all who chance to look. Chebel describes the street as one of the most erotic sites in the North African world, a place where seduction is everywhere apparent but where social mores and modesty forbid its outcome (1984: 133). This tension between desire and reserve is echoed in the designs themselves, which both elaborate and cover the body.

The Material Sign

Categorizing henna application as a "feminine art" is imposing a foreign definition on an activity that defies such facile categorization in the Moroccan context. Yet for an audience outside Morocco, the term does allow an ease of description and comparison of which I will take cautious advantage. For Moroccan women, inclusion of henna painting in the domain of art, however, is not as relevant as its inclusion in *taqalid,*[9] or "tradition." This tradition is actually dual: on the one hand, there is the centuries-old practice of daubing henna on the palms and the soles of the feet; on the other, the more recent custom (approximately three or four generations old) of material artistry in application. The first "tradition" is conceptual in nature, drawing on a large body of folk beliefs concerning the magical-medical properties of the henna plant as it is applied to the body in the form of paint or stain. The prophylactic uses of henna are many. Generally, henna protects against evil influences such as *jnun* and the evil eye, influences that lurk everywhere and must be rigorously guarded against. At one time, if anyone entered another's house with henna leaves or powder, they had to sprinkle some on the fire before they left in order to protect the inhabitants of the house from evil (Westermarck 1926). There is a particular abundance of henna lore surrounding childbirth. Before delivery a woman paints herself with henna so that in the event she dies in childbirth, she will enter heaven as a bride. The baby, once born, is rubbed with henna. Again, on the seventh day of the child's life, the day of the naming ceremony, both the mother and the child are daubed with henna. Given the vulnerable state of both mother and child during this period, it is not difficult to understand why precautionary measures are taken. Both of them need the protection and blessing that the henna plant affords.

The conceptual tradition has its counterpart in the domain of material culture. This tradition has synthesized other decorative art traditions, particularly tattoo and embroidery, and has emerged as a unique and distinctively feminine expressive form. No doubt henna has been used, much as red ochre, as a symbolic coloring substance in the places where it is indigenous—North Africa, Egypt, and parts of the Middle East. According to Field, archaeological evidence supports the fact that "henna has been used since the dawn of the historical period in the "Fertile Crescent." The modern custom of tinting the fingernails has its origin at least several thousand years before the dawn of the Christian era" (1958: 95). This sort of "tinting" is qualitatively different, however, from what is practiced now in many areas of the Arabized world. Modern henna application, in its decorative form, is much closer to tattoo than to a wash of color on the palms and soles of the feet, as was the custom in North Africa historically. Field reports that in 1800, Mungo Park described Moroccan women as being "stained" with henna on their feet and on their fingertips (1958: 140).

More recently, in 1932, Bourilly described "*la teinture au henne*": "A ces rites [of marriage] qui peuvent s'expliquer par un passage, il faut ajouter certains rites d'un caractère magique qui ont pour but de purifier les époux avant la consommation; qui ont but prophylactique, comme la *teinture* au henne . . ." (1932: 68, emphasis mine).[10] According to Bourilly, henna had a definite purificatory role in the marriage rites, but no mention is made of design. In fact, Bourilly (1932: 62) noted that the henna artist applied the henna "*sur les deux mains jusqu'au poignet*" (on the two hands until the wrist). It is possible, of course, that this application was decorative—employing motifs, that is—but it is unlikely, as no mention is made of them. This is true of most of the literature dealing with henna in North Africa during the nineteenth and early twentieth centuries: there is hardly any mention of designs. In Algeria, Naphegyi (1868: 129) describes the Arabs as having their fingernails dyed with henna. In 1914 Tremearne, observing customs in Tunisia, refers to the "staining of the bride and bridegroom" with henna. In Tripoli, Libya, the bride's hands were "covered" with red henna (Pfalz 1929: 221–27) and in Egypt, Sonnini (1798, 1: 291) describes Egyptian women's hands as being "dyed red" and refers to the practice of henna application as "daubing." There is little in the historical literature to suggest that henna application was anything but a wash of red stain on the hands and feet whose primary function was as a purifying and prophylactic substance. This is true for the countries mentioned as well as for nineteenth- and early twentieth-century Saudi Arabia, Jordan, Iraq, Turkey, and Afghanistan (Field 1958).

Whence, then, the intricate patterns laboriously applied to the hands and feet of Moroccan women today? One of the problems of examining as transitory an art as henna is that there exists no material upon which to base a historical story. It is virtually impossible to know what designs were used hundreds of years ago or if, indeed, there were any at all. Despite the fact that body painting in North Africa can be dated back to prehistoric times (recorded on the rock paintings of the Sahara [Searight 1984]), these paintings cannot verify the continuity or development of this ancient practice. The little that has been written about henna practices in the past suggests that its modern elaborate form is a relatively recent phenomenon. Just how recent it is impossible to say. Zohra told me that henna designs were popular in Marrakech and Fes when the French came (in 1912). "Our parents remember it, and we came into it," she said. She also said that Moroccan women abstained from decorating themselves with henna during the colonial period, as festive behavior would have been disrespectful during a time of occupation. When the French left in 1958, the following poem was popular:

bremu al-bnat
bremu bi al-ḥenna
Fransa mshet
wa al-Maghreb thena

turn around, girls
twine yourselves with henna
France has gone
and left Morocco in peace [lit., "health" or "calm"]

It is also possible that the art of henna developed even more rapidly during the colonial period in order to firmly establish a particularly Moroccan language of feminine adornment in contradistinction to the European influences that were infiltrating the Moroccan world. This would fit in with a general trend of traditionalism that characterized the period, but is, as yet, conjecture (Mernissi 1975).

Although henna designs are regional, there are similar motifs in most designs. They are all distinctively Moroccan, as can be seen by comparing them with Saudi Arabian or Indian designs. If, as Sijelmassi posits, most of the decorative arts in Morocco originally borrowed from tattoo motifs, then the influence is both a Berber and a feminine one: Berber because tattoo designs are in the genre of Berber art and feminine because tattooing in North Africa has long been primarily in and on the hands of women. To the extent, then, that tattooing has influenced henna and other decorative arts in Morocco, we have the imprint of a feminine aesthetic.

But tattoo motifs are not the only influences on contemporary henna design. The verb "to henna" is *naqasha,* whereas the henna artist is a *nqasha,* an "engraver" or "sculptor." Etymologically, this links henna to the plastic arts in Morocco, for a wood engraver or a sculptor in plaster is also called *nqash.* In fact, Zohra attributes the birth of today's elaborate henna designs to engravers in wood and plaster, whose art decorates traditional Moroccan architecture. According to Zohra, it was the wife of a *gabūs,* an engraver in plaster, who first began to decorate her hands with henna in ornate fashion: "She was looking and whatever he [her husband] did, she decorated in her hands [with henna]. And that's how henna design came about in Marrekech, that's the reason for it." Zohra tells a similar story about the origin of decorative henna in the city of Fes, where, she says, the influence was one of wood carving. Despite her acknowledgment of the male artistic influence, however, Zohra is also emphatic in her assertion that as far as henna is concerned, kul-ha jaya min ṭrrz, "it all comes from needlework" (or "embroidery"). This is remarkably clear in the examples of Fes embroidery, whose stitch is small, intricate, and geometrical, and Rabat embroidery, which uses a much larger (satin) stitch and is floral: the corresponding henna designs follow suit. Although the correspondences do not work across the board, the influence is clear. Zohra is quick to say that the plastic arts she mentions are older than embroidery traditions. Whether or not this is so is not essential to an understanding of henna design. What is essential, however, is that many Moroccan women attribute henna design to embroidery. This belief may be interpreted as a will to embrace henna art as a distinctly feminine one, with a feminine history.

Embroidery is a very important work for Moroccan women. Embroidered clothes and cloths are a part of a woman's marriage chest (*ṣinḍoq*), and her value as a wife symbolically increases if she possesses skill in needlework. Having a repertoire of embroidery designs and a tendency for industriousness elevates a woman among her peers. She not only has a skill that can make her money (women commission each other for embroidered pants, caftans, and other items), but she can also teach others what she knows and thereby command a certain authority. Having a favorable reputation among the female community is a particular asset in Morocco (Davis 1983). For Moroccan women, then, the correlation between embroidery and henna is significant; in correlating henna art with embroidery, Moroccan women define it, like embroidery, as a feminine art that confers status.

Henna application is practiced by women of all social categories in Morocco, encompassing both the "folk" (that is, the rural and working classes) and the elite. Although professional henna artists are the adepts in this medium, women and girls often "practice" on each other. Fineness of design, however, is reserved for those who can afford to hire the nqasha. (A professional henna artist is always hired for wedding ceremonies, regardless of class.) A distinction is to be made between henna as it is applied by a nqasha on ritual and ceremonial occasions and henna as it is applied by teenage girls on each other or by a woman on herself, without occasion other than desire for self-decoration with a grace-endowing substance. The nqasha perpetuates designs that have been codified or "traditionalized" according to region. These designs, although originating in one particular city or region, have now disseminated so as to form a pool from which henna artists of various regions may draw. Thus a bride from Marrakech may well be painted with a Fes design on one hand and a Rabat design on the other (for aesthetic reasons, no two hands are ever painted alike). Henna applied by the laywoman, on the other hand, does not necessarily conform to the traditional designs that accompany women's ceremony and ritual. In this realm henna "art" is much more spontaneous and is usually not as "fine" as the designs applied by the practiced hand of the nqasha. The traditional and the popular arts of henna are certainly mutually influential, the former representing formal conservatism (although, in actuality, some of the designs are quite new), the latter, formal innovation.

Dialogues and Genres

As implied earlier, there is a definite dialogue between the ephemeral art of henna and its indelible counterpart, tattoo. Even though henna is a transient art, its vocabulary strains toward images of permanency. Evoking the wood and plaster carvings so abundant in Moroccan architecture, the verb *naqasha,* literally "to engrave" or "inscribe," implies a solidity transgressed, a making unsmooth. A woman who is *manqusha,* "hennaed," is also traced with these semantic underpinnings: her boundaries malleable, her form unable to be glossed.

Historically henna has had a geographical distribution coinciding with tattoo practices (Field 1958: 4). That is to say, where henna is currently in use, there is a history of tattoo. This alone speaks of a necessary affinity and mutual influence between the two. Tattoo motifs are also highly salient in the henna designs themselves. Although tattoo was once more widespread in Morocco, it is now seen as a sign of backwardness, owing to a combination of religious disapproval and change of cultural aesthetic. Tattoos are so inauspicious that women use caustics to remove them, preferring the scar these caustics leave to the tattoo mark itself. The evidence of the negation of tattoo, its marked absence—the permanent scar—has itself become a (positive) symbol, expressing a rejection of a past aesthetic and a departure from a system of belief. Ironically henna reincorporates a similar aesthetic and belief system in an ephemeral, and thus less controversial, format. Because it is impermanent, so are its effects. Whereas the hadith (the reported sayings of the Prophet) says that on judgment day all tattoos will be removed with fire, henna requires no such drastic treatment. Henna thus permits the expression of female aesthetics and sexuality with impunity as well as providing an opportunity for renewal of the feminine community.

The fact that henna is used only on the hands and feet distinguishes it from the practice of tattooing, which uses more of the body—the face, neck, chest, torso, calves, and forearms, as well as hands and feet. Ebin calls attention to the fact that the hands and feet are the "outward means of communicating with the outside world and the concentration points of our nerves and sensitivity" (1979: 27). In traditional Moroccan society, the hands and feet are the visible parts of a body otherwise covered with a long *jellaba* and sometimes with a veil. The hands and the feet are the only body parts that have not somehow been mystified in the male-propagated discourse; they are the parts open to the exterior world, "*offert a l'inconnu et au risque*" (Maertens 1978: 54). Is it not appropriate, then, that these parts also be veiled in lacey "gloves" of henna? But there is an ambiguity here: the hands and feet are not hidden so much as they are disguised, and this disguise, capable of communicating many messages, is one that calls attention to itself. In masklike fashion, something is both hidden and revealed. Henna design changes the body into a text of many meanings.

Unlike tattoo, henna accompanies rites of passage such as birth, circumcision, marriage, and death. Among these, marriage is the most salient of the henna occasions.

Even the groom is dabbed with henna on his palms. Despite this practice, however, decorative henna is a particularly feminine phenomenon. Although men were once tattooed (identifying them as prisoners or musicians or in order to insure the survival of a male child [Searight 1984: 81–83]), tattoo among men has now all but ceased. Thus both body-marking practices are now attributes of the feminine world in Morocco and act to "mark off" one sex from the other.

Although tattoo and henna do not occupy the same ritual space, tattoo has largely been supplanted by henna application as a popular form of body marking. Levi-Strauss noted a similar transformation among the Caduveo. Tattooing and body painting served not only as emblems of culture for the Caduveo people but also as social markers and signs of rank: "The nobles bore, quite literally, the 'mark of rank' in the form of pictorial designs—painted or tattooed—on their bodies" (Levi-Strauss 1974: 161). Body marking among the Caduveo, as reported by Levi-Strauss, performed a dual function: it made the Caduveo able to cross the frontier from nature to culture, and it stratified that culture by conferring different social status on the inhabitants. Interesting and relevant to Morocco is the fact that tattooing eventually gave way to body painting, men eventually gave up the practice, and the representational art associated with men abdicated to the nonrepresentational designs of women. At the time of the publication of *Tristes Tropiques,* Levi-Strauss says that body painting had become simply a "pastime" for the Caduveo, although the "practice had once a much deeper meaning" (168). What Levi-Strauss does not address is the importance and meaning of this "pastime" for the women who practiced it. For him, this semiotic shift was rather a fall into secularization and trivialization. Furthermore, we have no clue as to what the indigenous interpretations of this shift were, or even if they viewed it as a shift.

Despite the truncated analysis of Levi-Strauss, his observations of the transition from permanence (tattoo) to impermanence (body painting) and the practice by men and women to women alone is pertinent to our concerns. A similar shift in Morocco suggests not an impoverishment of meaning, but a formal and semantic re-orientation of genre. Although tattoo and henna are contiguous rather than continuous, it is clear that henna has incorporated much of the significance once attached to tattoo (prophylactic benefits, luck, insurance against the evil eye), without incurring the negative associations.

Moroccan women are not consistently tattooed upon either puberty or marriage, though, at one time, many women were tattooed right before or after marriage. One woman told me that before her marriage, her future sister and mother-in-law forcefully abducted her and tattooed her wrists. Although this was reputedly done to make her more beautiful to her husband, the power expressed by the mother-in-law over even the physical appearance of her future daughter-in-law has impressive symbolic import. Although henna practices are never so drastic, the painting of the bride carries these messages of power relations as well.

In the Islamic context, henna and tattoo appear antithetical: tattoo is religiously disapproved in the hadith, whereas henna was used by the Prophet himself, and he encouraged its use (al-Nasa'i, vol. 8, Adornment: 139–40). The disapproval of tattoos in Islam as well as the growing numbers of country people immigrating to cities, where the practice is disdained, has caused a shift in signifiers so that henna art is functioning much as tattoos did in the past, with the extra advantages of religious sanction, impermanence, and semantic flexibility. Field (1958) confirms that the last one thousand years have seen a "marked" depopularization of tattoo as an art form. Henna, on the other hand, has flourished, particularly in Islamic countries. This has been helped by the fact that the Prophet Mohamed said henna was "the chief of the sweet-scented flowers of this world and of the next" (Lane 1871).

It is worth noting that the emblem of the hand is pervasive in Moroccan culture. The hand of Fatima, as it is called (Fatima was the Prophet's daughter), is found over door lintels, on favored animals (made with henna), in taxicabs, in market stalls, and in virtually every public place. It guards against the evil eye and is a generally auspicious symbol. For some, each finger represents a pillar of Islam (namely, faith, charity, prayer, fasting, and the profession of Allah and his Prophet Mohamed). Because henna art is associated primarily with the hands (only secondarily with the feet), this general hand symbolism is accessible and integral to it. In fact, when the hand of Fatima is wrought in metal, as in jewelry, it is done in filigree and somewhat resembles a hennaed hand. This accessing, albeit unintentional, of a larger social symbol adds another layer to henna's significance. Although tattoo is also found on the hand, its most prominent location is on the face, making it a less likely candidate for sharing the auspiciousness of the hand of Fatima symbolism.

The most common response to the question of the meaning of henna art is *ferḥa,* "joy," or, in more colloquial parlance, "happiness." This is an individual and a social happiness, an undoubtedly physical happiness, but also a much more complex psychological one. In the marriage ritual, the happiness belongs more to the family gaining a working, fecund member than it does to the bride at the moment of her inscription. Her

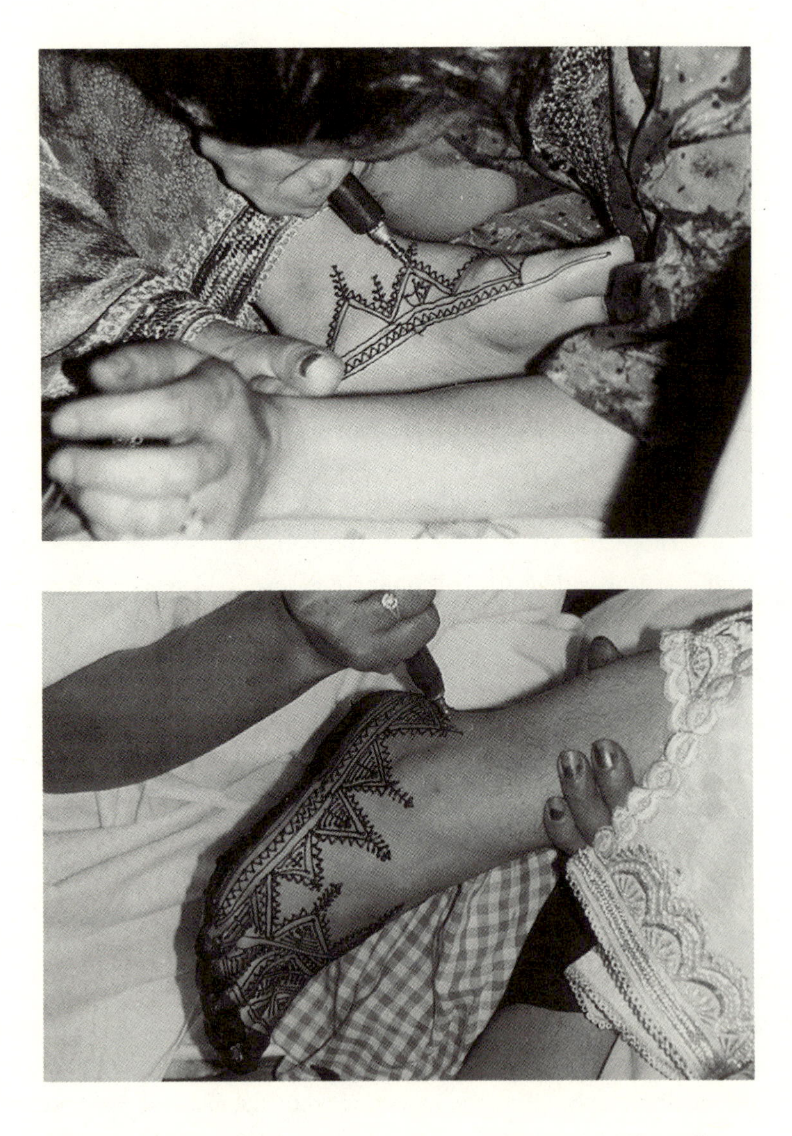

Fig. 1.3. The Painted Foot: After the feet are done, the bride loses the use of all her limbs until the henna is dry. Photograph by Deborah Kapchan.

enrollment, so to speak, into the category of wife is one fraught with ambiguity: she is about to become a sexual being (thus a social danger) but is also about to take possession of a new status that will, potentially, bring her greater social recognition and fulfillment via motherhood. During the nhar an-nqash, the bride is defined in relation to her impending position in the household of her future in-laws; that is, she is defined in relation to social prescription, in relation to a state not yet experienced. By de-ritualizing the nhar an-nqash, the secular henna ceremony helps women to make sense of this social rite of passage. The secular henna event, being authored by women, gives women back their bodies and allows them to refind the self offered to them by their feminine public. Renewal, in the broadest sense of the term, may be counted as a property of all henna events, whether it be the renewal (and reinforcement) of social structures in the dominant ideology, as in the wedding, or whether it be the renewal of particularly feminine concepts of self. The fact that henna application celebrates changes of life states such as marriage, birth, a son's circumcision, and even death serves to underscore henna's properties of renewal. Henna art elaborates on these internal changes by making them visible and public. This publication, as it were, of the woman's body serves not only to bear her into the dominant culture, but serves to define and even to rejuvenate that wider society by extending, symbolically, the renewing properties of the monosexual (private) henna occasion to a wider audience. The renewal resulting from the henna process may be said to be the constant in an otherwise ephemeral art.

Henna application acts as a cohesive in the feminine community, serving to strengthen as well as question social beliefs. It is clear that Moroccan women view henna as both a Moroccan and a feminine art form. It is, for them, an integral aspect of *taqalid*—a nexus of popular and religious folk beliefs, an occasion for feminine festivity, a celebration of the sexual body through its adornment, a means for incorporating baraka, and a gallery for the display of material artistry. The hennaed woman carries all of these messages. For the small group of women in attendance at the henna ceremony, the body re-presents itself, as the individual and physical body and as the gendered and the social body. The visibility of these private and public bodies calls into question their revisability and the power of the body itself to influence and alter its conditions.

Notes

1. Zohra is originally from Marrakech but moved with her family to Beni Mellal in the 1970s when her father, a government worker, was transferred there. As is the case generally in Morocco, Zohra identifies herself with the place of her birth. This is of particular relevance as *Marrokshi* are known for their henna designs.
2. For a discussion of the ambiguous nature of viscosity, see Sartre 1943: 696 and Douglas 1984: 38.
3. All blood is not equal, of course. The ritual slaughter of an animal, most always performed by a man, is an act that brings one closer to God by invoking Abraham's original sacrifice.
4. Girls usually attend many henna ceremonies and weddings before participating in their own.
5. Turner lists "nakedness or uniform clothing," "minimization of sex distinctions," "disregard for personal appearance," and "no distinctions of wealth," as properties of liminal beings (1969: 106). These categories directly oppose those of the bride in the Moroccan wedding ceremony.
6. Albeit with less frequency.
7. *Shikhat* are an anomalous category of women in Morocco. They are often, but not always, prostitutes. Women speak of them disparagingly, but not without some admiration and compassion in their voices. *Shikhat* are usually women who must support themselves and their children without any help. They are also considered "free" women, women with independence (thus the admiration). Some even manage to acquire property with the money they earn. Despite their low status in society, *shikhat* are highly visible at both private and public gatherings.
8. Almost homologous with the word *ḥenna* (the emphatic *h* is here a soft *h*) is the verb *hena,* "to be beneficial, wholesome, healthful." This is also played on in the linguistic context of henna use: see the poem quoted latter in the text.
9. *Taqalid* is a Moroccan term. In employing it, however, I take account of Hobsbawm's observation that "tradition" is invented in order to construct something that is invariant in the face of an often rapidly changing social environment (1983).
10. "To these [marriage] rites, which can be considered rites of passage, should be added certain rites with a magical character whose goal is to purify the brides before consummation, whose goal is prophylactic, such as staining with henna."

References

Abu-Lughod, Lila. 1986. *Veiled sentiments.* Berkeley: Univ. of California Press.

Bourdieu, Pierre. 1977. *Outline of a theory of practice.* Cambridge: Cambridge Univ. Press.

Bourrilly, Joseph. 1932. *Elements d'ethnographie Marocaine.* Paris.

Chebel, Malek. 1984. *Le corps dans la tradition au Maghreb.* Paris: Presses Universitaires de France.

Clark, Katerina, and Michael Holquist. 1984. *Mikhail Bakhtin.* Cambridge, MA: Harvard Univ. Press.

Davis, Susan Schaeffer. 1983. *Patience and power: Women's lives in a Moroccan village.* Cambridge, MA: Schenkman.

Davis-Floyd, Robbie E. 1985. The technological model of birth. *Journal of American Folklore* 100: 479–95.

Douglas, Mary. 1984. *Purity and danger.* London and New York: Ark Paperbacks.

Ebin, Victoria. 1979. *The body decorated.* London and New York: Thames and Hudson.

Field, Henry. 1958. *Body-marking in southwestern Asia.* Cambridge, MA: Peabody Museum.

Hambly, Wilfrid Dyson. [1925] 1974. *The history of tattooing and its significance.* Detroit: Gale Research.

Harway, Michele, and Marsha B. Liss. 1988. Arab mothers in Morocco: Responsibilities without rights. In *The different faces of motherhood.* Ed. Beverley Birns and Dale F. Hay, 101–17. New York: Plenum Books.

Herber, J. 1927. La main de Fathma. *Hesperis* 7: 423–25.

———. 1928. Tatouages curatifs au Maroc. *Revue d'Ethnographie et des Traditions Populaires* 9: 179– 87.

———. 1950. Tatouages Marocains. *Maroc Medical,* Nov.

Hobsbawm, Eric. 1983. Introduction: Inventing traditions. In *The invention of tradition.* Ed. Eric Hobsbawm and Terence Ranger, 1–14. New York : Cambridge Univ. Press.

Kanafani, Aida. 1983. *Aesthetics and ritual in the United Arab Emirates: The anthropology of food and personal adornment among Arab women.* Beirut: American Univ. of Beirut.

Lacoste-Dujardin, Camille. 1985. *Des mères contre les femmes: Maternité et patriarcat au Maghreb.* Paris: La Decouvert.

Lane, Edward William. 1871. *An account of the manners and customs of the modern Eygptians.* London: J. Murray.

Levi-Strauss, Claude. 1974. *Tristes Tropiques.* New York: Atheneum.

Maertens, Thierry. 1978. *Le dessein sur la peau: Essai d'anthropologie des inscriptions Tegumentaires.* Paris: Aubier Montaigne.

Maher, Vanessa. 1974. *Women and property in Morocco: Their changing relation to the process of social stratification in the middle atlas.* New York: Cambridge Univ. Press.

Medvedev, P. N. and M. M. Bakhtin. [1928] 1985. *The formal method in literary scholarship.* Trans. A. J. Wehrle. Cambridge, MA: Harvard Univ. Press.

Mernissi, Fatima. 1975. *Beyond the veil: Female dynamics in a modern Muslim society.* Cambridge, MA: Schenkman Publishing.

Messina, Maria. 1988. Henna party. *Natural History* 9: 41–46.

Munn, Nancy, D. 1973. Symbolism in a ritual context: aspects of symbolic action. In *Handbook of social and cultural anthropology.* Ed. John J. Honigmann. Chicago: Rand McNally and Co.

Naphegyi, Gabor. 1868. *Among the Arabs: A narrative of adventures in Algeria.* Philadelphia.

Nasa'i. N.d. *Sunan al-Nasa'i.* Cairo: Al-Matbara al Masriyyah bil Azhar.

Pfalz, Richard. 1929. Arabische hochzeitsbrauche in Tripolitanien. *Anthropos* 24: 221–27.

Roach, Mary Ellen. 1979. The social symbolism of women's dress. In *Fabrics of culture.* Ed. Justine M. Cordwell and Ronald A. Schwarz, 415–22. The Hague: Mouton.

Sartre, Jean-Paul. 1943. *L'Être et le neant.* 3d ed. Paris: Librairie Gallimard.

Searight, Susan. 1984. *The use and function of tattooing on Moroccan women.* New Haven, CT: Human Relations Area Files.

Sijelmassi, Mohamed. 1986. *Les arts traditionnels au Maroc.* Paris: ACR Edition, Vilo.

Sonnini, C. S. 1798. *Voyage dans la haute et basse Egypte.* Paris.

Stahl, Sandra K. D. 1983. Personal experience stories. In *Handbook of American folklore.* Ed. Richard M. Dorson, 268–76. Bloomington: Indiana Univ. Press.

Turner, Victor. 1969. *The ritual process.* Ithaca: Cornell Univ. Press.

———. 1984. Liminality and the performative genres. In *Rite, drama, festival, spectacle.* Ed. John J. MacAloon, 19–41. Philadelphia: Institute for the Study of Human Issues.

Van Gennep, Arnold. 1960. *The rites of passage,* trans. Monika B. Vizedom and Gabrielle L. Caffee. Chicago: Univ. of Chicago Press.

Westermarck, Edward. 1926. *Ritual and belief in Morocco.* London: Macmillan and Co.

2. *The Body in Water:* Women in American Spa Culture

SUSAN SLYOMOVICS

Drinking establishments known as water bars, bars that serve only bottled waters, have cropped up all over the United States. Although the first recorded water bar opened up in 1981 in Washington State, water bars are most numerous in California. According to Maureen and Timothy Green, authors of *The Good Water Guide*, Americans buy water for what it does *not* contain: calories, caffeine, and salt, whereas Europeans buy water for what it *does* contain: potassium, calcium, and magnesium (Garfinkel 1988: 6). Certainly the water that pours out of American faucets can never be labeled "cool" water: "Cool water comes in bottles . . . You would not drink tap water. It might be full of mercury, lead, zinc, plutonium, gold, frankincense and myrrh . . . Cool water is made by foreigners, or Americans pretending to be foreigners. It is French or Italian or Scandinavian with umlauts in the name" (Quindlen 1990: 4, 21).

I would like to apply this distinction of American absence versus European presence—and the American desire for a European presence mistakenly understood as absence—to the widespread phenomenon of spa resorts, of which water bars are an abbreviated urban variation.[1] Water bars are thematically and viscerally organized around the idea of ingesting water. Although a spa's existence depends initially on the presence of natural waters and springs in which bodies must be immersed, spas in America develop into other forms of recreation. A series of transformations takes place: American spas subordinate the supposed healing properties of natural water to the benefits of a spiritual and physical discipline. Along the way Jacuzzis and steambaths, and eventually bottled mineral water, serve as synecdochical reminders of the primordial waters.

I am also concerned with the ways in which the locally inflected, specifically American spa culture relates to a larger feminist discourse that seeks to understand the female body as a symbolic construct. In the ambiguous claims made by American spas, there is the familiar feminist opposition between existing for oneself as a subject versus existing for others as object. What do American women lack and what does American spa water not contain? Complex issues of gender, tourism, pilgrimage, and female self-image converge on the figure of the female body in water. My analysis owes much to the ideas of Michel Foucault, for whom social organization is a complex matter structured by sets of representational practices. In exploring the mixture of tourism and pilgrimage that attach to the idea of the female body taking the waters, I have attempted to disentangle these practices. When I quote women's writings about their spa experiences and juxtapose their accounts—written and visual spa advertisements laid side by side on the same page of a magazine—I also draw upon the work of Judith Williamson to decode the messages conveyed.

The word *spa* originally referred to a European water-oriented therapy popularized in the town of Spa, Belgium, although spas did not originate there. In America the meaning of the word has expanded exponentially. Currently any facility that applies soothing and healthful treatments to individual parts of a body at rest in a hotel, a department store, or rural retreat is a "spa." A spa may be an exercise room and a sauna located in a downtown hotel; a $37 million health and fitness complex such as the Canyon Ranch in Lenox, Massachusetts; or San Francisco's Shangri-la, located in Nordstrom's department store, offering a full roster of services both in and out of the water. There are new age spas providing training in Eastern philosophies, yoga, tai chi, visualization, hypnotherapy, homeopathy, and biofeedback, and offering courses in human potential and self-realization. A few spas are devoted exclusively to mental well-being.

I should add that not all American spas are expensive resorts with a largely female clientele. There are simple pools, undeveloped springs, murky watering holes, and inexpensive motels with tepid swimming pools clustered around hot springs throughout the Western and Rocky Mountain states. The U.S. Geological Survey mentions some 434 thermal springs in Idaho, Montana, Wyoming, Colorado, and New Mexico, with 400 more in California, Utah, and Nevada (Brown 1977: 96). The main reason for their continued popularity is the belief in the healthful properties of their water (Shalinsky 1985: 32-58).

Male Absence versus Female Bodies/Female Voices

Travel agent surveys claim that 85 percent of the clientele at upscale American spas are women.[2] The subject of women's overwhelming presence and men's noteworthy absence at spas can even be openly addressed in advertisements. Advertising campaigns boldly confront the issue of spa resorts' notorious manlessness by either directly assuaging male fears or coaxing female readers into a fantasy of improved marital relations resulting from frequent and therapeutic spa attendance.

Crucial to our understanding of how advertisements work is their capacity for creating new meanings, what Judith Williamson calls "the work of the *signifiers.*" Williamson studies the "content" of advertising form in a semiotic-structural analysis in which a signifier (material object) appearing in an advertisement, though theoretically indivisible from its signified (meaning) because the signifier-signified constitute the indivisible sign, is interpreted in the light of the ideological and social conventions in which it is embedded (Williamson 1978: 17–19). Advertising systems endow form (the signifier) with meaning; hence, it is capable of feats such as playing on and reversing the prevailing American notion that only women go to spas. In the November 1989 issue of *Esquire* magazine ("man at his best"), a glossy advertisement spread was devoted to answering this daring question: "Are you man enough for a Spa?" Answer: "You bet your loofah" (Boghurst 1989). The advertising strategy repositioned spas as places for male health and fitness by reassuring male readers that spas such as Safety Harbor in Florida are "not for wimps . . . there's a distinctly macho feel to Safety Harbor Spa." The signifiers of unregenerate masculine aggression were photographs of sweating, muscled boxers supported by the advertising copy: "It's probably the boxing ring that serves as the centerpiece of one of the gyms or the fact that Safety Harbor has become the 'in' spot for boxers in training."

Another marketing strategy, one featured in the quarterly newsletter published by the Bonaventure Spa in Fort Lauderdale, is the arbitrary declaration of March as "men's month" (Hewitt 1990: 3). Acknowledging the difficulty of persuading "your 'significant other'" to indulge in the complete spa experience with the targeted female reader, the advertising copy scripts a scenario for the solicitous wife to manipulate her apprehensive mate, to show her concern, and to have the proverbial last word:

> "Care to join me at the spa?" she asks. "I'm too busy at the office these days to break away," he explains. "You'll always be busy," she counters. "Besides an escape from the pressures will do you a world of good." "I don't want to be the *only* man in a spa filled with women." Well now you can reply that the Bonaventure has developed an innovative health and fitness program specifically created for the modern business man.

Male fears of being identified with a pampered but obdurate female body also thematically organize writings about spas produced by women journalists. Anne O'Malley titles a subsection of her spa survey for the *New York Times* "facials, No. Hiking, Yes." She quotes a spa client named Danny Thomas, a forty-year-old life and health insurance agent from Alaska. These biographical details signal to the reader that the speaker is a male in the prime of life, presumably in great shape because he is from rugged Alaska, someone professionally aware of his own and everybody else's mortality: "Thomas . . . was in New York on a business trip recently and decided to go to the New Age Spa in Neversink, N.Y., for a few days of hiking in the Catskill Mountains. 'I'm not interested in herbal wraps or facials,' he said. 'But it's nice to be able to go hiking in an environment where my meals are prepared and I have a room to sleep in'" (O'Malley 1989: 50). For Thomas going to a spa is not only about *dépaysement,* a rural retreat from urban stress: his vacation includes a second order of escape, one that removes him from the spa premises. Surely this is an extreme example of the male attraction to the spa environment but not to its avowed purposes.

Even as early as 1775 a visitor's description of spa life surveyed the patrons of Warm Springs in Standing Stone Valley near the Juniata River in Pennsylvania and noted that the whole place was "an asylum for all impatient women in cases of barrenness . . . [as well as including] unmarried Virgins of various ages." Women lacking children and husbands flocked to colonial-era spas, where their presence was prescribed to compensate for the "absence" in their lives. Indeed, medicinal spas may be considered precursors to contemporary resort spas. Arriving in the New World with a traditional predilection for English spas such as Bath, English colonists profited from Native American instruction in the therapeutic qualities of medicinal springs. We have historical attestation that Bostonians were patronizing nearby Lynn Springs in 1699. It seems that in a strict Puritan atmosphere, the pursuit of health rather than pleasure lent legitimacy to family vacations (Sutton 1976: 6, 1).

Although the pursuit of health remains a constant theme of American spa-going, the absence of children and, frequently, men at spas is treated ambivalently in contemporary advertising. On the one hand, as if to mimic the structure of repeated media images depicting isolated, naked female figures in water, spas promote a woman's narcissistic obsession with her body shape as a solitary activity best undertaken away from stressful family life. On the other economic hand, male clients increase spa revenues. Although female attendance at spas is the perceived norm, the implicit ideology of the contemporary spa alternates dizzyingly between reconstituting the conjugal couple in spa isolation far from societal pressures and, conversely, detaching the female in order to return her to the family strengthened and rejuvenated. A *New Yorker* cartoon lays bare the unstable foundations of the modern American family. While serving dinner to her husband, children, and grandchildren, a matronly, bespectacled grandmother announces: "Thank you all for coming. Starting next year, Mother's Days will find me at the Desert Palm Spa" (Reilly 1990: 37). Our annual national holiday glorifying motherhood is spatially relocated from the site of the traditional family dinner table (high in cholesterol, fat, calories, and stress) to the low-calorie, high–complex carbohydrate, organic spa cuisine. Is Grandma's transformed life-style, one in which she immerses herself in water with or without her family's consent, a deliberate absence from her family role, the invention of new celebratory traditions consonant with changes in American family life? Or is it a rediscovery of the female body long obscured by layers of maternal demands?

Not only do the bodies at spas belong primarily to females but so, too, do the narrative voices that we hear and read in women's magazines. Contemporary accounts of American spa life are a subgenre of travel writing, though they also include ethnographic descriptions derived from the participant-observation school of anthropology. In terms of literary typology, writing about spas is characteristically a topic for female writers. They employ the experiential first-person pronoun, the convention that informs that the narrative is that of the sinner's confessional, and the publication venue is frequently in the pages of upscale magazines specifically targeted to the female reader, such as *Cosmopolitan, Vogue, Savvy, New Woman, Self,* and so forth. Women's spa writing, comparable to what Clifford Geertz calls the "inscription of action" (what does the ethnographer do? "*He writes it down*" [Geertz 1973: 19; emphasis in original]), is cast in a confessional mode. What I mean by the confluence of the female and the confessional voice is that even when an article in a women's magazine features a subject such as automobiles, the female author's approach emphasizes her personal experience of the automobile by framing her encounter with it in autobiographical terms: the attitudes she brings to the act of buying or her feelings about pricing and shopping for a car, along with many allusions to her history as either a tomboy whiz kid car mechanic or a dithering, unmechanical bimbo who miraculously conquers inert machinery. In other words, not only the subject of spa-going but also its place of publication in women's magazines (and I include the travel and leisure sections of newspapers) imposes a confessional mode on the writing.

One structuring narrative strategy is to view your own flesh-and-blood reality as distinct from your writing self, in fact, from who you really are. The writing self views specific body parts, currently thin thighs and a muscle-toned, "cellulite"-free rump, noting the various profound mortifications visited on the flesh from a vantage point outside the body. Art historian Rosamund Bernier introduces her *Vogue* article on California's Cal-A-Vie Spa by evoking the existence of a geographically distant, eternally estranged body transformed into the sum of its statistical, physical capabilities by the uncanny science of weight control:

> There is a machine three thousand miles away that knows all too much about me, and certainly more than I would care to reveal, even to my best friend. It goes like this. You step on to a treadmill that is moving at a very smart pace. Devices have been attached to one's body that are in cahoots with a computer, which has already been fed with personal details. Age, weight, measurements—all are somewhere inside it, together with my address, my occupation, and for all I know my unlisted telephone number.
>
> Green lights go off and on. Wheels whir. And then, with what I consider an arrogant flourish, it spits out three sheets of paper filled with startling (to me) information about percentage of fat (humiliating), my lean body mass, and (in pounds avoirdupois) my extracellular water, my intercellular water, muscle, and—very laconic, this—other. ("Other" means bones, etc.) Finally, there is that most dour of all statistics: total fat in pounds. I'm not giving that away. (Bernier 1989: 150)

The body is separated from the soul, a psychophysical feat that manages to conjoin two seemingly disparate phenomena: the spirituality of pilgrimage travelogues and the symptomatology of schizophrenia. In diverse journalistic testimonials, the focus of intense longing and the goal of the spa investigator's journey is not the soul's union with the divine presence in Jerusalem, Mecca, or Lourdes; rather, the soul hovers anxiously above the recalcitrant flesh, and it is the body, not the soul, that is etherealized and rendered insubstantial.

Another example is a personal narrative by Mary Cantwell, with strong religious overtones remindful of pilgrimage accounts, which appeared in the April 1988 *Vogue* travel section. She identifies her sinful, gluttonous nature with the depression brought on by seasonal bingeing:

> It was not until I spilled the canned fruit cocktail down my front that I realized the extent of my depression. True there had been warning signs—bags of Oreos showing up in the groceries, brownies eaten by the row—but it took the Del Monte cascade to open my eyes . . . It seemed clear as I watched the diced pears and the halved cherries rolling down my chest that to get back on the right track I would have to separate myself entirely from the wrong one. Which is why I left New York at its giddiest, a few weeks before Christmas for a spa. (1988: 238)

Cantwell successfully sheds pounds at the spa. She provides detailed descriptions of her physical privations only to despair over the ultimately unredeemable nature of her flesh:

> Am I now four months later a reformed character? Not entirely. I ride my stationary bicycle grudgingly. But I am giving much thought to my pelvic tilt and even more to finding the right exercise class. Oreos have not passed my lips and the two pans of brownies I baked at Christmas were given to friends. Given that—and for God's laziest woman that's a lot—it's fair to say I am, at last, back on the track. (1988: 238)

The spa-goer's quest necessarily entails splitting the mind from the body for an unattainable physical ideal. The self, the metaphysical or spiritual self, materializes in the physical body. The physical body must now literally display its owner's conception of it. Yearning for the ideal form, coupled with longing for the sacred site where the transformation will take place, underlies Cantwell's article, the headlines of which play with the word *resort:* "Spas are no longer the last resort when you need to lose a few pounds, they've become a new kind of resort, the ultimate travel rest and recreation when you are longing to get away from it all." The context gives the cliché "getting away from it all" a new and precise meaning: getting away from your own body by transforming it into a tourist site to be explored, conquered, colonized, and played with.

Pilgrims and Spa-goers

Spa-going, as opposed to pilgrimage, tries to traverse the distance between the person in the body and the "real" you by going away spatially in order to find a lost self hidden

"I'M STILL AT THE RANCH!"

"Canyon Ranch was the most incredible vacation! I'm back two months and I can't believe how great I still feel. That's what's so wonderful about Canyon Ranch—it really stays with you.

They showed me how much fun I can have just taking care of myself. I make every day like a day at the Ranch. I'm exercising and eating right, setting priorities, taking time for me. Not just because it makes sense, but because it feels so good.

Going there was one of the smartest things I ever did. And with a Canyon Ranch so close, I can take some short spa getaways before my next vacation!"

For reservations and information call 1-800-726-9900.

Canyon Ranch®

HE SPA THAT NEVER LEAVES YOU.℠

YON RANCH IN THE BERKSHIRES℠: BELLEFONTAINE, KEMBLE STREET, LENOX, MASSACHUSETTS 01240

CANYON RANCH TUCSON: 8600 EAST ROCKCLIFF ROAD, TUCSON, ARIZONA 85715

ENJOY OUR 35% LOWER SUMMER RATES IN TUCSON.

Fig. 2.1 The Fabricated Body: Canyon Ranch.

under layers of fat rather than sin. Even if you must leave the spa and return to the world of temptation and ever-expanding flesh, the advertising of Canyon Ranch Spa bills it as the "spa that never leaves you." One magazine layout shows an elegantly dressed woman standing in a telephone booth (the contemporary confessional?) and gushing into a telephone receiver in the language of the reformed addict: "I'm still at the ranch. It's been almost four months since my vacation at Canyon Ranch. I can't believe how great I still feel. I've been to other spas and have always relapsed. I went back to the 'old life' within a week of getting home."

Another in the series of Canyon Ranch ads shows two women excitedly shrieking the same phrase, "I'm still at the ranch!" A city background obviously contradict their words, but those words are made flesh by commitments that have been maintained despite worldly temptations. The three women in the two advertisements are dressed in white linen "resort" summer outfits. They exude the stylish elegance of wealthy women, fortyish and slender, and all three display enough ecstatic and kinetic energy to whirl them off the page. The pictures speak of sophisticated urban environments surrounding the material body while the text alludes to a nonmaterial etherealized body. The ads colonize the body by representing a body etherealized and thinned to transparency explicitly in pictures and implicitly in text.

The advertising brochure circulated by another spa, the famous, fabulously expensive La Costa Spa in Carlsbad, California, emphasizes its supramundane, extratemporal qualities: "At La Costa the world disappears." What is the seeker left with when the everyday world, as promised, disappears? Not the self, but the body appropriated to represent a notion of the self about which La Costa makes this promise: "Here your body is warmed, soothed, soaked, massaged, oiled, cooled, perfumed, pampered and indulged with the most exotic and effective treatment." La Costa calls itself the "elegant escape." Like pilgrimage, spa-going involves a journey, preferably to a remote, sacred area; geographic distance; serious dieting; programmed exercise; therapeutic collapse in the waters; and temporary escape from the everyday, the ordinary, and the sinful. The sinful, however, is equated with the solid matter of the female body.

Spa enthusiasts share other characteristics with pilgrims. The pilgrim as well as the spa-goer steps out from mundane life into a more sacred dimension, a dimension that reestablishes a link to symbolic realities underlying the American religious tradition. In the case of spa-goers, the tradition is rewritten in secular terms: we are all out of shape because we are all sinners. Consider, for example, the writing found in *The Spa-Finder,* the first comprehensive catalog of spas. Its author, Jeffrey Joseph, creates the verb *to spa* from the noun *spa* in order to describe a watered-down version of new age existentialism and new world democracy:

> The joy of spa-ing is the joy of renewing your commitment to be the best you can become. In fact spa-ing is really about *becoming*. Becoming fitter, stronger, trimmer forever. Becoming centered, energized, and ready to deal with all the dilemmas of daily life without overloading on stress . . . Families and friends of inveterate spa-goers share before and after stories in praise of the fall-out benefit after spa-ing. Mommy has a better sense of humor about Koolaid stains on the beige berber rug when the spa vacation is a regular part of her health and wellness plan . . . And these days a spa vacation can be one of your best travel buys . . . that's one of the wonderful things about the spa experience—from secretary to chairman of the board, *everyone* looks the same in leotard and sweats. And when you're trying to stretch that final fraction of an inch or make it through the last five minutes of afternoon aerobics, you'll find that the superficialities of daily life drop away and very special friendships are made. And that's the great joy of spa-ing, *sharing*. (Joseph 1988: 4)

This closely approximates Victor Turner's description of pilgrimage as an existential or spontaneous *communitas* in which a change of location also heralds a joyous, communal experience that transcends normal societal structures and class differences (1969: 134–50). Or as Marion Laffey Fox (1990: 113) reports on the Lodge at Cordillera, a twenty-eight room mountain retreat in Edwards, Colorado, "[The instructors] emphasized the spa is a process—not a quick fix." However, it is a disembodied self, a self that treats the body as an object, that experiences the so-called processual, communitas-producing sensibility of the spa. Indeed, asks Katharine Young, what other solution is there for all those disembodied selves? The disembodied self that experiences democratic intimacy with others is soon reinserted into an etherealized, purified, and symbolic body (Katharine Young, letter to author, Oct. 16, 1990).

I claim that the spa ethos encourages a perception of the body as a site of pilgrimage that shares the attributes of the tourist experience. Tourism conquers and colonizes exotic foreign sites for personal consumption. Like pilgrimage, it removes the body from its usual surroundings, promotes travelers' camaraderie among strangers, and promises

Fig. 2.2. The Naked Body: La Costa.

self-knowledge. Viewing selected tourist sites is said to be a transforming experience. Touring selected parts of one's body splits the physical body from the perceiving, viewing self. Spas begin with the grand tour of the entire physical body, but most female spa-goers are deeply concerned about altering individual segments, such as a rounded stomach or bulging buttocks. The results of detaching parts of one's physique in order to sculpt and landscape one's flesh as if it were Futureland in Disney World bring about several paradoxical conflations. In what follows I discuss native costume, notions of touristic authenticity, founding legends, and the souvenir, topics around which the contradictory notions of tourism and pilgrimage are organized.

Native Costume: The Naked Body

Both tourist and pilgrim can go native and dress in the local costume. In spa resorts this costume is a lack of dress, primarily nudity, which brings together the disparate, fantastical utopias characteristically implicit in tourism and pilgrimage. Nakedness represents the state of innocent, youthful, unpolluted childhood, the Garden of Eden in which souls were perfect and (we can now conjecture) bodies were perfectly formed. In her travel article on European spas, Judith Shulevitz quotes Goethe, "who spent sixteen summers in Czech spa towns, [and] wrote his wife from Carlsbad (now Karlovy Vary in Czechoslovakia), 'I feel as if I'm in some paradise of innocence and spontaneity'" (Shulevitz 1989: 16).

We were expelled from the Garden and admonished that by the sweat of our brow shall we labor. It is a mark of Jeffery Joseph's marketing genius that he has reinterpreted these ancient words as a call to self-punishment in a pursuit of a life made whole and new: the sweat of our brow is the shared water coursing down our flesh and drenching our sweatsuits.

The current spa fashion for skinny, muscled bodies shows clearly the necessity of difference in producing meaning. When nourishment was uncertain and starvation widespread, a plump woman and wife was a mark of luxury. What we now consider an overweight woman was not just a symbol but an indexical sign of a life of leisure, a status marker distancing the rich from the masses. Now skinniness stands for the same things—leisure, wealth and distance—because it suggests abundant resources for leisure and travel. Keep in mind that many spas charge their clients as much as $2,500 per week.

Europeans see a yearly cure not as a luxury for a moneyed class of women but as a staple of middle-class family life. In many European countries it is covered by national health insurance.

Focusing on the colonized, naked female body prepared as a tourist or pilgrimage site, writers discuss the ways it can be appropriated and transformed by physical suffering. Francine Du Plessix Gray, for example, describes her visit to a French spa and contrasts its pampering and hedonistic European schedule with the exertions that typify American spas, claiming, "It took me several days to shed the Puritan hang-up that I was not suffering enough to merit any sense of well-being" (Gray 1987: 180). The precept that suffering is good for character formation is translated into purely physical terms: suffering ennobles the body by making it thinner.

Whenever European and American spas are compared and contrasted, American ones are typically said to be populated with wealthy, exercise-crazy female tourists, whereas European spas evoke family, the cultured conversation of pilgrim-aesthetes, and the absence of suffering: "In Europe, a spa is a place where guests relax, sip mineral water and listen to string quartets; picture Marcello Mastroianni in the movie *Dark Eyes.* In this country it used to be a place where rich women were pampered, massaged and prudently exercised" (Wells 1989: 75–76). Rosamond Bernier notes condescendingly the behavior of guests in a California spa as opposed to the civilized comportment of those in a French spa:

> I found the contrast between Quiberon—where my husband and I have been several times—and Cal-A-Vie hugely amusing. In Brittany good manners call upon one to ignore the other clients. Famous people, from cabinet ministers to movie stars, pad around in their Porthault bathrobes as if Siegfried's *Tarnhelm* had made them invisible. At the end of a week of bobbing up and down in the communal exercise pool, shoulder beside shoulder, thigh beside thigh, a very slight inclination of the head—"Bonjour Monsieur" "Bonjour, Madame"—is the most that is allowed. In the Quiberon dining room, nothing but food is discussed . . . Naturally the French find it a trial to do without bread. As for doing without wine, *n'en parlons pas!* At Cal-A-Vie everybody was immediately on a first name basis. Everyone appreciated the food, but apart from one or two nostalgic references to junk food, there was never a word about food in the abstract. The great subject of conversation was real estate . . . Nobody missed bread, but only a few could

> stomach the whole bottle of mineral water that we were meant to drink every day at room temperature. "Whoever drank water without ice?" (Bernier 1989: 160)

The American body is conceived of as an outer envelope, to be immersed in water, its external material casing manipulatable, and its geographical contours shaped from the outside. Unlike their less-friendly European counterparts, American spas encourage their clientele to lose weight in an environment of camaraderie: "The supportive atmosphere does create an environment that encourages friendship. Taking an early morning hike with sixty strangers helps you make friends quickly" (Asher 1990: 236). These friendly feelings are reminiscent of an American boot camp and are very different from the hushed, reverent accents of European families on pilgrimages to spas where immersion in water that has no harmful properties and, more important, ingestion, the absorption of the water's beneficial qualities into the body, are the twin sacraments.

The Quest for Authenticity

Spas, like pilgrimage sites or tourist venues, have what Dean MacCannell has called the "touristic need for authenticity" (1973: 590). Authenticity, the real thing, like the perfect body, is out there—we just cannot get our hands on it. For this reason, in order to provide the necessary touristic and pilgrimage authenticity, American spas, whether wealthy or funky, draw upon two principal kinds of founding legends: American Indian creation myths or European legends of ancient miraculous waters transplanted to the New World. Brochures from Saratoga Springs spas, for example, describe how the Iroquois regarded the local curative waters as an important element in the process by which the world was created. In fact, a cursory survey suggests that Native Americans stopped regularly for spiritual and physical rejuvenation at many of the 834 thermal springs listed in the U.S. Geological Survey. Spa advertisements inform us that many spa locations were considered sacred ground and evolved into neutral territories in which tribal antagonisms were suspended. Taos, New Mexico, claims the oldest spa in the country, one first frequented by the Pueblo Indians in the Edenic past preceding the coming of the Spaniards. Jane Fonda's Laurel Springs is said to be situated on holy Chumash Indian ground (Des Barres 1990: 112). Such legend making, however contrived, does reflect a long and dishonorable history of the federal government's purchasing thermal springs from tribes such as

Every three thousand years or so, Italian waters make a special contribution to health and beauty.

Many millennia ago, in the days of the Roman Empire, Caesar sent his wounded soldiers to a volcanic spring in Tuscany, Italy. To soak in the warm, mineral and plankton-laden waters. To bathe in the natural pools and cascades. To take the cures Nature herself offered up. To heal. Soon, others found the waters to offer new life. And a spa sprang up. Called Terme di Saturnia. Three thousand years later, a second spa has arisen from the same waters. A spa that combines their essence with ancient therapies and modern American fitness techniques. A haven called the Doral Saturnia. At Doral Saturnia, Terme di Saturnia's fango mud treatments and hydrotherapy peacefully coexist with electronic exercise equipment and stress management classes. Strong, experienced hands give facials and massages in private rooms, while others operate bio-feedback equipment and demonstrate the preparation of Doral Saturnia's Spa Cuisine. The same sumptuous fare based on a revolutionary caloric and "fat point system" of nutrition is enjoyed in the spa's two elegant restaurants. The blend of old Italy and modern America permeates the spa. From the 48 guest suites, where the touch of a finger can fill a marble bath or switch on the VCR. To the courts where the ancient sport of lawn bowling is practiced only steps from the modern games of golf and tennis at the adjacent Doral Hotel and Country Club. It took hundreds of the best minds from the world's best spas to create Doral Saturnia, but it can serve as sanctuary for no more than 96 guests at any one time. We urge you to write or phone for more detailed information on the spa and its rapidly dwindling available dates. Soon. Another spa like this may not arise from Italian waters for another three thousand years.

Doral Saturnia

INTERNATIONAL SPA·RESORT

8755 N.W. 36th St., Miami, FL 33178
800-331-7768 • in FL 800-247-8901 • 305-593-6030

Fig. 2.3 The Colonized Body: Doral Saturnia.

the Shoshone and Arapaho of Wyoming in the 1890s (Shalinsky 1985: 41–42). Part of the bloody inheritance of American colonialist expansion was to wrest these sacred waters from the natives, perhaps, I suggest, in order to perpetuate a newer colonialization process over another large dispossessed group, namely, women.

As an example of a European-transplanted legend, what Umberto Eco has movingly described as the phenomenon of "hyperreality, an American constant, the philosophy of immortality in duplication, the past preserved in full-scale authentic copy" (Eco 1986: 15), there is the case of the Doral Saturnia Spa Resort in Miami, Florida. Expensive, full-page color advertisements placed in numerous upscale magazines relate the spa's history: "Many millennia ago, in the days of the Roman Empire, Caesar sent his wounded soldiers to a volcanic spring in Tuscany Italy. To soak in the plankton-laden waters, to heal, etc. Soon others found the waters to offer new life. And a spa sprang up called Terme di Saturnia." Note where the hyperreal slippage in logic is inserted: "Three thousand years later a second spa has risen from the same waters." How is this tale geographically and geologically possible? Like William Randolph Hearst's imitation Renaissance castle at San Simeon, California, the Doral Saturnia Spa in Florida is only worth visiting if it is guaranteed to be simultaneously authentic and a copy of a European original.

Not only the waters and therapies but also the decor of spas are revivals of the European tradition. Surroundings that combine ancient Roman and Renaissance Tuscan elements contribute to spa-goers' fantasies of aristocratic luxury. In one advertising image from Doral Saturnia Spa, a woman clad in a flowing pastel toga pours water from an earthenware jug onto the bare back of a second seated naked lady, who arches her body ecstatically backward to receive the magical streams of water. The two women are enveloped in lush clouds of pink-gray steam. The advertising grants the viewer privileged access to an intimate feminine scene between mistress and maid. The female nude, so long the object of Western painting, is offered as a product to be purchased—if we accept the possibility that an everyday female body can be transformed into an ethereal work of art.

The Souvenir Body

Like the tourist and the pilgrim, the spa-goer becomes the heroine of her own adventure: her growth and self-mastery consist of dominating the flesh. The touristic souvenir from the adventure is intangible but corporeal. The pilgrim returns with her heart and spirit altered, whereas the spa-goer returns with a tan, slimmed body. Both are temporary victories, subject to sinful relapse, and require eternal vigilance and calendrical revisitation.

Pilgrimage implies attendance and devotion to chosen sacred sites and to the act of repeating the pilgrimage journey; tourism thrives on one-time journeys to a series of exotic vacation spots. Spas are populated by "spa junkies" and "aerobic overachievers," and food critic Gael Greene believes that recursive spa attendance is quasi-religious in nature. Broken "impassioned fitness vows" must be revived, reintegrated into the psyche, and practiced assiduously: "I become attached once again to the same ten pounds I have shed a hundred times or more. And I must race off to a spa for a shot of enforced discipline. Spas are like psychotherapy. You have to keep discovering the truths you already know until your unconscious surrenders." Her experiences, chronicled in *New York* magazine, are couched in psychological-religious terminology that reinforces the notion of communitas as a therapeutic practice. She describes not only her own efforts but also those of two relapsed companions, because, as she points out, "penitence wants company" (Greene 1988: 42). Spa-going partakes of the qualities of both tourism and pilgrimage just as "a tourist is half a pilgrim, if a pilgrim is half a tourist" (Turner and Turner 1978: 20).

The major attraction at spas, whether they are considered tourist or pilgrimage sites, or somewhere in between, is an abundance of water to surround the body. In rites performed by pilgrims, water has healing properties and contains God's blessing; in Christian ritual it cleanses the soul in the sacrament of baptism (Turner 1974: 203). In contrast, American spa waters are miraculous not for what they contain but for their instrumentality, what they permit you to do to the external surfaces of the body.

Immersed in the water, the female body is perceived to be both beautiful and unclean, a source of pleasure but also a source of evil and pollution. In his study of German culture through its folklore, Alan Dundes points out the German attachment to spas and notes the paradoxical nature of mud baths: the healing powers of water depend on the application of mud. The very notion of a mud bath, to bathe in mud in order to become clean, is part of a particular clean-dirty paradigm in which holiness/cleanliness are at one end of the continuum and impurity/dirt are at the opposite end (Dundes 1985: 16). Do American spas place the female body at the impure and polluted end? Mary Douglas (1966: 154) tells us that a polluting person is always wrong because she has developed a wrong condition. In American spa culture, the external manifestation changes over time—once it was wrong to be skinny, now it is an impurity to be too fat. In both cases, however, the wrongful or sinful condition is femaleness.

ANOTHER WORLD ANOTHER WORLD ANOTHER WORLD ANOTHER WORLD ANOTHER WORLD ANOTHER WORLD

S A T U R N I A

The ancient rituals have mysterious, rejuvenating powers.

Perhaps it's the wealth of rare minerals in the waters at Saturnia. Or the life-giving volcanic plankton. Or the uncommon combination of extracts and mineral salts in the purifying Fango mud.

Whatever the reason, bodies respond to the naturally occurring elements of Saturnia. And have thrived on them since Roman times.

The hands of those who administer these treatments are sure and gifted. Even the touch of the cascading waters is magical.

Revivifying therapies are as much a part of Saturnia as the challenges prescribed in our sophisticated fitness methods—from a rhythmic aerobics class to a rousing set of tennis. Much as the daily diet is a celebration of both body and senses.

While the powers of Saturnia may remain enigmatic for all of time, its benefits to both man and woman are irrefutable. To experience them for yourself, simply phone 800-331-7768.

ANOTHER WORLD ANOTHER WORLD ANOTHER WORLD ANOTHER WORLD ANOTHER WORLD ANOTHER WORLD

Fig. 2.4. The Souvenir Body: Saturnia.

French and American Responses

In the letters to the editor section of *New York* magazine, Mary Anne Cohen, director of the New York Center for Eating Disorders, pleads with journalist Gael Greene, author of the previously cited article on spa weight loss. Cohen considers Greene a role model for many women and urges her to live with her fluctuating ten pounds: "[Gael Greene's] humorous struggle is only the tip of the iceberg for millions of women whose self-esteem revolves painfully around what the scale pronounces each morning. If the scale shows the wrong number (as it invariably does), it will be, for many women, a day of dieting, fasting, bingeing, throwing up, laxative abuse, and/or overwhelming feelings of worthlessness" (Sept. 19, 1988, 10).

Psychologists and social workers such as Cohen point out that American women are taught to judge themselves against an ideal body image that is unattainable except by the slimmest, the most fit, and the most muscular. To counter prevailing ideologies glorified in spas, where a fat, penitent female body must be made to suffer, columnist Jane Brody surveys the new world of "body image workshop" therapies (Brody 1988: B14). What is particularly striking about techniques utilized by body-image therapists to help women love their bodies is the manner in which they replicate, overlap with, or mirror spa exercises. Brody cites the work of psychologist Marcia Germaine Hutchinson, whose book *Transforming Body Image: Learning to Love the Body You Have* counsels women that "in a relaxed state, participants 'converse' with the parts of themselves they deplore and eventually come to accept those parts as they are." The body may be perceived as sinful or fat or normal and fat, in either case the physical envelope is chopped into its constituent, detachable parts, which the body's owner either rejects or accepts, depending on whether she attends a spa or a body-image workshop: "Draw your own body in the nude, marking with red the areas you feel bad about; then be extra kind to your red parts" (Brody 1988: 14).

Additional recommendations for fostering a good body image are culled from a list of activities found in *The Melopene Journal,* a newsletter on women's health issues. Brody cites the first item, "Adopt an activity that is a good stress for your body like yoga, meditation, fast walking, bicycling or swimming," which is no different from any spa exercise regime. The second suggestion, to "write poems describing your feelings about your body, or keep a journal of the feelings you sometimes cover up by eating," amounts to the exercise of a confessional journal. The third suggestion is to "visit a museum or peruse an art book that depicts nude female sculpture and paintings from past eras when rounded, even plump, women were the societal ideal." It is accompanied by a line drawing of Botticelli's Venus emerging from the half-shell. The black and white illustration, attributed to Jill Karla Shwartz, accentuates Venus' large thighs and hips and is narrowly cropped to focus on the goddess' plump physique. The same Botticelli Venus is quoted in advertisements for the Doral Saturnia Spa in Florida but with markedly different intentions. Botticelli's complete uncropped painting is reproduced in a lavish color advertisement: a clothed servant tries to throw a coverlet over Venus' naked body as the gods endeavor to preserve her nudity by blowing gusts of wind. Venus' thighs, singled out in the body-image workshop article, do not seem disproportionately plump within the context of the entire painting. In spa advertising, Renaissance Italy, like ancient Rome, is magically transposed to modern America. Finally, another item in the body-image workshop list urges us to "indulge in body-pleasing activities such as massages, luxurious baths or clothing that makes you feel especially good." In other words, visit a spa where feelings of body worthlessness are guaranteed to be reinforced.

To muddy the waters further, some French feminists, especially Hélène Cixous, see water as the quintessential feminine element, continuous with the secure amniotic world of the mother's womb: "We are ourselves sea, sand, coral, sea-weed, beaches, tides, swimmers, children, waves" (Cixous 1980: 260). For Cixous it is "within this watery space that the female speaking subject is free to move from one subject position to another or to merge oceanically with the world" (Moi 1985: 117). Whereas in America the body is a nonporous casing, water is the absence of evil properties (merely instrumental), and the self is disembodied, the French-European body is pervious to water that contains and transmits healthful properties. But is the European self embodied?

The body in the water can either be construed as a French utopian vision of what water *does* contain of the feminine, reestablishing a spontaneous relationship to the physicality of the female body, or it can be viewed for what it does *not* contain. In the latter case it is a just another form of American commodification, in which the notion of health is domesticated into beauty, fitness into sexuality, and presence into absence. Thinness is equated with wealth and status, water with pollution and dirt, and all of us woman are complicit once again in our own degradation.

Notes

1. This is an expanded version of a talk delivered at the American Folklore Society annual meeting, Cambridge, Massachusetts, October 26–30, 1988. I am grateful to my father, Josef Slyomovics, who grew up in the spa town of Carlsbad (Karlovy Vary), Czechoslovakia, and who believes in the efficacy of spa cures, thereby providing me with a lifetime of fieldwork experience at European and North American spas. For their critical readings I thank Katharine G. Young and Brooks McNamara.
2. Figures are from Jeffery Joseph, president of Spa-Finders, a New York travel agency devoted exclusively to spa travel (also qtd. in Asher 1990: 236). Although most writers counsel that spas are not the place to initiate a romance, I cannot resist citing the article about the wedding of two (self-described) driven health fanatics who tied the knot at a New Jersey spa. As their wedding presents to each other, they booked separate massages (Staples 1989: 50–53).

References

Asher, Liza Galin. 1990. Spa-ing around. *Cosmopolitan,* May, 236–40.

Bernier, Rosamond. 1989. Images: Cal-A-Vie. *Vogue,* Dec., 150–60.

Boghurst, John. 1989. Are you man enough for a spa? *Esquire,* Nov.

Brody, Jane E. 1988. In quest of a healthy body image that can liberate women from societal images. *New York Times,* Oct. 20: 14.

Brown, Constance. 1977. But it's always hot springs time in the Rockies. *Smithsonian Magazine,* Nov., 91–97.

Cantwell, Mary. 1988. Spas—the pleasure principle. *Vogue,* Apr., 238–40.

Cixous, Hélène. 1981. The laugh of Medusa. In *New French feminisms: An anthology.* Ed. Elaine Marks and Isabelle de Courtivroon. New York: Schocken, 245–64.

Des Barres, Pamela. 1990. I was a (pretty) good sport at the Jane Fonda spa. *Cosmopolitan,* Mar., 110–14.

Douglas, Mary. 1966. *Purity and danger: An analysis of pollution and taboo.* London: Routledge & Kegan Paul.

Dundes, Alan. 1985. *"Life is like a chicken coop ladder": A study of German national character through folklore.* New York: Columbia Univ. Press.

Eco, Umberto. 1986. *Travels in hyperreality.* Trans. William Weaver. New York: Harcourt Brace Jovanovich.

Fox, Marion Laffey. 1990. The lodge at Cordillera: An antidote to real life. *Vis-à-Vis,* Aug., 113.

Garfinkel, Perry. 1988. Quaffing the waters in the latest California bars. *New York Times,* Apr. 13, C1, 6.

Geertz, Clifford. 1973. Thick description: Toward an interpretative theory of culture. In *The interpretation of cultures.* New York: Basic Books, 3–32.

Greene, Gael. 1988. Losing it again. *New York,* Aug. 29, 42–46.

Gray, Francine Du Plessix. 1987. In Quiberon, a pleasure spa. *Vogue,* Dec., 180–84.

Hewitt, Shannon. 1990. March is men's month. *Bodytalk: The Quarterly Newsletter of the Bonaventure Resort and Spa,* Feb. 3.

Joseph, Jeffrey. 1987. The joy of spa-ing. *The spa-finder.* New York: Jeffrey Joseph's Spa-Finders Travel Arrangements.

MacCannell, Dean. 1973. Staged authenticity: arrangements of social space in tourist settings. *American Journal of Sociology* 79: 589–603.

Moi, Toril. 1985. *Sexual/textual politics: Feminist literary theory.* New York: Methuen.

O'Malley, Anne. 1989. A bit of pampering, close at hand. *New York Times,* Oct. 15: 50.

Quindlen, Anna. 1990. Cool water. *New York Times,* Sept. 30: 21.

Reilly, Donald. 1990. Cartoon. *New Yorker,* May 14: 37.

Shalinsky, Audrey C. 1985. Thermal springs as folk curing mechanisms. *Folklore Forum* 18: 32–58.

Shulevitz, Judith. 1989. A sampling of spas: Where to take the waters in Czechoslovakia and Hungary. *New York Times,* Nov. 26: 16.

Sutton, Horace. 1976. Resort life in the colonies. *New York Times,* July 4: 1, 6.

Turner, Victor. 1969. *The ritual process: Structure and anti-structure.* Ithaca, NY: Cornell Univ. Press.

———. 1974. *Dramas, fields, and metaphors.* Ithaca, NY: Cornell Univ. Press.

Turner, Victor, and Edith Turner. 1978. *Image and pilgrimage in Christian culture.* New York: Columbia Univ. Press.

Wells, Linda. 1989. Spa life. *New York Times,* May 7: 75–76.

Williamson, Judith. 1978. *Decoding advertisements: Ideology and meaning in advertising.* London: Marion Boyars.

Boundary/Transgression

Preserving the propriety, integrity, and continence of its outer surface permits the construction of the body as an object. The self, conceived as enclosed in, perfused through, or constituted by the body, takes on this continent imagery. The self is embodied. At the same time, the body is taken as a microcosm that incorporates, replicates, or represents certain aspects of the macrocosm. The cosmos is likewise embodied. Breaches of the boundaries of the body in "Hamlet" threaten not only the embodied self but also the conceptual order the body represents. Fragmentations of the body portend the vicissitudes of the state as well as of the person. The self exteriorized on the spectacular body, especially the body of the king, is opposed to the self interiorized in the introspective figure of Hamlet. An antimony is set up in the play between spectacle and introspection, between a discourse of surfaces and a discourse of interiors, between the apparent and the hidden. Puns embody this antimony. Specifically, they sustain the hidden double, the taboo, improper, grotesque, obscene character of the subversive, inversive other discourse. *Hamlet* explores the complexity with which the body is appropriated by cultural discourses.

Bodily exuviae, as Mary Douglas calls them—sweat, spit, snot, shit, piss, smegma, semen, secretions, tears, milk, pus, and blood—transgress the boundaries of the body. These ambiguous substances are both part of the body and apart from it. The Hakka Chinese blood bowl ceremony focuses on a substance at once deeply infused with personhood and profoundly taboo. The ritual expiates bodily transgressions after death. Its efficacy depends on messages transmitted in a seance through a medium, who in her own person, transacts the boundary between the land of the living and the realm of the dead.

Bodily transgressions represent symbolic ones.

3. *When Nothing Really Matters:* Body Puns in *Hamlet*

PHYLLIS GORFAIN

In this most cerebral of Shakespeare's tragedies, characters voice a remarkable array of body images that show how the body forms the basic medium through which they must think and act. Characters refer to many body parts, including some seldom mentioned in the theater, such as eyelids, arteries, heels, and teeth; more significantly, characters repeatedly use particular images—eyes, ears, brain, tongue, face, hand, and heart (Hunt 1988)—to express ideas about communication, perception, and power. Several important recent studies of *Hamlet* have focused on this extraordinary body imagery as critics have combined the insights of older literary analyses (Charney 1969; Clemen 1951; Donawerth 1984; Muir 1964; Spurgeon 1935; States 1973; Wentersdorf 1978) with poststructuralist and materialist perspectives on the production of meaning (Barker 1984; Hunt 1988; Goldberg 1988).

Yet these literary studies of *Hamlet*'s corporeal imagery have not examined the peculiar impact of this script in the theater when characters, who speak so incessantly of the body, appear, as they must do, in the real bodies of actors. Nor has the attention to body images fully recognized how these characters—especially Hamlet—frequently produce puns using these images, thereby anatomizing the incarnation of meaning in physical sound.[1] Their puns are also often reflexive, acknowledging the ways sound and semantics collide. Such puns implicitly comment on the way they deconstruct language by detaching abstract meaning from the body of sound. In this discussion of the ways body puns in *Hamlet* confront the nature of expression, I am not making a historical argument about Elizabethan or Stuart ideas about language in general, nor about a larger theory of language enclosed dramatically within *Hamlet*. Recent studies of Elizabethan language theory caution against imposing a modern philosophical distrust of language onto Renaissance theories of language (de Grazia 1978) but also emphasize the considerable contemporary controversy concerning linguistic and communicative limits. The ambivalence toward rhetorical fictions and communication through gesture, body, writing, and other signs resulted in a variety of views that Shakespeare amply illustrates, perhaps nowhere more energetically than in *Hamlet* (Donawerth 1984). In calling attention to the astonishing energy of particular reflexive puns, I will focus on how they reflect on the problematic relationship between the intellectual production of meaning and the physical body through which ideas must be expressed in precise social situations in the world of *Hamlet.*

For example, some very revealing body puns in *Hamlet* occur during times of salutation and leave-taking. In dramatized, as in actual, social situations, these encounters are occasions for formulaic performances, as speakers position their bodies and social statuses using terms of address, rituals of deference or recognition, and conventional body language—such as clasping hands, bowing, embracing, threatening with a sword, or twirling a bonnet. When puns or other wordplay capsize conventional expectations at these perimeters of social definition, they register profound comments on the construction of social meaning through language and the body. If these puns also stress positions and bodies, they reflexively denote the principal markers of disorder in this playworld.

At the same time, puns within greetings and farewells—at the boundaries of social events—reach out beyond the limits of the world of Elsinore to reflect on the larger Elizabethan context. In 1600 succession was a threat to the delicately balanced settlement between many kinds of contested authority—religious, philosophical, and economic. The difficult juncture between one ruler and the next made the problem of succession increasingly evident in the aged body of the heirless queen (Tennenhouse 1987: 80–81).

As puns echo against past words, they similarly block the linear progress of language through a creative recursivity. These brief moments of memory or stasis resonate with issues of succession and usurpation as well as with many other images and incidents of hesitation, pause, paralysis, and interruption in the play. In the theatrical enactment of speech, puns further underline the problematics of sovereignty or privileged space, because they operate at two levels, within the enclosed dramatic world of the play and beyond that world, in the extradramatic dimensions of the theater and the globe for which it is a microcosm. In drama, all language must be spoken aloud. Every word—and every pun—heard by characters in the world of the play is also heard by audiences in the world of the theater. Indeed, as some words may rehearse other words the audience has heard, but that a character has not, they are ironic puns produced for us by the play, not by the character. In Shakespearean drama, where characters frequently speak directly to the audience, straddling the line between stage and house, other puns may be deliberately spoken by a character only to us and not for other characters. As puns reverberate with other signifiers—including physical objects and events on stage—they establish a connected and complex multiple drama of meanings through play.

The resulting pattern of serious wordplay in *Hamlet* expressly targets certain bodies—of the king and of women—as physical entities and sites of mystical value. Real bodies are at stake, but the issue is their status as the symbolic texts on which culture can be inscribed. Shakespeare's society held both types of bodies, in an elaborate corpus of lore and ideology, to be fundamental sources of life and purpose. Moreover, in a society in which social order depended on hierarchies, statuses, and differences, these bodies marked for rank and gender particularly exhibited social significance, although anatomical and biological differences between male and female bodies were regarded as homologically identical (but evaluatively asymmetrical). The prevailing Renaissance gynecology made women's reproductive organs the diminutive and inverse replica of men's (Greenblatt 1988: 75–86; Tennenhouse 1987: 78). Gender differences and political hierarchies were therefore entangled when the bodies of women of higher rank were treated as naturally superior to those of lower-status males but as inferior to the male bodies in their own class. The crucial and vexed differences of rank and gender—which Elizabethan and Stuart ideology held as absolute, given, and natural—were exposed by puns as positional, questionable, and cultural.

The Reformation doctrine of the king's "two bodies," which emerged in England during the reign of Henry VIII and after the break with Rome, was developed to enable a secular monarch to serve as the sacred primate of the Church of England. More precisely, the doctrine distinguished between the body natural—the mortal body of a king, subject to infirmity, aging, and death—and the body politic—the immortal mystical body of kingship (Axton 1977; Kantorowicz 1957). The body politic had corporate perpetuity while occupying a temporary corpus: "The King is a Name . . . which shall endure . . . as long as the People continue . . . and in this Name the King never dies" (judicial opinion of 1560, qtd. in Axton 1977: 14). When the king died, the juncture between these two ontological realms was encapsulated in the paradoxical announcement, "The King is Dead! Long Live the King!"

The body of woman, as a construct, was also utilized as a map of moral order. This symbolic system was codified in a doctrine of conduct promulgated in the burgeoning number of etiquette books specifying the ideal manners for Christian gentlewomen.[2]

Very much in keeping with Mary Douglas's theories about body orifices as a systematic set of openings with which to incarnate symbolic zones of social threat and security, danger and purity were attributed to whatever the lady saw, spoke, heard, ingested, or was penetrated by. Measured and knowable through the integrity of her body as a site of ambiguity, her personal integrity was a key to family honor, reliable inheritance, and succession.[3]

When Gertrude, who is both the queen of Denmark and Hamlet's mother, seems to Hamlet to have betrayed her vows to her dead husband, Hamlet's father and the king, by marrying Hamlet's father's brother within two months of the funeral; and when the two of them occupy the ruling positions of Denmark, the symbolic aspects of the bodies of woman and monarch, and of the language and symbols based on them, become particularly distressed. Appropriately, in Hamlet's first line alone, he yearns, "O that this too too solid flesh would melt" (1.2.130).[4] Then he learns a ghost has appeared, with a "figure like [his] father" (1.2.199); that same night it speaks to him, explaining it is still embodied, unable to find rest in its grave because it was murdered, unshriven, when at rest. The armed figure relates the narrative of his murder in curdling physical detail and warns the prince that his uncle/stepfather/king has usurped his position—on the throne and in the royal bed of Denmark—by poisoning King Hamlet through his ears. The ghost now pours into the ears of his son the news that "the serpent that did sting thy father's life" (1.5.39) has

> . . . given out that, sleeping my orchard,
> A serpent stung me. So the whole ear of Denmark
> Is by a forged process of my death
> Rankly abused . . .
>
> (1.5.35–38)[5]

The counterfeiting of signs, the frailty of women, the corruption of the kingship, and the mortality of the body pose for Hamlet an epistemological dilemma in which meaning cannot be sustained by its material texts. Denmark, which names both the land and its king, has been poisoned through its ears by lies; Hamlet's despair visualizes the framework of time as a broken body: "The time is out of joint: O cursed spite / That ever I was born to set it right.—" (1.5.189–90). Joined metaphors personify the body politic and the edifice of state as Hamlet imagines himself the physician who must reset both its twisted joints and abused frame to restore chronology and proper succession.

Hamlet's virtuoso punning accordingly breaks the linear progress of language through time, as if halting discourse for static moments of reflexive play. As the puns assault difference, likeness, and rank, they accurately encapsulate the same structural and historical tensions that arise when meaning must be incorporated in material signs. Such play with words deconstructs the polyvalency and mortality of symbols, which possess both an abstract level of signification and a material dimension of being. Physical symbols locate ideas in a naturalized experience and simultaneously interpret experience in abstraction (Geertz 1973; Turner 1974). Symbols make matter matter.

As soon as the play opens, it places these problems of assuring succession and stable meaning at the margins of the Danish state. The first line of the play is a salutation as a challenging question, "Who's there?" (1.1.1).[6] We soon realize the speaker is a relief guard at the frontiers of Elsinore. Yet his military challenge does not elicit the expected answer: if the second speaker were a countryman, he would supply his name or a statement of allegiance; if the speaker were the enemy, he would utter some form of challenge. Surprisingly, although it is not spoken by an enemy, the succeeding line contests the first:

> Barnardo: Who's there?
> Francisco: Nay answer me. Stand and unfold yourself.
> Barnardo: Long live the king!
> Francisco: Barnardo?
> Barnardo: He.
>
> (1.1.1–5)

Not yet relieved by his successor, the guard Francisco finds his replacement has just usurped his right to question who's there. Conventional forms have been thoroughly inverted as guard and guarded against become transposed through fear and error. Francisco cannot perform, but must reassert, the authority of his position at this uneasy junction between shifts and at the exact line between one day and another, for Barnardo will soon announce the time, "'Tis now struck twelve. Get thee to bed, Francisco" (1.1.7), as he takes up his office.

Barnardo's reply, "Long live the king!", states his fealty to the king's two bodies and demonstrates that Francisco does not seek an individual identity but an identification of group affiliation. The "king" who is to live long refers immediately to Claudius, but also ironically acknowledges the dead king's body, which has been much too lively. We quickly learn these sentinels are as much on guard against that dead king's wandering body as they are on guard to protect the living king's corporate body, which, as a mystical entity, the mysterious ghost challenges.

The demand that the first speaker "stand and unfold" himself also immediately sounds the first of the play's many images that exploit the disclosure of body parts as a metaphor for the disclosure of personal identity and the enclosure of social identifications. The figure of speech presents the announcement as an unfolding; politically aligning oneself is poetically equated with opening a folded paper or unwrapping a piece of cloth such as a hood or a mantle. To name oneself is to dismantle. Naming oneself is then like opening oneself as a book, or a sheet of paper, which is unfolded in order to be read. The metaphor assimilates making identity to making the self socially legible; the self is disclosed as if it were a social body that can be literally known.

The guards arrange for their exchange as the other arrivals approach. Barnardo thinks he recognizes the voice of one of the new sentries: "Say, / What, is Horatio there?" (1.1.18–19).[7] Horatio, almost as witty as his best friend, Hamlet, replies, "A piece of him" (1.1.19). The questions and answers show us that this scene takes place in the dark, where sound, not sight, must be used to detect presence, and where language must indicate identity. Although Horatio speaks only metaphorically, in a kind of understatement typical of his character, an actor can make this remark a literalized metaphor by holding out his hand, a piece of himself, perhaps all of him that shows in the dark. Creating such a visual body pun comments on how handshakes, welcomes, and naming are tropes that establish social identity as partial and metonymic. However the line is performed, with a body gesture or not, the wordplay will always be spoken, and the surprising wit at this edgy moment immediately testifies to the anxiety of the guards as Horatio verbally amputates a piece of himself. His insistence that he can introduce only a "piece" of "Horatio" illustrates the difficulty of establishing identity at the seams of any social encounter.

Throughout the play other boundary-making forms of salutation and valediction are disrupted in this diverting way, through either mistake or play. Both techniques reveal the uneasy borders in this usurped state and call attention to our position within the theater but outside the stage. Such games with openings and closings—often punning on images of the body—display the dilemma of creating a body of knowable social acts in a disjoint body politic.

Hamlet, in particular, exercises ritualistic greetings and farewells to disrupt how the court defines roles, frequently through his non sequiturs to underline questions of succession. Because the king is a regicide and the royal marriage is, for Hamlet, incestuous (Rosenblatt 1978), Hamlet surely experiences torment in his simultaneous position as prince, son, and nephew. He therefore seizes moments of arrival and departure to defy the ways folk forms perform and constitute social relationships. For example, in Hamlet's initial appearance, when the king first tries to contain the prince's subversive silence and persistent mourning, Claudius fulsomely recognizes him by more than one kinship term. But Claudius ironically thereby voices the surplus of relationships he has created by marrying his brother's wife. Thus when he approaches Hamlet with the salutation, "But now, my cousin Hamlet, and my son—" (1.2.64), Hamlet succinctly denies this definition of their relationship: "A little more than kin and less than kind" (1.2.65). In the early printed texts, no stage direction indicates how this subversive reply is spoken. Is it an aside to the audience from the edge of the stage? Does Hamlet aim it directly to the king with full eye contact? Or does he audibly mutter this to himself? The actor must make that choice, and how he positions his body as he utters Hamlet's famous first line will show how aggressively or meditatively Hamlet introduces this friction into Claudius's oily management of the state.

The brilliant puns on "kin" and "kind," however they are visibly performed, oppose the bodily kinships of sound and blood to moral differences, exaggerating the likenesses of sound and their differences of significance to contest the likeness between situational and essential "kindness." Such wordplay also reflexively comments on itself; it shows how the kinship of sound in wordplay can deform social relationships. Punning underlines the very distinctions Claudius abrogates through his hasty and incestuous marriage, a marriage that combines what should be mutually exclusive. By adding terms to his prior kinship with Hamlet and with Gertrude as uncle and brother, the marriage violates proper distinctions of kinship and time; Hamlet's punning replicates this multiplication of signification and breach of difference.

Hamlet's technique of punning to transgress rituals of greeting and farewell is perhaps most comic as Hamlet disorders nearly every contact he has with the officious courtier Polonius, who correspondingly exploits every encounter he has with Hamlet as either a spying opportunity or as a mission of state supervision. At one point defeated by Hamlet's contestive verbal games, Polonius tries to extricate himself by employing a customary farewell: "My honourable lord, I will most humbly take my leave of you" (2.2.207–8).[8] Hamlet does not let him get away so easily: "You cannot sir take from me anything that I will not more willingly part withal; except my life, except my life, except my life" (2.2.209–10).[9] Hamlet's play with both words and social forms literalizes leave-taking. Hamlet's joke treats the leave that Polonius wants to take as if it were a bodily part Polonius had deposited with him and that he now gratefully returns.

The Prince also extends the boundaries of this discourse all the way to the extremes of his own life and death. He offers to cooperate in the social ritual of returning some inanimate part of Polonius, his "leave," but refuses to share his animate "life." The near-rhyme employs the body of sound to pun on the difference between a life and a leave. Only with dead rituals can we take our leaves, suggests Hamlet, playing on the dead metaphor in Polonius's parting remark. Hamlet's wordplay revives a hidden point in leave-taking rituals. The prince's refusal to give his life in this punning context warns that unless we are careful, these daily points of etiquette can disintegrate the essential wholeness of our selves. The language of "parts" as Polonius de-parts proclaims how parting socially defines the social parts we play while the punning questions to what extent we can compartmentalize our selves.

If Polonius adds to his obsequious remark by ceremoniously bowing or carefully walking backward facing the prince, whatever Hamlet does with his body—and the actor must do something even if he just stands still—will be a reaction to Polonius's movements and will indicate even more about how Hamlet dissects a social formula to lay bare the perplexities of making identity through language and the body. Such self-conscious punning thus anatomizes puns as well as leave-taking itself.

For example, when Hamlet leaves for England, where Claudius is arranging to have him assassinated, he serves up a royal insult in his farewell to the king: "Farewell, dear mother" (4.3.45–46). Actors playing the prince often add a little—or even a big—good-by kiss right on the king's lips. In such a performance, the actor playing Claudius will have the king react physically as well as verbally to this mistake. His line insists, "Thy loving father, Hamlet" (4.3.47), but his body may physically recoil from the kiss. In this double message, he makes evident his lie. Even if these lines are not so physicalized, Claudius's verbal objection to Hamlet's mistake about his gender, his title, and their relationship enables the prince to correct his correction. Hamlet then proceeds with the kind of utterly logical but nonsensical syllogism in which Shakespeare's fools specialize. He explains, "My mother. Father and mother is man and wife, man and wife is one flesh, and so, my mother. Come, for England" (4.3.48–49).[10] Before Claudius can reply, Hamlet is out the door.

Claudius's next line, spoken to his guards after Hamlet has vanished, uses a body metaphor to regain political mastery through physical containment: "Follow him at foot" (4.4.57). Hamlet's farewell—which trifles with ideas of identity, gender, and the body—subverts the authority of the king by subverting the authority of folk sayings and church doctrine. He parodies the sanctimony that would sacralize sexual intercourse, making of it a mystical union of "one flesh." Hamlet's final farewell, "Come, for England," points up the sudden removal of his flesh from this cozy union and completes the verbal duel in which he has exploited the religious fiction of one flesh in marriage to question Claudius's own bodily and moral integrity. Hamlet manipulates wordplay about the body at the very moment his body is being forcibly taken in exile. The unruly prince leaves the king without his own final reciprocal line of farewell, and Claudius can recover his rule only by coercive physical power. In a sense Hamlet forces the king's hand. The king's physical response then belies its own inadequacy. Hamlet's insurrections against language, custom, and folk belief cannot be confined through the constraint of his body.

Ophelia, in her madness, replicates these same problematic greetings and farewells. Ironically duplicating Hamlet's subversion of gender difference and hierarchy in a disruptive farewell, Ophelia departs the court by saying politely but inappropriately, "Good night, ladies." Like Hamlet's, her term of address feminizes her audience, dominated by a king who rules by virtue of his gendered authority. Earlier, her upsetting entry to the court was verbally expressed in her challenging question, "Where is the beauteous Majesty of Denmark?" (4.5.21). Her abrupt opening, like the question ("Who's there?") that commences the play, epitomizes the difficulty of locating self and others in a state where the former king's body in the figure of a ghost invades the territories his subjects defend in the name of the king. Ophelia's question is wonderfully puzzling as it plays with the literalization of majesty in the ambiguous body of either the king or queen. Neither body really contains the "the majesty," although regal trappings can awe viewers in the theater of power enacted in Renaissance courts. In using the hyper-correct "beauteous," Ophelia also mocks the surely exaggerated efforts to embody majesty in this illegitimate regime. Her wordplay repeatedly deforms folk forms and rituals to substitute mistaken terms for their likenesses. These mistakes mock the essential usurpation that has created missing majesty and a false likeness at the center of a counterfeit court.

Her body disordered,[11] Ophelia may seem mad, "incapable of her own distress" (4.7.178), as Gertrude appropriately frames it later. Her violations of decorum in speech, dress, and body assault the feminine code in which we have seen her carefully instructed. In so doing, Ophelia acts out the hidden turmoil in the court, for her brother and father have governed her conduct as an index of her family's honor and to maintain class and gender hierarchies. Ophelia may seem to perform her potentially dangerous acts without self-reflexivity, but actors can choose a greater degree of self-awareness. Even more significantly, they can show how seriously the court registers the threats her remarks and body can pose, and the construction of Ophelia's madness may be performed as a function of the court or patriarchal design.

However self-consciously she uses her body, others respond to Ophelia's danger by minimizing her, by referring to her as if she were an irrelevant "nothing," by textualizing her behavior, or by subjecting her to surveillance as a perilous gap into which meanings can be inserted. The problem of her "nothingness" magnifies but also thereby displays how images of women serve as empty texts for patriarchal projections, why women pose such a semiotic danger for patriarchal regulation of interpretation.

For example, before Gertrude grants entry to the transformed Ophelia, a male character warns the queen that "[Ophelia's] speech is nothing, / Yet the unshaped use of if it doth move / The hearers to collection" (4.5.7–9).[12] The advisor goes on to tell the queen that Ophelia's body language, her nonverbal "winks and nods and gestures," speak to her audience "their own thoughts.... though nothing sure" (4.5.11–13). In response, Gertrude herself metaphorically reduces the alarming ambiguity of Ophelia's actions by calling her behavior a "toy" (4.5.18).

Gertrude's nominal subjection of Ophelia's threatening disorder soon dissolves once she has witnessed Ophelia's performances of song snatches, her customary awards of folklorically decipherable flowers, and her fragmentation of other popular genres. Ophelia is then accommodated by taking her as a sentimentalized text, "A document in madness, thoughts and remembrance fitted" (4.5.176), as Laertes articulates it for the court. He also feminizes her anger: "Thought and affliction, passion, hell itself, / She turns to favour and to prettiness" (4.5.183–84).[13] Yet Laertes also paradoxically acknowledges that "this nothing's more than matter" (4.5.173). The implicit wordplay in "nothing" and "matter" equates semantic sense and material sensation, as if to suggest that it is a mistake to think that mere matter means nothing. The ambiguity in the pun admits that abstract ambiguous signs, like Ophelia's "nothing," may carry more semantic weight, matter more, than does matter. Puns on "nothing" and "matter" accentuate how the court tries to suppress, through the concept of "nothing," the volatile sexual, political, social, and gender matters released by Ophelia.

One of Hamlet's most celebrated punning dialogues also combines puns on "nothing" and "matter" in connection with Ophelia. The elaborate wordplay aggressively reveals the misogyny that courtly euphemism masks. Many previous studies have discussed this incident, but I want to pursue a new matter: the way reflexive punning allows the play to examine how assaults on verbal order violate the body of sound, folk conventions, rituals of greeting and farewell, and other contained bodies—in this case, women's chastity. Hamlet performs his famous punning feat at the edges of another social juncture, just as the court is arranging itself to hear the play. Hamlet disarranges social order by asking Ophelia where he can place himself:

> Hamlet: Lady, shall I lie in your lap?
> Ophelia: No, my lord.
> Hamlet: I mean, my head upon your lap.
> Ophelia: Ay, my lord.
>
> (3.2.99–102)[14]

As if to suggest that Ophelia has mistaken his question by taking it as the obscene pun it is, the Folio Hamlet seems to profess innocence by talking directly about the problem of interpretation as he specifies his meaning: "I mean, my head upon your lap." Of course, the actor also could perform this phrase as an outright sexual suggestion, because "head" was also a sexual entendre, referring to maidenhead, the prepuce, testicles, or the penis (Colman 1974: 198; Partridge 1960: 126; Rubinstein 1984: 122). Actors, however, usually make his strategy more maddening. If he seems to chasten what he implies is Ophelia's bawdy error—she is supposedly the one with a dirty mind if she takes his straightforward question as a sexual innuendo—he inflicts a double message of polite sociability and offensive suggestion.

Even more elaborately, Hamlet also could be alluding to morality plays where "a youth, by lying in the lap of a temptress, puts himself in her power and is betrayed" (Jenkins 1982: 294). The insinuations go even further than these various levels of language play. Real bodies are also in question, and the concern is where to put them physically and socially. What does the actor show Hamlet doing when he proposes laying his head—and which one—in Ophelia's lap? Does he just glance at her knees, or fix his gaze higher? Does she sit on the floor or on a stool, so does his suggestion mean that he will forgo a chair and rest on her? How does he do so?

And when Ophelia, at least in the Folio, apparently acquiesces to the supposedly sanitized second request by agreeing, "Ay, my lord," does she prepare her lap by straightening her dress, patting her thighs provocatively, or visibly locking her knees together under her garments? At the same time, her verbal affirmation affords Hamlet a new opportunity to unfold her closed language whatever she does with her legs. In the Folio he places in her "ay," as the Quarto Hamlet places in her earlier "no," his own layered puns as he plies her with more questions:

> Hamlet: Do you think I meant country matters?
> Ophelia: I think nothing, my lord.
> Hamlet: That's a fair thought to lie between maids' legs.
> Ophelia: What is, my lord?
> Hamlet: Nothing.
>
> (3.2.102–6)

Linguistic historians believe that "nothing" was probably pronounced in a way that made it sound like "noting," both of which were then pronounced in the same way as was "nutting."[15] "Nothing" was therefore available as a pun with "noting," to make notes or sounds, and, by extension, with "noting" as "pricking notes" on the lute, an instrument associated with amorous wooing. "Noting" was also associated with making a "note," which had several meanings. A "note" referred to the zero symbol as well as to the letter *O*, which could stand for an orgasmic groan. "To note" meant to inform; a "note" was a stigma, so a "notable" characteristic signified a defamatory trait. In addition, if used singularly, "note" could refer to a penis, for a "prick" was a musical note. Because "note" and "nut" were interchangeable aurally, two notes could refer to testicles. "Nothing" also formed a homonym with "nutting," a folkloric slang term for sexual intercourse. There is some evidence that "nothing," as another lexeme, might well have served as a slang term for a woman's vulva, genitals, as opposed to a male's "thing." As an iconic hand gesture, the sign for "nothing" is a closed circle, a zero or cipher, or a "naught," for which "note" was a homonym as well as a synonym. In these ways, "nothing" and "note" linked images of woman's sexuality with puns on "naught" and "naughty." Because "nothing" simultaneously refers to the "noting" (making of sound) about "nothing" (sexual intercourse), it is also about punning about such naughtiness. As a term that reflexively puns on its own making of sound into sense, which speaks of how noting it makes naughty meanings, "nothing" infinitely puns on its ability to generate endless puns out of naught.

Therefore when Hamlet asks Ophelia if she thought he meant "country matters," he continues the punning association between nothing and matter, extending the reflexive exploration of how puns use matter to create meaning out of nothings. The pun on "country" (which could be spelled "cuntrie") suggests, in such a complex context, that women's orifices—their mouths and "cunts"—stand for the sites in which communication is reproduced. Simultaneously these are also marked as the sites where the problem of restricting meaning is also located. Promiscuity in language and sex become equated problems as Hamlet projects his anger about deception onto Ophelia, who becomes for him a symbol of all false notes. So he must reduce all her words into a sign of "nothing."

Hamlet's complex alliance of the two puns on "country" and "matters" hints that Ophelia's thoughts of nothing may be filled with at least seven country matters: genital organs, genital secretions, acts of animal husbandry, barnyard sounds, coital sounds, country quarrels, and, reflexively, coital quibbles. In Shakespeare's theater, where a boy actor played Ophelia, the pun on "nothing" as the fair thought between "a maid's legs" makes even further ironic gestures toward the many things men, women, actors, and audiences think may be between their own or others' legs, and the "nothings" exchanged by Hamlet and Ophelia can represent a very replete set of naughty notings.

If Ophelia tries to maintain a semblance of bodily integrity through chaste speech, saying "nothing," Hamlet penetrates the fissures of her silence. When Ophelia insists she did not understand Hamlet in a naughty sense—"I think nothing"—the actor playing Ophelia needs to decide if she knowingly puns. Even if she does seize Hamlet's own strategy in a brave self-mockery, Hamlet arrests the paradox in her words, for even as she speaks of her thoughts as unspeakable, Hamlet again takes her word about closed subjects as a small opening in which to insert another pun. After all, her verb "think" governs a direct object "nothing," which names what she thinks, voicing denial instead of vacuity, and in that denial Hamlet can insist matter lies: "That's a fair thought to lie between maid's legs." His entry into her attempt at closure is a symbolic act that exposes the gaps in any representation, particularly any show of feminine modesty. Just as the nunnery to which he would relegate Ophelia might denote a monastery or refer to a brothel (Jenkins 1982: 282, 493–96), so any female word can be taken as its opposite by misogyny. An actor may play Ophelia as engaging in a very witty exchange with Hamlet, as strongly opposing his assaults, or as trying to appear innocent or reticent. No matter how she is played, Hamlet's strategy prevails. He has the last word. Hamlet's special license follows from both his position as Prince and his antic disposition, which is tolerated because the court does not hold him responsible for this apparently uncontrollable condition. His bawdy wordplay then makes Ophelia's language and body into objects on which a privileged male speaker can impress his purposes, robbing her of her power to govern matters.

Teasing out meanings by separating sounds from sense through puns becomes the linguistic and social equivalent to playing with body parts. Whether this tickling of language through the body also can tickle the body through language, it becomes obscene when it offends the dignity of the body and social relationships. Obscenity, like all forms of pollution, depends on violating social boundaries, and to the extent this reflexive play with language remains play—is taken as "no offense" by those who respond to it—it can prick the social fabric rather than tear it apart. The erotics of such playful violence then titillates rather than degrades the bodies of women and language.

The language about language and the body makes clear to the characters themselves that speech play performs both aggressive and erotic symbolic actions. Actors must then decide how some choices can make the symbolism of the dazzling punning more or less evident. They may show this, in part, through the ways they have Ophelia and the rest of the court respond to Hamlet's verbal aggressions. For example, when Ophelia later tries to check another harassing move by Hamlet, she repeats a word: "You are naught, you are naught, I'll mark the play." The repetition, played imaginatively, could signal that the second "naught" puns on the first. In insisting on substituting the play for the object of her attention, Ophelia may be saying the play is more than the naught she then suggests Hamlet is. Is her rejection of Hamlet's naughtiness teasing? Or is her reply indignant and reproving? Does she deliver it as a parry in a verbal duel in which she claims a part?

Even if the term is not played as a pun with which Ophelia deliberately twits Hamlet in the world of Elsinore, it may be heard as a pun for the audience. At the theatrical level, Ophelia's wordplay can show us the play we mark (*Hamlet* or "The Mousetrap" or both) is logically contrasted to its own wordplay, which is "naught." Yet if this is also performed as Ophelia's conscious pun, such doubling of signs directly in her mouth allows her to take control of the cultural suspicion about all forms of female duplicity and to defy her marginality by seizing the very "naughtiness" to which her speech and body have been reduced.

Only in Ophelia's self-destructive madness—or her self-directed show of madness, depending on how it is played—does she sustain the power to use herself as a spectacle and so to subvert the chaste silence to which she has been relegated. Her quotations of traditional speech, folk sayings, proverbs, folk songs, blessings, fragments of myths and tales use broken forms and puns to appropriate others' speech in the same way as Hamlet has done with his puns.[16] Yet her derangement, whether feigned or not, lacks the open self-declared reflexivity of Hamlet's strategically stated lunacy. The court grants her madness the same immunity it allows to play, but a different respect than is accorded to the player-of-madness, Hamlet.

Hamlet exploits this impunity during an amazingly condensed exchange with Claudius; again he refuses to cooperate in a relationship as Claudius attempts to enact a courtly greeting. Claudius enters the court to view the play Hamlet is presenting and addresses the prince:

> Claudius: How fares our cousin Hamlet?
> Hamlet: Excellent, i' faith, of the chameleon's dish; I eat the air, promise-cramm'd—you cannot feed capons so.
> Claudius: I have nothing with this answer, Hamlet, these words are not mine.
> Hamlet: No, nor mine now.
>
> (3.2.82–87)[17]

Claudius's conventional greeting, "How fares . . . ?" resembles his address to the prince in the first court scene, but this time he uses a single kinship term. Nonetheless, "cousin" cannot restrain Hamlet's punning disruptions of relationship. Hamlet's wild punning is here more esoteric as he rejects Claudius's greeting as a social form. Hamlet's cryptic response usurps Claudius's question about how he fares and responds as if it were not a formulaic greeting, but a literal question about his diet. Hamlet's appropriation of the king's greeting reinterprets every aspect of his uses of language.

Claudius's question, like his greeting in act 1, scene 2, enacts what anthropologists call a *ritualistic phatic inquiry.* Such customary greetings are not information-seeking speech acts. They are performative genres that display and constitute social relationships. The greeting enacts a social bond that Hamlet repudiates by his bizarre answer. Using an ancient bit of folklore that chameleons eat air, Hamlet also plays on the "unnatural" folk practice of fattening degendered male roosters, capons, for feasts. Cleverly combining these motifs, Hamlet registers a complex complaint: he implies that while he is being prepared for slaughter at the court, he is being emasculated without any productive function, as if he were a capon. Unlike a capon, however, he is being stuffed only with airy promises about being heir, as if he were a chameleon.

In the flash of these allusions, Hamlet issues a coded threat. By identifying himself with the chameleon instead of the capon, he suggests that if he must eat air, he also has the protean coloring of the chameleon and can change his complexion with each breath. So the chameleon prince hints that if he is a cousin to the king, then the king is a related chameleon, one who changes his verbal complexion for each audience (Webber 1976; Calderwood 1985: 81–82). Removing Claudius's social mask, Hamlet protests the innocence of his greeting as well as any kinship with Claudius. The prince treats the salutation as a reference to eating habits and thus inverts the notion of eating as he also unbares the consuming aggression of Claudius's schemes. In refusing to take his place as cousin, and through non sequiturs denying the fictions of succession, Hamlet's punning substitutes himself as the fare for a courtly repast. Hamlet appropriates folk expressions, beliefs, and the speech of others to choose his own alterations, not to be castrated but to castrate the expressions of others.

This remarkable wordplay openly airs court hostilities over Hamlet's succession, over his being kept at court deprived of his education and independence, and now over who owns the language of the court. As puns use the paradoxicality of play, they can deny responsible or single meanings. More than other forms of wordplay, punning forms a contestive ground on which not only the interpretations of words but also the very possession of language are at stake. The struggle for possession of language represents a struggle for domination of the situation; in redefining the linguistic exchange, the punster can recast an entire social event.

Claudius tries to oppose this reduction of his speech to "nothing" (96) by refusing to accept Hamlet's reply as a reciprocal answer. His contestive reply claims that Hamlet has stolen his words. Yet Hamlet denies that he any longer possesses the king's speech. Once spoken, he implies, words are not owned. Repelling the court's policing in the form of polite greetings, Hamlet exercises play as a way to forestall politic exchange. He starves discourse by refusing to incorporate the king's language. He thus remains a socially inedible body. In the impunity of performed madness and play, Hamlet uses parodic folklore to undo official languages, carnivalizing the body politic and refusing all forms of incarnation and consumption by others.[18] This aggressive inversion of who serves whom, whose language belongs in whose mouth, and who eats whom surfaces again when Hamlet's wordplay resists another greeting by Claudius.

Following the murder of Polonius, Hamlet must be chased down and brought as a prisoner before Claudius. The king opens his third interaction with the prince with an outright interrogation, no longer bothering with courtly inquiries couched as greetings. Like all investigation in Elsinore, his direct question asks, "Who's there?" The repeated queries about social and personal identity exemplify an obsessive concern about the disposition of "the body," whether they be questions about the movements of King Hamlet's ghost, Hamlet's antic disposition of his body and manners, the place of missing majesty in Denmark, the proper rites for Ophelia's body, the "revolutions" enacted in the grave as various skulls are turned out to make room for a new tenant, or, at the end of the play, the rites enacted to make a text of Hamlet's corpse. At this point, Rosencrantz and Guildenstern have already asked Hamlet three times what he has "done with the dead body" (3.4.5, 3.4.7., 3.4.22), and as soon as he appears before Claudius, he is met by the same demand:

> Claudius: Now Hamlet, where's Polonius?
> Hamlet: At supper.
> Claudius: At supper? Where?
> Hamlet: Not where he eats, but where a is eaten. A certain convocation of politic worms are e'en at him. Your worm is your only emperor for diet: we fat all creatures else to fat us, and we fat ourselves for maggots. Your fat king and lean beggar is but variable service, two dishes, but to one table; that's the end.
> Claudius: Alas, alas.
> Hamlet: A man may fish with the worm that hath eat of a king, and eat of the fish that hath fed of that worm.
> Claudius: What dost thou mean by this?

> Hamlet: Nothing but to show you how a king may go a progress through the guts of a beggar.
>
> (4.3.16–29)[19]

Hamlet's answer functions as a riddling question, so Claudius must play Hamlet's riddling partner instead of his interrogator. When Hamlet provides the answer to his own riddle, his solution relates another of his foolish narratives, this one a homily about the future of all bodies. However evidently well-attended the king, no tributes due him can reserve his body from the table at which all other bodies are eventually served. On that plane, the body is no mystified corporate body politic but a diet for a convocation of worms. If the funeral baked meats furnished forth the marriage tables, Hamlet's inventive puns on diets, progress, worms, and convocations turn another table on Claudius. The prince invokes carnivalesque folk ideas about the recycling of life to transgress the lines of kingly protocols and progresses, lineages and hierarchies. He now transcends his earlier puns on the politic diets of capons, chameleons, and kings. Hamlet's riddle shows all fatting—whether with air or court favors—serves the same cosmic end. Hamlet's grotesque carnival humor inserted into the grim center of court discourse uses body puns to undo all courtly cover-ups of death. His antic disposition, which he says means "nothing" (l. 28), deposes the king—decomposes the mystified two bodies and all polite discourse in a carnivalesque bodylore of the lower regions.

Hamlet's antic disposition uses evasion as a way to play back to the court a mirror of its own depositions, but it gradually changes to a more direct acceptance of the body and its mortality as his confrontations with dead bodies lead him toward a more fatalistic and less self-conscious engagement with action. Before he achieves that sense of responsibility for his deeds, he relies on his puns about bodies to turn tragic mistakes into double takes. He tries to undo, through language, the finality of death, in a different kind of punning with endings. For example, when he discovers he has killed Polonius behind the screen, instead of the spying king he expected, Hamlet's puns screen the finality of his mistake:

> Thou wretched, rash, intruding fool, farewell. I took thee for thy better. Take thy fortune.
>
> (3.4.31–32)[20]

In the deliberate mistaking of these puns, Hamlet can reinterpret but cannot reverse the finality of death. Hamlet's ironic compliment to his unintended victim, "I took thee for thy better," (or "betters," as in F) and his deliberately ambiguous farewell, "Take thy fortune," create a cynical parallel between his taking of Polonius's life and Polonius's now passive ability to "take" for himself the fortune that Hamlet has given him. Yet in this grotesquely punning farewell, Hamlet's grief also may be evident.

The polyvalence of the puns admits the tragic difficulty of knowing how to take anything cloaked behind the interventions of signs. Yet the puns, in a form of serious play, would make this tragic mis-take deliberate and the object of wit. These puns name the recurrent predicaments of the play: how to deal with the violent "taking" of lives, how to know "who is there," and how to position oneself with others whom one fears to be "like." Issues such as these become critical at moments of meeting or separation. Hamlet's farewell to Polonius puns on all the differences and likenesses that Hamlet keeps trying to draw.

Finally only Polonius's corpse is left to take away. As Hamlet does so, he puns again:

> Mother, good night. Indeed, this counsellor
> Is now most till, most secret, and most grave,
> Who was in life a foolish prating knave.
> Come sir, to draw toward an end with you.
> Good night mother.
>
> *Exit Hamlet tugging in Polonius.* (3.4.214–18)[21]

The circumspect "grave" counselor into whom Hamlet has transformed the prating knave is now full of gravity. Hamlet himself must lug the body away, a fact that the unusually vivid stage direction in the Folio makes clear. However lightly he puns, his wordplay cannot relieve the heavy task of disposing of this body. The job remains a reality he must physically "draw toward an end." The theatrical actuality of the dragging out the body of Polonius, like the actuality of ceremonially carrying on Ophelia's body (both live actors playing dead) for her maimed rites, places the real gravity of the body centrally next to the consoling rites and puns that would reinterpret death for cultural recuperation.

Hamlet learns this best in the graveyard when he confronts the dead body as debris, as bones to be jowled to the ground. There he meets his match in the clown/gravedigger, who outwits Hamlet in the literalizing mistakes and carnivalesque perspectives Hamlet has used to discompose others. The returned prince opens his exchange with the gravedigger with a question-greeting we now recognize as typical in *Hamlet*:

> Hamlet: Whose grave's this sirrah?
> Clown: Mine, sir.
> *(Sings)*
> O, a pit of clay for to be made
> for such a guest is meet.
> Hamlet: I think it be thine indeed, for thou liest in't.
> Clown: You lie out on't, sir, and therefore 'tis not yours. For my part, I do not lie in't, yet it is mine.
> Hamlet: Thou dost lie in't, to be in't and say 'tis thine. 'Tis for the dead, not for the quick: therefore thou liest.
> Clown: 'Tis a quick lie, sir, 'twill away again from me to you.
>
> (5.1.99–108)[22]

When language and death blur the boundaries between what is a quick lie and what lies dead, wordplay gains antic mastery over the loss of distinctive meanings, possessions, identities, classes, occupations, and genders:

> Hamlet: What man dost thou dig it for?
> Clown: For no man, sir.
> Hamlet: What woman then?
> Clown: For none neither.
> Hamlet: Who is to be buried in't?
> Clown: One that was a woman, sir; but rest her soul, she's dead.
>
> (5.1.109–14)

The gravedigger's dead literalism paradoxically forbids reductive interpretations. His mundane replies expose the worldly vanity in our fashioning of signs. Like the stubborn soil and the irremediable fact of death, the material humor of the clown buries differences in a gay sameness that decomposes fine distinctions. The lower realm of the grave triumphs over the privileged level of values and social power, uncrowning its differences. As the gravedigger makes the body the fundamental site for the unmaking of absolute and relative meanings, so his surprising wordplay overturns any absolute sense, making the materiality of sound the fundamental problem in the making of significance.

In his last speech, as he bids farewell to us all, Hamlet has at last committed the bodily act of regicide by accepting his own body and its irreversible actions. He is also dying, surrounded by a stageful of dead bodies (four people are killed by poison within the last ten minutes of the play). As he dies, his concern is again with righting the body and time through the lineage of meanings, shows, and stories that will succeed him:

> You that are pale, and tremble at this chance,
> That are but mutes or audience to this act,
> Had I but time, as this fell sergeant death
> Is strict in his arrest, oh I could tell you—
> But let it be. Horatio, I am dead,
> Thou livest; report me and my cause aright
> To the unsatisfied.
>
> (5.2.313–19)[23]

Refusing this job as orator, for which his name destines him, Horatio reaches for the poisoned wine to join his beloved prince in death. Hamlet must again implore him:

> O God, Horatio, what a wounded name,
> Things standing thus unknown, shall live behind me!
> If thou didst ever hold me in thy heart,
> Absent thee from felicity awhile,
> And in this harsh world draw thy breath in pain
> To tell my story.
>
> (5.2.323–27)[24]

Hamlet's request has clearly recast the ghost's plea for filial revenge as a way to remember the mutilated body of time, state, and of the king's name. The body, breathing in pain, will use that same breath to speak. Life and speech are simultaneously necessary to heal the wounded name and reverse the history of murderous revenge. A new succession, of retold stories, requires actors to live; this new ethic replaces the lineages of revenge, which doom actors to retributive deaths. "To tell" can work as a pun meaning both "to relate" and "to count." Narrative telling will thus replace the arithmetic of the ledger book as forgiveness and play transform the law of talion as a way of telling the past. In revenge, no count makes the score even; in the storytelling of this play, the endlessness of retaliation changes into the open-endedness of related stories as a way to heal the social body.

Yet before Horatio's story can "satisfy" those who are "pale and tremble" at "things standing thus unknown," Fortinbras orders that another voice speak for Hamlet's wounded body:

> Let four captains
> Bear Hamlet like a soldier to the stage,
> For he was likely, had he been put on,
> To have proved most royal; and for his passage,
> The soldier's music and the rite of war
> Speak loudly for him.
> Take up the bodies. Such a sight as this
> Becomes the field, but here shows much amiss.
> Go bid the soldiers shoot.
>
> (5.2.374–82)[25]

The new ruler takes possession of the corpse to write his own values on the body politic. He erects his own hierarchies and rites to set time right. Fortinbras, whose name is a body epithet, strong-in-arms, ends the play by ordering a ritual that will raise Hamlet's body to another stage. This procession creates a legible text: the soldier's rites bear away the actor's body representing Hamlet's newly mystified corpse, which Fortinbras would use to generate a new lineage of meanings in his military image (Charney 1969: 19–21).

Whatever takes place at that offstage platform on which Hamlet is to be shown can only be imagined. In that unseen potentiality, the multiple meanings of the show we have watched will always intersect in a contest for the rite/right to authority. There puns, stories, play and carnival vision will compete with these stated constructions of value. By the close of the play, the question of how to "take up the body"—physically and morally, verbally and symbolically—has been so thoroughly complicated by the puns on bodies and how and where to "take" them, that no stage, just as no political realm, whatever its embodied metaphors may be, can fully contain the body's dispositions. The dramatized attempt to confine those meanings has been the tragic problem the puns encapsulate through their decomposition of the openings, closings, and boundaries of social and bodied forms.

Notes

1. The list of works considering puns in *Hamlet* nearly coincides with the list of works about *Hamlet,* but some of the most significant for this study have been: Sigurd Burckhardt, *Shakespearean Meanings* (Princeton, NJ: Princeton Univ. Press, 1968), 24–26; James Calderwood, *To Be and Not to Be: Negation and Metadrama in "Hamlet"* (New York: Columbia Univ. Press, 1985); Maurice Charney, *Style in Hamlet* (Princeton, NJ: Princeton Univ. Press, 1969); Lawrence Danson, *Tragic Alphabet: Shakespeare's Drama of Language* (New Haven, CT: Yale Univ. Press, 1974); Madeleine Doran, *Shakespeare's Dramatic Language* (Madison: Univ. of Wisconsin Press, 1976); Margaret Ferguson, "*Hamlet:* Letters and Spirits," in *Shakespeare and the Question of Theory,* ed. Geoffrey Hartman and Patricia Parker (New York: Methuen, 1985), 292–309; Andrew Gurr, *Hamlet and the Distracted Globe* (Totowa: Humanities Press, 1978); Terence Hawkes, "Telmah," in *Shakespeare and the Question of Theory,* 310–32; Frankie Rubinstein, *A Dictionary of Shakespeare's Sexual Puns and Their Significance* (Salem, NH: Salem House, Merrimack Publisher's Circle, 1984), 121–26; and David Wilbern, "Shakespeare's Nothing," *Representing Shakespeare,* ed. Coppelia Kahn and Murray Schwartz (Baltimore: Johns Hopkins Univ. Press, 1980), 244–63.
   David Bevington's *Action Is Eloquence: Shakespeare's Language of Gesture* (Cambridge, MA: Harvard Univ. Press, 1984) does consider many of these issues in theatrical terms but does not focus on body imagery per se, or on language play; Alan Dessen's *Elizabethan Stage Conventions and Modern Interpreters* (Cambridge: Cambridge Univ. Press, 1984) emphasizes not only actor's bodies and movements but also other visible stage properties as he examines the production of meaning through physicality and iconographic imagery on stage; in his discussion of several important image patterns in *Hamlet,* he also does not center on body images or wordplay.
2. Many works consider the primary documents and their gender implications, and among the most important for this study are Norbert Elias, *The Civilizing Process* 1, *The History of Manners,* trans. Edmund Jephcott (New York: Urizon Books, 1978); Suzanne W. Hull, *Chaste, Silent, and Obedient: English Books for Women 1475–1640* (San Marino: Huntington Library Press, 1982); Ann Jones, "Nets and Bridles: Early Modern Conduct Books and Sixteenth Century Women's Lyrics," in *The Ideology of Conduct: Essays in Literature and the History of Sexuality,* ed. Nancy Armstrong and Leonard Tennenhouse (New York: Methuen, 1987), 39–72; Ruth Kelso, *Doctrine for the Lady of the Renaissance* (Urbana: Univ. of Illinois Press, 1956); Ian Maclean, *The Renaissance Notion of Woman: A Study in the Fortunes of Scholasticism and Medical Science in*

European Intellectual Life (New York: Cambridge Univ. Press, 1983); Peter Stallybrass, "Patriarchal Territories: The Body Enclosed," in *Rewriting the Renaissance: The Discourse of Sexual Difference in Early Modern Europe,* ed. Margaret Ferguson et al. (Chicago: Univ. of Chicago Press, 1986), 123–42; Keith Thomas, "The Double Standard," *Journal of the History of Ideas* 20 (1959): 195–217; and Linda Woodbridge, *Women and the English Renaissance: Literature and the Nature of Womanhood, 1540–1620* (Urbana: Univ. of Illinois Press, 1984).

3. Other influential works that treat the semiotics of the female body in Renaissance literature include Leonard Barkan, *Nature's Work of Art: The Human Body as Image of the World* (New Haven, CT: Yale Univ. Press, 1975) and Nancy Vickers, "Diana Described: Scattered Women and Scattered Rhyme," *Critical Inquiry* 8, no. 2 (Winter 1981): 265–79.
4. This and all subsequent quotations from the text will use the *New Cambridge Shakespeare,* ed. Philip Edwards (Cambridge: Cambridge Univ. Press, 1985). References are to act, scene, and line. Like most modern editions, this is a composite text, combining and correcting the three distinctive early printed texts (no manuscript exists) of the play. The first, Quarto One (Q1), 1603, is much shorter than the others, and it has been argued—although this is a controversial point—that it is an abridged version of Shakespeare's play produced for playing in the provinces. The second, Quarto Two (Q2), is dated 1604 in some copies and 1605 in others, and is often considered to be the most reliable version; that it is based on a Shakespeare manuscript, however, remains a speculative point. This is the text on which Edwards most often relies. The third early printed text appeared in the first collection of the dramatic works of Shakespeare, the First Folio, 1623 (F). This shorter version is missing several passages from Q2 (adding up to 222 lines), but adding a few not in Q2 (totaling 83 lines). Current textual controversies—about the relationship of these texts to one another, to Shakespeare's original papers, and to the theater—represent very important methodological and epistemological problems (see Edwards's introduction to the Cambridge edition and recent essays by Trousdale, Urkowitz, and Werstine listed in this chapter's References). I will, therefore, note textual differences, because they may be significant in any interpretation one makes of the text, but I will comment on these variations only if I see them as especially relevant to this article.
   In this quotation, "Solid" is in F; "sallied" appears in Q2 and Q1.4. This line, which the editor has divided (to create a complex metrical unity with other phrases), appears as one line in both Q2 and F.
5. Line 35: "my" is in Q2 and Q1; "mine" appears in F.
6. Line 1: "Who's" is in F; "whose" appears in Q2.
7. This line, which the editor has divided (to create a complex metrical unity with other phrases), appears as one line in both Q2 and F.
8. Line 207: "honourable lord" is in F; "Lord" appears in Q2. In the same line: "most humbly" is in F; no adverb appears in Q2.
9. Line 209: "will" is in F; "will not" appears in Q2. Line 210: "Except my life, except my life, except my life" is in Q2; "except my life, my life" appears in F.
10. Line 49: "and so" is in F; "so" appears in Q2.

11. The famous stage direction for Ophelia's entrance, in Q1, "Enter Ofelia playing on a Lute, and her haire downe swinging," provides a vivid set of stage body images that Dessen, 36–38, has identified as conventional on the Elizabethan stage to signify madness, particularly female distraction. Elaine Showalter, "Representing Ophelia: Women, Madness, and Responsibilities of Feminist Criticism," in *Shakespeare and The Question of Theory,* 77–94, offers a fine account of the ways visual images of Ophelia's madness as marked by her body, gesture, and dress have formed paradigms for the embodiment of female madness in English and American history.
12. Horatio provides this information in F; a gentleman provides it in Q2; the report is absent from Q; in either case, a male advises Gertrude that Ophelia's speech is a "nothing."
13. Line 183: "affliction" is in F; "afflictions" appears in Q2.
14. Lines 101–2, from "Hamlet: I mean" to "lord," are in F; the lines do not appear in Q2.
15. For questions of pronunciation and puns, see Fausto Cercignani, *Shakespeare's Works and Elizabethan Pronunciation* (New York: Oxford Univ. Press, 1980); Eric Partridge, *Shakespeare's Bawdy: A Literary and Psychological Essay and a Comprehensive Glossary* (New York: E. P. Dutton, 1960).
   Also see discussions of the specific term *nothing* in E. A. M. Colman, *The Dramatic Use of Bawdy in Shakespeare* (London: Longman Group, 1974), 15–18, 163–64, 204–5; Hilda Hulme, *Explorations in Shakespeare's Language: Some Problems of Lexical Meaning in the Dramatic Text* (London: Longman's, 1962), 78–80, 136–37; Helge Kokeritz, *Shakespeare's Pronunciation* (New Haven, CT: Yale Univ. Press, 1953); M. M. Mahood, *Shakespeare's Wordplay* (1957; reprint, London: Methuen, 1965), 183; Frankie Rubinstein, *A Dictionary of Shakespeare's Sexual Puns and Their Significance* (London: Macmillan Press, 1984), 171–73; and David Wilbern, "Shakespeare's Nothing," in *Representing Shakespeare,* ed. Coppelia Kahn and Murray Schwartz (Baltimore: Johns Hopkins Univ. Press, 1980), 244–63.
16. See also Carol Thomas Neely, "Documents in Madness," *Shakespeare Quarterly* 42 (1991): 315–38.
17. Line 87: the Folio line reads, "No, nor mine. Now my Lord" (Hamlet here would probably turn to address Polonius). Q2 reads: "No, nor mine now my Lord."
18. For discussions of carnival language and images in literature of the early modern period, see works such as Barbara Babcock, "The Novel and the Carnival World: An Essay in Honor of Joe Doherty," *Modern Language Notes* 89, no. 6 (1974): 911–37; Mikhail Bakhtin, *Rabelais and His World,* trans. Hélène Iswolsky (Cambridge, Mass: MIT Press, 1968); Michael Bristol, *Carnival and Theatre: Plebeian Culture and the Structure of Authority in Renaissance England* (New York: Methuen, 1985). Also see my article, "Toward a Theory of Play and the Carnivalesque in *Hamlet,*" *Hamlet Studies* 13, no. 1–2 (1991): 25–49.
19. Line 19: "a is eaten" is in Q2; "he is eaten" appears in F. Line 20: "politic" is in Q2 and not in F. Line 21: "ourselves" is in Q2; "our selfe" appears in F. Lines 24–26: From "Claudius: Alas . . . that worm" is in Q2 but not F.

20. Line 32: "better" is in Q2; "betters" appears in F.
21. Line 216, "fool" is in F; Q2 reads "most foolish." The remarkably vivid stage direction is from F; Q2 reads "Exit."
22. Line 99: "Sirrah" is in Q2; "sir" appears in F. Line 101: "Oh" is "O" in F; "Or" appears in Q2. Line 102, "For . . . meet" is only in F and does not appear in Q2. Line 104: "'Tis" is in Q2; "it is" appears in F. Line 105: "yet" is in Q2; "and yet" appears in F. Line 106: "'tis thine" is in F; "it is thine" appears in Q2.
23. Line 318: "cause aright" is in Q2; "causes right" appears in F.
24. Line 323: "O God" is in Q2; "oh good" appears in F. Line 324: "shall live" is in F; "shall I leave" appears in Q2.
25. Line 377: "royal" is "royall" in Q2 and Q1; "royally" appears in F. Line 378: "rite" is "right" in Q2; "rites" appears in F. Line 380: "bodies" is in Q2; "body" appears in F.

References

Armstrong, Nancy, and Leonard Tennenhouse, eds. 1989. *The violence of representation: Literature and the history of violence.* London: Routledge.

Axton, Marie. 1977. *The queen's two bodies: Drama and the Elizabethan succession.* London: Royal Historical Society.

Babcock, Barbara. 1974. The novel and the carnival world: An essay in honor of Joe Doherty. *Modern Language Notes* 89 (6): 911–37.

Bakhtin, Mikhail. 1968. *Rabelais and his world.* Trans. Hélène Iswolsky. Cambridge, MA: MIT Press.

Barkan, Leonard. 1975. *Nature's work of art: The human body as image of the world.* New Haven, CT: Yale Univ. Press.

Barker, Francis. 1984. *The tremulous private body: Essays on subjection.* New York: Methuen.

Bateson, Gregory. 1972. *Steps to an ecology of mind.* New York: Ballantine Books.

Bevington, David. 1984. *Action is eloquence: Shakespeare's language of gesture.* Cambridge: Harvard Univ. Press.

Bristol, Michael. 1985. *Carnival and theatre: Plebeian culture and the structure of authority in Renaissance England.* New York: Methuen.

Burckhardt, Sigurd. 1968. *Shakespearean meanings.* Princeton, NJ: Princeton Univ. Press.

Calderwood, James. 1985. *To be and not to be: Negation and metadrama in "Hamlet."* New York: Columbia Univ. Press.

Cercignani, Fausto. 1980. *Shakespeare's works and Elizabethan pronunciation.* New York: Oxford Univ. Press.

Charney, Maurice. 1969. *Style in Hamlet.* Princeton, NJ: Princeton Univ. Press.

———. 1988. *Hamlet's fictions.* London: Routledge.

Clemen, Wolfgang. 1951. *The development of Shakespeare's Imagery.* Cambridge, Mass: Harvard Univ. Press.

Colman, E. A. M. 1974. *The dramatic use of bawdy in Shakespeare.* London: Longman Group.

Danson, Lawrence. 1974. *Tragic alphabet: Shakespeare's drama of language.* New Haven, CT: Yale Univ. Press.

de Grazia, Margreta. 1978. Shakespeare's view of language: An historical perspective. *Shakespeare Quarterly* 29: 374–88.

Dessen, Alan. 1984. *Elizabethan stage conventions and modern interpreters.* Cambridge: Cambridge Univ. Press.

Donawerth, Jane L. 1984. *Shakespeare and the sixteenth century study of language.* Urbana: Univ. of Illinois Press.

Doran, Madeleine. 1976. *Shakespeare's dramatic language.* Madison: Univ. of Wisconsin Press.

Douglas, Mary. 1966. *Purity and danger: An analysis of pollution and taboo.* New York: Praeger Press.

Edwards, Philip, ed. 1985. *Hamlet, prince of Denmark.* By William Shakespeare. Cambridge: Cambridge Univ. Press.

Elias, Norbert. 1978. *The history of manners.* Trans. Edmund Jephcott. Vol. 1. New York: Urizon Books.

Ferguson, Margaret. 1985. *Hamlet:* Letters and spirits. In *Shakespeare and the question of theory.* Ed. Hartman and Parker, 292–309.

Geertz, Clifford. 1973. Religion as a cultural system. In *The interpretation of cultures.* 87–125. New York: Basic Books.

Goldberg, Jonathan. 1988. Hamlet's hand. *Shakespeare Quarterly* 39 (3): 307 -27.

Gorfain, Phyllis. 1991. Toward a theory of play and the carnivalesque in *Hamlet. Hamlet Studies* 13 (1–2): 25–49.

Greenblatt, Stephen. 1988. Fiction and Friction. In *Shakespearean negotiations: The circulation of social energy in Renaissance England,* 66–93. Berkeley: Univ. of California Press.

Gurr, Andrew. 1978. *Hamlet and the distracted globe.* Totowa: Humanities Press.

Hartman, Geoffrey, and Patricia Parker, eds. 1985. *Shakespeare and the question of theory.* New York: Methuen.

Hawkes, Terence. 1985. Telmah. In *Shakespeare and the question of theory.* Ed. Hartman and Parker, 310–32.

Hull, Suzanne W. 1982. *Chaste, silent, and obedient: English books for women 1475–1640.* San Marino: Huntington Library Press.

Hulme, Hilda. 1962. *Explorations in Shakespeare's language: Some problems of lexical meaning in the dramatic text.* London: Longman's.

Hunt, John. 1988. A thing of nothing: The catastrophic body in *Hamlet. Shakespeare Quarterly* 39 (1): 27–44.

Jenkins, Harold. Ed. 1982. *Hamlet.* By William Shakespeare. London: Methuen.

Jones, Ann. 1987. Nets and bridles: early modern conduct books and sixteenth century women's lyrics. In *The ideology of conduct: Essays in literature and the history of sexuality.* Ed. Nancy Armstrong and Leonard Tennenhouse, 39–72. New York: Methuen.

Kantorowicz, Ernst H. 1957. *The king's two bodies.* Princeton, NJ: Princeton Univ. Press.

Kelso, Ruth. 1956. *Doctrine for the lady of the Renaissance.* Urbana: Univ. of Illinois Press.

Kokeritz, Helge. 1953. *Shakespeare's pronunciation.* New Haven, CT: Yale Univ. Press.

Maclean, Ian. 1983. *The Renaissance notion of woman: A study in the fortunes of scholasticism and medical science in European intellectual life.* New York: Cambridge Univ. Press.

Mahood, M. M. 1957. *Shakespeare's wordplay.* London: Methuen.

Muir, Kenneth. 1964. Imagery and symbolism in *Hamlet. Etudes Anglaises* 17: 353–63.

Partridge, Eric. 1960. *Shakespeare's bawdy: A literary and psychological essay and a comprehensive glossary.* New York: E. P. Dutton.

Rosenblatt, Jason. 1978. Aspects of the incest problem in *Hamlet. Shakespeare Quarterly* 29: 349–64.

Rubinstein, Frankie. 1984. *A dictionary of Shakespeare's sexual puns and their significance.* Salem, NH: Salem House, Merrimack Publisher's Circle.

Showalter, Elaine. 1985. Representing Ophelia: Women, madness and the responsibilities of feminist criticism. In *Shakespeare and the question of theory.* Ed. Hartman and Parker, 77–94.

Spurgeon, Caroline F. E. 1935. *Shakespeare's imagery and what it tells us.* Cambridge: Cambridge Univ. Press.

Stallybrass, Peter. 1986. Patriarchal territories: The body enclosed. In *Rewriting the Renaissance: The discourse of sexual difference in early modern Europe.* Ed. Margaret Ferguson, Maureen Quilligan, et. al., 123–42. Chicago: Univ. of Chicago Press.

States, Bert O. 1973. The word pictures in *Hamlet. Hudson Review* 26 (3): 510–22.

Tennenhouse, Leonard. 1987. Violence done to women on the Renaissance stage. In *The violence of representation,* ed. Armstrong and Tennenhouse, 77–97.

Thomas, Keith. 1959. The double standard. *Journal of the History of Ideas* 20: 195–217.

Trousdale, Marion. 1990. A second look at critical bibliography and the acting of plays. *Shakespeare Quarterly* 41 (1): 87–96.

Turner, Victor. 1974. *Dramas, fields, and metaphors: Symbolic action in human society.* Ithaca: Cornell Univ. Press.

Urkowitz, Steven. 1986. "Well-sayd olde mole": Burying three *Hamlets* in modern editions. In *Shakespeare study today.* Ed. Georgeanne Ziegler, 37–70. New York: AMS Press.

———. 1987. "Thy strange mutations make us hate thee": Textual and thematic variants in Shakespeare's multiple text plays. Unpublished essay.

———. 1988. Good news about "bad" quartos. In *"Bad" Shakespeare: Revaluations of the Shakespeare canon.* Ed. Maurice Charney, 189–206. Madison, NJ: Fairleigh Dickinson Univ. Press.

Vickers, Nancy. 1981. Diana described: Scattered women and scattered rhyme. *Critical Inquiry* 8 (2): 265–79.

Webber, Joan. 1976. *Hamlet* and the freeing of the mind. In *English Renaissance drama: Essays in honor of Madeleine Doran.* Ed. Standish Henning, Robert Kimbrough, and Richard Knowles, 76–99. Carbondale: Univ. of Southern Illinois Press.

Wentersdorf, Karl P. 1978. *Hamlet:* Ophelia's "Long Purples." *Shakespeare Quarterly* 29: 413–67.

———. 1983–84. Animal symbolism in Shakespeare's *Hamlet. Comparative Drama* 17(4): 348–82.

Werstine, Paul. The textual mystery of *Hamlet. Shakespeare Quarterly* 39(1): 1–26.

———. 1990. Narratives about printed Shakespearean texts: "Foul papers" and "bad quartos." *Shakespeare Quarterly* 41(1): 65–86.

Wilbern, David. 1980. Shakespeare's Nothing. In *Representing Shakespeare.* Ed. Coppelia Kahn and Murray Schwartz, 244–63. Baltimore: Johns Hopkins Univ. Press.

Woodbridge, Linda. 1984. *Women and the English Renaissance: Literature and the nature of womanhood, 1540–1620.* Urbana: Univ. of Illinois Press.

4. Drinking the Blood of Childbirth: The Reincorporation of the Dead in Hakka Funeral Ritual

Maxine Miska

Because all societies do not have the same concept of the body and its extension in the world, it follows that they do not have the same concept of what happens to the body at death. In fact, the shape of death in a society is like a shadow, a projection of its ethos. As Richard Huntington and Peter Metcalf point out, "The issue of death throws into relief the most important cultural values by which people live their lives and evaluate their experiences. Life becomes transparent against the background of death, and fundamental social and cultural issues are revealed" (Huntington and Metcalf 1979: 2). Furthermore, the disposition of the body and whatever nonmaterial parts inhabit it is related to the finality with which death is viewed, and the degree of interaction between living and dead. In some societies death is not considered an instantaneous break with the living but an ongoing metamorphosized relationship, a process of successive transformations over time of the constitutive parts of what had been a person.

In traditional China, death is considered a reorganization into new configurations of the yin-yang balances that comprise the body.[1] Among the Hakka-speaking Chinese living in Taiwan, death does not mark the dissolution of family bonds, but their transformation.[2] In this patrilineal, ancestor-worshipping society, the dead become ancestors who are worshipped and nurtured through sacrifices by the family, and as ancestors, they bestow blessings upon their descendants.[3]

In order to become an ancestor, a person's body at death undergoes a metamorphosis: it separates into various components that undergo further transformations. The corpse is buried in an individual grave for five to seven years, during which time the polluting aspect of the body, the flesh, disappears into the earth. Then the potent parts of the corpse, the bones, are exhumed.[4] The bones are reburied in a collective tomb, where they will bring blessings to the family by collecting the cosmic currents flowing through the earth.[5]

In addition to the corpse, ten souls are released at death. Seven of these, called *phak,* return to the earth after death, but unless they take on demonic form, they do not participate in the ongoing relations between living and dead. The three remaining souls, *fun,* are the aspects of a person that continue after death. They correspond to the simultaneous paths that a dead person takes on the road to ancestorhood. One of the souls is a continuation of the personality that must pass through the sufferings of hell, be judged, and then reincarnated as a new person. A second resides permanently as an ancestor in the ancestor hall and heaven. This soul is prayed to during home sacrifices and becomes part of the corporate ancestor that the family worships. A third soul resides at the grave and is associated with the worship of graves at the Qing Ming festival, when families bring sacrifices to the family tombs and clean up the graves.

These potent aspects of the body after death—corpse and souls—can be both beneficial and dangerous. For example, members of the family whose horoscopes clash with the time of encoffining must absent themselves or risk being harmed by the proceedings. If the corpse is not handled properly, if the burial and the coffin are not comfortable (if, for example, the coffin does not contain sufficient layers of cloth), if the proper amenities are not provided to the spirit through paper facsimiles of money, food, clothing, and vehicles (burned as a way of transporting them to the spirit world), the realignment of living and dead, the process of establishing a beneficial ancestor, will not proceed smoothly. There may be sickness, bad luck, or infertility in the family.

The task of the funeral ceremony is to see that these aspects of the person are reordered in such a fashion that the relationship is favorable to both living and dead. The funeral ceremony involves a series of ritual dramatizations led by Taoist priests that transfer the various parts of a person's multiple soul and body into nondangerous relationships with the living. Through these various rituals, the souls find their proper abodes and the family helps their dead relative through the punishments of the underworld to rebirth. These rituals enable the dead person, both corpse and spirit, to be transformed into a beneficial ancestor rather than an unhappy, troublesome ghost.

This chapter focuses on one specific ritual within the Hakka funeral ceremony that is always performed for a woman who has borne children. It is called "breaking the blood bowl" (*ta hiet-phun*). In her passage through the underworld after death, any woman who has given birth is imprisoned in a pool of blood. This is the blood that flowed from her body into the earth after childbirth. This blood is considered polluting to the earth, and the woman will suffer in the pool unless she is helped by her descendants.[6]

The ritual, as I saw it performed, involves setting up a small stool in the courtyard, under which sand is piled. Painted duck eggs and colored pennants are arranged in the sand. A bowl filled with wine is placed in the center of the sand pile beneath the stool.[7] This stool with its flags and sand represent a fortress guarded by demons of the underworld. Imprisoned within the fortress is the soul of the dead woman, wallowing in a pool of blood, represented by the bowl of wine. In order to secure her release, her descendants drink the bowl of wine, symbolically drinking the blood in the pool of hell. Once done, her soul is released from this torture and her passage through the underworld to rebirth is expedited.

The Symbolic Meaning of Women's Blood in Hakka Folk Religion

The blood of childbirth has a specific meaning and function within the ritual itself. In this ritual, living and dead are linked together in order to be irrevocably separated. They are linked by building a ritual model, the bowl of wine, and establishing a magical equivalence between it and the blood pool in hell. Drinking the wine is equivalent to draining the blood pool. The completion of this act breaks a link between living and dead—the link of the blood of childbirth. This blood is anomalous; it belongs neither to mother nor child, yet it was once part of both. The blood was absorbed into the earth and thus into the underworld. By means of the ritual, the blood is symbolically reincorporated into the descendants. All corporeal remains of the deceased are now fully segregated into the grave or transformed into part of the living, and the spiritual aspects of the soul can move onward to rebirth.

Wine is used in other contexts within Chinese folk religion as a means of neutralizing or removing negative influences. Emily Ahern describes the function of wine in the funeral ceremony for expunging parts of the corpse and preventing the dead from returning to harm the living: "In the rites of second burial held six or seven years after death, if the flesh on the body has not decayed, wine is spilt onto the corpse to make the flesh rot. In the funeral ceremony, wine is applied to eradicate the presence of the dead as a corpse among the living, for the rite of pouring wine immediately precedes the removal of the coffin from the graveyard" (Ahern 1974: 298–99). The blood bowl ritual is the opposite of childbirth. In birth the excorporation of blood gives life. In the breaking the blood bowl, the incorporation of blood by the children gives death, that is, allows the soul to move on to successive existences.

Menstrual blood, which the Hakka treat the same as the blood of childbirth, is considered dirty blood and is buried or put in latrines to be incorporated into the earth. The earth is considered dirty itself. The rivers, too, are polluted by women washing clothes contaminated by these discharges. I heard one story of a woman who while walking outside suddenly miscarried, filling a stream with her blood. It was believed that she was subsequently punished by the river god with insanity. Like many polluting substances, menstrual blood is both powerful and dangerous (Douglas 1966: 116). A menstruating woman is unclean and cannot pray to the gods. According to Elliott (1955: 48–49), if a menstruating woman is present at certain ceremonies involving the possession of a *dang-ki* (male spirit medium) by the gods, the success of the ritual is placed in jeopardy.

In an essay entitled "The Power and Pollution of Chinese Women," Ahern explores the question of why women are considered polluting (1975: 193–214). She reasons that a woman's fertility increases the family by bringing descendants to it, but it also threatens the unity of the extended family by creating children who are loyal to their mother and might be persuaded to break off from the extended family. Women are outsiders from the viewpoint of a patrilineal system, and are therefore both a necessity and threat to its continuance.

Ahern also finds that the polluting properties of death are similar to those of blood; mourners are prevented from praying to the gods, and the ancestor tablets and images of the gods are covered during the funeral period to prevent their contamination by pollution emanating from the corpse. Following Mary Douglas's analysis, pollution involves things being out of place, crossing boundaries, out of order (1966: 12–16). The gods, who represent order, are very sensitive to pollution. Ahern finds that the higher gods are invariably worshipped by men, whereas the lower gods and ghosts (who are considered unclean) are worshipped by women, who are themselves periodically unclean. The corpse leaving the family is a polluting object, and care is taken that the dead person is reintegrated as an ancestor in an orderly fashion and so does not become a hungry ghost with no one to take care of it (the epitome of disorder). In this system, however, birth is more polluting than death because it involves crossing both family boundaries (increasing membership) and bodily boundaries (through the mother's vagina). The existential dilemma expressed through pollution and its close association with birth and death is, according to Ahern (1975: 190), "How can we keep families pure and homogeneous and their members united and loyal when, in order to grow, they need outsiders (women with competing loyalties and children whose loyalties are unformed) and when, in addition, all family members must eventually die?"

Ahern adds that

> it is no accident that women rather than men are considered outsiders, and that the children women they bear must be anchored to their families by elaborate ritual means. It is because the kinship system is focused on male lines of descent that women are depicted on the boundaries, breaking in as strangers. It may be events that are polluting rather than women *per se,* but polluting events are events that intrude new people or remove old ones in a male-oriented kinship system. (Ahern 1975: 213)[8]

Although Ahern does not believe that men intentionally use the negative representation of a woman's reproductive power as a way of obscuring its importance, she does mention the blood bowl ritual as a striking example of the negative transformation of an essential and a valued event, one that pays an inverted tribute to the importance of women's reproductive power.

The Story of "Mu-lian Saves His Mother"

As one might expect, this underlying contradiction between women as a necessity to the continuance of the family and a threat to its patrilineal focus is reflected in the major myth connected with the blood bowl ceremony. When I asked informants specific questions about the funeral rituals, they volunteered the explanation that all funerals must imitate the myth "Mu-lian Saves His Mother." Others mentioned Mu-lian as both a general response to why funeral rituals are performed and an explanation of the blood bowl ceremony: "When a person dies, we must perform funeral rituals. Those who don't know, ask, 'Why do we do these rituals? What good does it do?' One who knows, says, 'Why do we do funerals?' It is because of the breaking of the blood bowl. She who bore us, large and small, so that after dying she won't be drowned in the blood pool. Like 'Mu-lian Saves His Mother,' we undergo great difficulties for her.

Mu-lian was a Buddhist priest who in popular folklore descended into hell in order to save his mother from the tortures of the underworld. In some versions of the tale, such as the one collected by Wolfram Eberhard, the mother had been greedy in life and had killed and eaten many animals. After death she is severely punished for these transgressions. As soon as Mu-lian brings his mother back to the earth, she pulls a carrot up and eats it to satisfy her appetite. Mu-lian, fearing his work will be undone, cuts off his finger and inserts it in place of the carrot, accounting now for the red color of carrots (Eberhard 1965: 8–9). The cutting off of a part of the body for the sake of one's parent occurs in other Chinese stories of filial piety and alludes to the Confucian idea that one's body is a gift from and belongs to one's parents.

In a different version of this story, which I collected from a Taoist priest who performed the blood bowl ritual at local funeral ceremonies, Mu-lian's mother was a devout Buddhist vegetarian tricked by Mu-lian's younger brother into eating dog's meat disguised in a meat bun. Consequently Mu-lian becomes a Buddhist adept and uses his techniques to open the gates of hell and save his mother. He lessens her sufferings, just as the purpose of the funeral ceremony is to lessen the sufferings of the soul. Werner quotes a literary source of the story of Mu-lian, involving a vegetarian mother who gradually began to like meat and finally killed and ate the house dog. Mu-lian rescued her through the intervention of many monks and the application of spiritual power (Werner 1969: 309). Mu-lian serves as a prototype for the male Taoists priests that officiate at the funeral ceremony. This, then, is the overt meaning of why "Mu-lian Saves His Mother" is an explanation of the funeral ceremony.

In more than one version of the Mu-lian story, including the ones I collected, dog's flesh is mentioned as part of the mother's transgression. It is interesting that dog's meat is specified, because the consumption of any kind of meat would constitute a breach of vegetarianism. There is a clear association of dogs with ghosts and demons. From ancient times dogs' blood and bodies have been used for exorcism (De Groot 1972, 6: 1007–9), According to Hakka informants, dog's blood is used to exorcise ghosts, and according to Ahern (1975: 197), "black dog's blood" is a euphemism for menses and is used for this purpose.

In Dore's description of the ceremony of the bloody pond, *hsueh-hu,* the link between Mu-lian and the blood of menstruation and childbirth is even clearer. Dore translates a warrant that Buddhist priests have that allows them to perform the ceremony. The document describes how Mu-lian found the bloody pond in which many women were suffering and asked the ruler of Hades, Yen-wang, why their husbands were not also immersed. Yen-wang replied, "They are here because in giving birth to children they have discharged polluted blood which offends the Spirits of the Earth. Moreover, they have washed their bloodstained clothes in rivers and streams, whence men and women draw this contaminated water, and make therewith tea, which they afterwards offer to the gods." Mu-lian asked how he could rescue his mother from the bloody pond. He was told that rescue could be attained by honoring one's parents, worshipping the Buddhist trinity, and reciting the ceremony of rescue with a prayer he was given (Dore 1966, 1: 84–87).

The Mu-lian story is not historically the model for the blood bowl ritual, of course. The myth and ritual are fitted together a posteriori due to the basic thematic similarity of children assisting in the reintegration of their parents after death. According to Dore, Mu-lian is of Indian origin, a retelling of the story of Maudgalyayana, a disciple of Sakyamuni, who delivered his mother from hell (Dore 1966, 1: 86–87). The Chinese versions of the story contain the Buddhist elements of Mu-lian being a monk and of Mu-lian's mother being punished for the transgression of killing animals and eating meat. Versions quoted by Dore and Werner also include Mu-lian using the spiritual powers of other monks and other Buddhas to release his mother. This combines with the folk religious element of Mu-lian finding his mother in a bloody pool and with the Confucian element of *xiao,* filial piety, as Mu-lian's motivation, rather than a general caring for the suffering of mankind.

This assimilation of an Indian story into a Chinese context is also the reason informants described the funeral ceremony as imitating the actions of Mu-lian. According to Werner, Mu-lian has become associated with the Chinese god Ti-tsang Wang, the ruler of the underworld who oversees souls on their way to rebirth. Ti-tsang Wang is an overlord of hell who could have achieved Buddhahood but, moved by compassion, chose to rescue spirits caught in the torture of hell and make their passages easier (Werner 1969: 497–98). In performing rituals to ease the passage of the soul, the Chinese family is imitating the actions of Ti-tsang Wang.

The breaking the blood bowl is at one level a transformation or reenactment of the story of "Mu-lian Saves His Mother," the myth serving as a model for the ritual. But at another level, the myth as an explanation of funeral ceremonies lies in an inverse relationship to those ceremonies.[9] In the myth the mother must be rescued from the consequences of a sin involving the incorporation of a forbidden substance (eating meat), whereas in the ritual the mother must be rescued from the consequences of a sin involving excorporation of an unclean substance. Her children rescue her by the symbolic incorporation of this unclean substance. It is significant that this myth, which informants used to explain the funeral ceremonies, is about a mother and son rather than a father and son. The obligations are not conceptualized in terms of patrilineage or filial piety toward one's male seniors, but in terms of pollution and motherhood. In other words, ceremonies that seek to establish ancestors who will benefit a family conceived of as focused around a patrilineage is explained by a myth concerning a mother, her son, and blood.

The Myth of the Origin of Ancestor Tablets

Linking a mother and son through the blood of childbirth is also central to a myth I collected concerning the origin of the ancestor tablets, the focus of patrilineally based worship. The ancestor tablets are wooden plaques on which are inscribed the names of the generations of male ancestors and their wives. The tablets are placed on the altar of the ancestor hall or on a shelf in the main room of the house. Only sons and their wives are recorded. Daughters born into the family marry out and are inscribed on their husband's tablets in another home. The tablets are the physical representation of a household's ancestors, ideally an unbroken line of males.

The following myth was told to me by a widow in her fifties who had spent several years as the assistant to a female spirit medium. It is important to mention that her knowledge and interest are somewhat specialized, and that this story, although known to other members of the community, would not generally be given as an explanation of ancestor worship, as was the story of Mu-lian as an explanation of funerals. This story describes the origin of ancestor tablets:

> There was a mother, her son was not filial. The son was extremely unfilial. He didn't know how to be, since no one had taught him. His mother carried a basket of rice for him to eat—it is just as in the story of "Mu-lian Saves His Mother." If she was late in giving him his lunch, he beat her. If she was late in giving him dinner, he beat her. No one had taught him [filial piety].

> One day as she was carrying his food over, the son was watching her carry the rice from a distance. He saw a lamb drinking milk; it knelt down in gratitude [as it nursed] for the milk. He was moved by it and said, "The lamb can kneel down in gratitude to thank his mother's kindness, and I don't even know enough to thank my mother." He saw the lamb and himself and thought about it. "I have also learned to be filial. Hereafter, when my mother brings me food, I won't hit her."
>
> He understood that he should go to meet his mother. He saw her coming from afar carrying food, so he wanted to meet her. His mother thought he was going to beat her again, so she quickly jumped into the pond. Her son jumped into the pond to find her. He found a piece of wood. He took the wood. Alas, he only found a piece of wood. "I don't know if this is my mother." His mother was afraid of being beaten by him. She thought he was coming to beat her. "Alas, he is going to beat me again." So she jumped in.
>
> He went to search and found a piece of wood. He didn't find his mother. He brought back the piece of wood and pricked it, with an awl he pricked it. "If I prick it and there is no blood, then it isn't my mother." He pricked it and a lot of blood gushed out. Today the ancestor tablet is made of this wood.
>
> After she died, he then became filial. Before his mother died he wasn't filial. Only after his mother died did he understand having filial piety. He really understood reforming and was filial to his mother.

Because this is a myth about the origin of an important cultural institution, the story probably implies not only the invention of ancestor tablets but also the development of filial piety. The son didn't know how to behave because no one had taught him. The cultural values did not yet exist, and he had to learn them from nature and apply them to human society. He learned them, in fact, by observing the nurturing act of a mother animal and her offspring, rather than from the teachings of a father.[10] It makes sense that ancestor tablets and filial piety should be thought of as connected. In fact, the story ends with the statement that the son only understood filial piety after his mother had died. The narrator of the story says, "It is just as in the story 'Mu-lian Saves His Mother.'" She is, at the level of surface structure, referring to the son rescuing his mother from the pond, but at a deeper structural level referring to the fact that both myths concern the origins of practices concerning death and ancestors. What is most striking about this myth, of course, is that the story about the origin of the symbol of the patrilineage—the ancestor tablets—contains no fathers. The tablets' origin is a mother, and, more precisely, a mother's transformed body. The proof of the transformation is the blood, which spurts out when she is pricked with an awl. This blood, representing her reproductive powers as both bride and mother, illuminates the biological facts of birth versus the ideology of patrilineage, an opposition of nature and culture.

Through structural analysis of this myth, a series of pertinent oppositions emerge (Levi-Strauss 1967: 202–28). The terms used to analyze this myth are important categories present in Hakka folk religion, the opposition of yin/yang, and *wu xing,* the five elements. The basic expression of opposing forces in Chinese folk religion is that of yin and yang. The Chinese universe is not divided according to distinctions of essence and attributes, mind and body, spirit and matter, or culture and nature, but rather is conceived of as balances between balances, of configurations of yin-yang oppositions. Yin and yang form a set of contrasts and correlatives. Yin is associated with the moon, females, dark, wet, shadow, and death. Yang is associated with the sun, males, light, dryness, the sunny side of mountains, and life. This does not mean that men are yang and women are yin, but that men: women: : yang: yin. Each man and each woman have both forces within them, and the body itself involves the balancing of yin-yang forces. The five elements—wood, fire, earth, metal, and water—mutually produce and destroy each other, and these transformations and combinations constitute the phenomenal world.

If we look at the myth in terms of oppositions of yin and yang, we can see that in the beginning of the myth, yang predominates over yin in the sense that the son predominates over the mother. At the end of the myth, yin predominates over yang, in that the son has repented and begins to honor his mother. But a transmogrification has taken place, so that the object the son now worships is a piece of wood he fashions into ancestor tablets. The meaning of the yin-yang opposition has also shifted, so that now yin takes precedence over yang, in the sense that the dead (ancestors) have precedence over the living. The wood being pricked with an awl is important beyond its obvious sexual meaning in that it merges fertility and ancestor worship. The son in a sense has sexual intercourse with the ancestor tablets or the patrilineage, the woman's body being obscured through transformation. Because this is a myth, it is also possible for the analyst to wonder whether the events portrayed are a primal incest, through which later normal family relations began once the son had learned filial piety and begun to worship ancestors. The crucial obfuscation occurs when yin takes on the meaning of the dead rather than woman, and yang takes on the meaning of living rather than man. Likewise, the movement from nature to culture involves the son discovering filial piety through the natural model of a lamb kneeling to suckle, and establishing the cultural model of ancestor worship involving fathers and sons.

The second set of pertinent oppositions found in the myth is that of the five elements—metal, water, earth, wood, and fire—the constitutive substrata of the Chinese universe. The element earth is implicated in the beginning of the story, where the son is out working the fields and sees the lamb nursing. The second element is water, the pond into which his mother jumps to escape his wrath. The third element is wood, into which his mother is transformed. The fourth element is metal, the awl that pricks the wood; and the final element, which is only implied, is fire, an essential part of worshipping ancestors (in lighting incense and burning paper sacrifices). The movement of these elements is from earth to fire. The earth is associated with natural relationships—the ewe grazing as her lamb nurses, also, in this case, a female image. The fire is associated with the cultural act of ancestor worship, an act associated with males. The movement from earth to fire also represents the movement of the dead as corpse to the dead as ancestor.

The passage through the myth is from natural relationships to cultural ones. The process of learning filial piety is within the realm of nature: the son learns the proper ordering of generations and then runs to greet his mother, causing her to jump into the pond out of fear; but the establishment of ancestor worship involves the cultural transformation of the mother through the intermediary elements of water, wood, and metal. Wood occupies the crucial transitional spot in the myth. When she is transformed into wood, the mother is both dead and alive. She is no longer the son's living relative but still has the essential characteristic of life, blood. A woman's body and her blood are the mediator between life and death.

Through the mediation of filial piety, however, there is an asymmetry in the structure of the myth. The myth begins with the mother (yin) in an improper subservient relationship with her son (yang); then, through the mediator of filial piety, that relationship is reversed. Through the woman's transformation into wood, the final relationship is the son (yang) in a subservient relationship—not to his mother—but to his ancestors (yin). (See fig. 4.1.)

The myth brings out the paradox in a system in which sons are defined culturally by descent from one parent, the father, though born (naturally) by a mother.[11] In ideal terms, the kinship system is a line of males, but in practice one cannot avoid the absolute fact of motherhood. The natural relationship of birth competes with the ideological relationship of ancestor worship. Myth and ritual are dialectically related. The rituals focused around the ancestor tablets are patrilineal, whereas the myth explaining the origin of the tablets concerns a mother-son relationship.

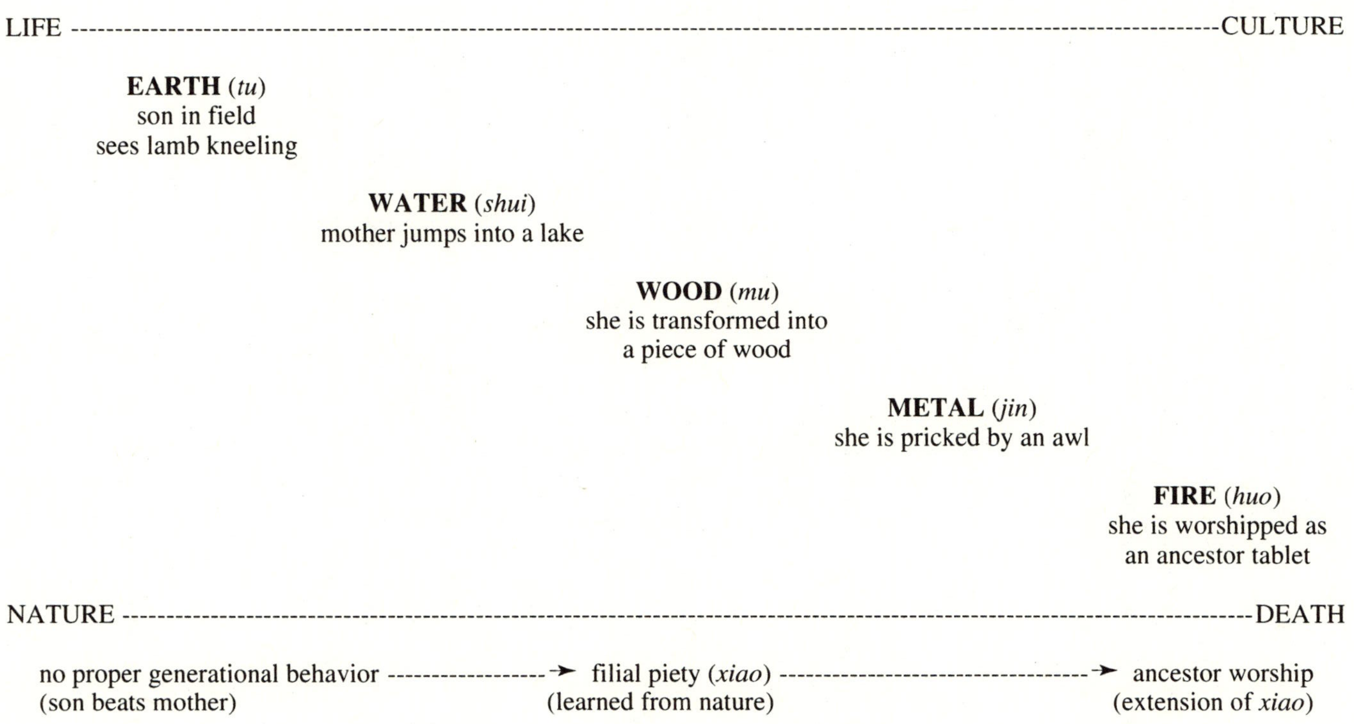

LIFE -- CULTURE

EARTH (*tu*)
son in field
sees lamb kneeling

WATER (*shui*)
mother jumps into a lake

WOOD (*mu*)
she is transformed into
a piece of wood

METAL (*jin*)
she is pricked by an awl

FIRE (*huo*)
she is worshipped as
an ancestor tablet

NATURE -- DEATH

no proper generational behavior (son beats mother) ----------→ filial piety (*xiao*) (learned from nature) ----------→ ancestor worship (extension of *xiao*)

Fig. 4.1. The Transformed Body: Structure of "The Origin of the Ancestor Tablets."

There is also a dialectical relationship between how motherhood is valorized in myth and how it is valorized in ritual. At the mythic level, homage is paid to the primacy of female fertility and the absolute character of childbirth, but at the ritual level motherhood is expressed in negative terms. An inversion has taken place, so that women's fertility is expressed in negative terms as a type of pollution that is absolved through the intervention of male Taoist priests, for whom Mu-lian serves as the prototype.

There is perhaps a sense in which the worship of ancestors is like an inverted worship of women. Could we say that the transformation of a woman's body into ancestor tablets symbolizes the displacement of homage to women for their fertility into homage to ancestors who bring good fortune, including fertility? It is true, for example, that Mu-lian has become the god who generally nurtures and assists the dead. But there is not enough evidence to speculate whether inverted myths about fertility point to some prior form of worship that overtly honored women's fertility. It is sufficient at this point to suggest that there is a tension between the orthodox "texts" of rituals and the stories associated with them.

The Hakka Seance

If, indeed, these myths point to a major contradiction in Hakka culture, one would expect that contradiction to be present at other levels of interaction as well. This proves to be the case. Although I had been introduced to the blood bowl ceremony as one of many rituals performed during the funeral, my attention was drawn to it while I was engaged in a case study of another funeral ritual, the seance. Seances are performed as a regular part of the funeral ceremony at specified intervals, usually forty-nine days, one hundred days, and one year after the death, or at the time of reburial in the family tomb. Seances may also be performed if there is some problem in the family, such as infertility or bad fortune. The purpose of the seance is to find out if the deceased is content or requires some assistance from the living. The family also hears about the other departed relatives and receives moral advice from the dead person, but the primary purpose is to see that the needs of the deceased are satisfied. In seances held after a funeral, the spirit of the departed specifically comments upon the effectiveness of the rituals and sacrifices. The spirit medium engaged by the family in these seances is always female and blind. The seances are private events attended by close family members and held either in the dead person's chambers or the living room.

After a lengthy process of elucidating the dead and living relatives and ascertaining the dates of birth of the departed spirit and various family members, the medium with the help of spirit familiars is able to locate the correct soul. The members of the family then light incense and invite the spirit to return home. The spirit enters the body of the medium, who has been in trance communicating with the spirit world, then speaks to the assembled family through the body of the medium.

In the family whose seances I studied, a seance was held for the eighty-six-year-old matriarch of the family, Tshia Mui-moi. On returning to speak, she stated, "When I went to the domain of the dead, the blood bowl hadn't yet been totally purified. You should make another blood bowl for me." She went on to say that this lack of purification had increased her suffering and impeded her progress. She told them that she was not a bad person in her lifetime, and that she had cultivated her virtue (similar to gaining karma through good deeds), but that the ritual had not been adequately performed:

> I, a whole life time, had virtue. It is not that I lacked virtue, it is just that the blood bowl was not purified properly. Have you heard? . . . To die and then do [the ritual] is more difficult to obtain [results]. To die and then do it, it is more difficult to purify the blood bowl. I had many children. I had many birth fluids. Have you heard?

She went on to say that the Taoist priest paid more attention to other rituals than to the blood bowl, and so now the family must take care of her by finishing the purification.

The matriarch's comments function to remind the family of its indebtedness to her and of her inextricable presence in the family. An ancestor's power lies in his ability to bestow or withhold blessings, and the matriarch's complaints are an assertion of that power. This power, of course, is couched in terms of mutual love and affection, because the family not only fears and wishes to appease the spirit but also are moved by her plight and wish her to be happy. The blood bowl ritual is, in fact, conceived of as a way of expressing filial piety toward their mother.

All of this is of a piece with the analysis presented in the two myths. What is curious, however, is that the blood bowl also played an important role in the seance held for the matriarch's son, who died three years earlier. It is interesting that the blood bowl should be part of a seance for a man. In that seance, the spirit medium made several attempts but could not locate the soul of the deceased eldest son. With much embarrassment, the family finally had to admit that they had given the medium the wrong information during the search for the soul. The man was survived by the matriarch of the household, whom he called mother, but the family had not told the medium that she was not the biological mother. The woman who had given birth to the son had died soon after childbirth. The matriarch, who was the second wife, had raised him. She was the only mother the other children had known. As was frequently the case in those times, the first wife was an adopted daughter-in-law who the man had not chosen for himself, and the second wife was a woman he had chosen and loved. The first wife was adopted into the family as a young girl for the express purpose of eventually marrying a son of the family. To the son it was like marrying his sister.[12]

After the family admitted that their beloved matriarch was not the biological mother of the eldest son, the medium was possessed by his spirit. He berated the family for neglecting his mother and described in detail how much she had been suffering in the blood pool, because they had not adequately performed the ritual of breaking the blood bowl. The family argued with him, telling him he could not be sure it was his mother, but he continued to berate them and to recapitulate his mother's pitiful state. The family had no choice but to listen.

The plea for a repetition of the blood bowl ceremony by the spirit during a seance is not idiosyncratic to the seances I observed. When questioned in an interview, the Taoist priest who officiated at the funeral ceremonies mentioned that during the seances held after a funeral for a woman, the family often learns that her spirit is still suffering in the blood pool and requires that her children perform the ritual again. In his description of the "Bloody-Pond" ceremony, Doolittle says, "Sometimes it is performed several times on the death of the mother of a family of children. This is one way by which they manifest their *filial love* for the deceased" (Doolittle 1966, 1: 196–97). The two rituals—the seance and the blood bowl—are in some way linked. The importance of the blood bowl ritual in these seances does not derive from the specifics of family history but is another manifestation of the underlying contradiction in the mythos of Hakka ancestor worship.

The Seance as a Women's Ritual

The seance is the only portion of the funeral ceremonies presided over by a female ritual specialist. When the spirit returns, she begins with an address to the women present: "You, sisters, daughters-in-law . . ." The seance is a woman's ritual, whether the departed soul is male or female. The public events of the funeral, including the ceremony of the blood bowl, are presided over by male ritual specialists, but the private portion of the ceremony is controlled by a female medium and a largely female audience. Mu-lian is the prototype for the male priests, and in a sense, Mu-lian's mother serves as a prototype for the female section of the ceremony, bringing the absolute fact of her blood as a measure of filial piety. Failure to appease the demands of this blood through filial acts can interfere with the tidy canalization of the parts of the dead person, spiritual and material, which are essential to the smooth passage from elder to ancestor. The rituals women perform include private rituals such as the seance, and sacrifices to the hungry ghosts who are spirits that have not been taken care of properly. The god in charge of these spirits is Ti-tsang Wang, who is really Mu-lian. Mu-lian—who took so much pity upon the fate of his mother in the underworld that he found a way to help all women polluted by giving birth—is, by extension, the god who pities and controls the other spirits caught in suffering.

This awareness of woman's blood as gateway to life and death, and of women as mediating the passage between living and dead, is exemplified in a story told by Tshia Mui-moi's granddaughter concerning the matriarch and her relation with the ghost of the first wife (the biological mother of the eldest son). Both women were pregnant at the same time, but the first wife died shortly after childbirth. Both sons were nursed by Tshia Mui-moi. Nursing two sons at once was not easy, and she worked in the fields as well. She raised both children as her own, but the spirit of the dead woman returned to haunt her. At night it would come and make loud noises and shake the old-style canopy bed to scare her. Tshia Mui-moi threatened her, saying, "I take care of your son as though he were my own, and yet you keep frightening me. I won't take care of him anymore." The ghost was softer, but still followed her, even when she moved to the mountains. The matriarch got mad and said, "If you keep this up I will throw dog's blood on your grave [so that the spirit can never rise again]!" The ghost left her alone.

The ghost may be haunting the matriarch out of jealousy, or even attachment, to her child, but as her son's seance indicated, her spirit certainly cannot rest until the fact of her motherhood is acknowledged through the blood bowl ceremony. The opposition emphasized in this story is between *yong,* raising a child, and *kiung,* giving birth to a child. This opposition is similar to the one mentioned with regard to the myth of the ancestor tablets, kiung: yong: : nature: culture.[13] Ahern mentions that black dog's blood is a euphemism for menses, but because dog's blood itself is used to exorcise ghosts, it is difficult to know which substance is meant in the matriarch's threat. The power of woman's blood is such that it can both give life to human beings and kill ghosts. As in the blood bowl ritual itself, a woman's menstrual blood can be used to control the wanderings of the parts of the soul after death and before rebirth. It is the source of human birth and can be the source of spiritual annihilation.

The Muting and Amplification of Contradictions

Although both the myth-ritual opposition and the references to the blood bowl ceremony in the seances contain the opposition of motherhood and patrilineage, they function very differently. The ceremony of the blood bowl acknowledges the importance of women's fertility in a negative and inverted form. In contrast, by examining the myths associated with the funeral rituals, we can see the importance of women's fertility in the origin of cultural institutions. In myth, the contradiction between patrilineage and the absolute fact of birth is laid bare. What is treated negatively in the ritual is placed in a more positive light in myth. Considered as a complex, the myth and ritual form a dialectic that mirrors the tensions in the family system. At the same time, because the myth of the origin of the ancestor tablets is only a remote referent for the funeral ceremony, the effects of the contradiction are muted. Furthermore, myths about the origins of cultural institutions and culture heroes are not immediate models or daily referents for the Hakka in the way that stories are about famous historical figures who later may have been worshipped as gods.[14] The segregation of this contradiction into two generic forms—myth and ritual—thus obscures its force.

Much the opposite happens when the blood bowl ritual is mentioned in the seances. The request for additional blood basin ceremonies calls the attention of the assembled family to the fact of motherhood. It also requires that the family go to the expense of performing additional rituals at the behest of a female medium. The nesting of references to the blood bowl ritual in the seance ritual thus functions to reinsert this contradiction between establishing a new ancestor in the male-focused system of worship and acknowledging the importance of women's fertility (symbolized by her blood). In the same way, the nesting of references to the birth of the eldest son brings out the contradiction between motherhood as a blood relationship and motherhood as raising children. The process of nesting one ritual (the blood bowl) within another (the seance) allows the tensions in the family system to be expressed. Two complimentary operations are at work here: the segregation of a contradiction in two generic forms (myth and ritual), which represent two experiential domains, in order to obscure the tension; and the nesting of one genre within another—the blood bowl ritual within the seance ritual—to amplify the contradiction.

Conclusion

It is worth recapitulating the extensive journey beyond the boundaries of the woman's body that the blood of childbirth has undergone. Discarded after the birth as a polluting substance, this blood seeps into the earth and enters the underworld, where it is eventually reunited with the spirit of its owner but in an inverted form: rather than being excorporated from the woman's body, it encompasses her body, drowning her. The blood has left the domain of the living and entered a transitional domain. That blood is symbolically reincorporated by her descendants who, by drinking the wine during the blood bowl ritual, make it part of their bodies, allowing their mother to pass through the punishments of the underworld to rebirth. It is thus part of the process by which the potent blood-and-flesh aspects of the body are neutralized so that the bones and spirit can be metamorphosized into ancestorhood. This blood of childbirth is a link between generations—it can never return to the mother, but is absorbed by her offspring. Although it seems that the blood of childbirth can thus be tidily disposed of, it is, in fact, not so easily eradicated, a fact to which the frequent requests for blood bowl ceremonies attest.

In the blood bowl ceremony itself, the contradiction between the ideology of patrilineage and the natural fact of motherhood is present in a passive form, a remote mythological referent that stands in opposition to the actions of the male Taoist priests performing the ceremony. In the seances performed by female mediums, however, this contradiction is active, as the medium asserts the necessity of performing the ritual again and bringing the absolute fact of motherhood, symbolized by the blood of childbirth, before the assembled family. The ritual symbol of the blood of childbirth is thus strategically deployed in the only section of the funeral rituals presided over by a female ritual specialist.

The rituals of death are not only a reflection of the ethos of a society. In the ritual transformations the body undergoes after death—in the process of the dissolution of its living configuration and reemergent metamorphosis—parts of the body can represent conflicting ideologies. These ideologies are encoded in distinct genres that, in their complex relationship in a ritual event, enact the contradictions in the society.

Notes

1. This paper is based on research in Taiwan sponsored by the U.S. Department of Education and the National Institute of Mental Health.
2. Hakka is one of the major dialects of the Chinese language. The Hakka are one of the two major groups of Chinese to have colonized Taiwan.
3. A complete description of ancestor worship may be found in Ahern 1973, Jordan 1972, and Wolf 1974.
4. For a description of this process, see James L. Watson, "Of Flesh and Bones: The Management of Death Pollution in Cantonese Society," in Bloch and Parry 1982.
5. For a complete description of *feng-shui,* see Needham 1956: 359.
6. Doolittle describes the "Bloody-Pond" ceremony performed for married women and (some say) only for women who die in or after childbirth. Rev. Justus Doolittle, *The Social Life of the Chinese* 1 (1865; reprint, Taipei: Ch'eng-wen Publishing, 1966), 196–97.
7. The word *phun* denotes "basin" in Hakka, and according to Dore refers to the basin used to catch the fluids at birth (see Dore 1966: 86).
8. Freedman (1967: 98) states that "in Chinese domestic life, married women are seen by men to be the ultimate source of trouble . . ."
9. Levi-Strauss discusses the inverse relationship of myth and ritual. He is investigating how the myths and rituals of contiguous populations may be inversely related, that is, how the inversion of one group's myth may be found in the ritual of a neighboring group. I am using his idea of inverse relationship but applying it to myths and rituals within the same culture in order to demonstrate how the underlying contradictions in a society can be deciphered by examining the entire myth-ritual complex surrounding a rite of passage. See Levi-Strauss 1967: 229–38.
10. The motif of the lamb kneeling to the ewe is also found in the popular cycle of stories known as the "Twenty-four Acts of Filial Piety."
11. Also see Levi-Strauss 1967: 212 on being born from one and born from two in his discussion of the Oedipus myth.
12. This practice is described in depth in Wolf 1972: 171–90.
13. The analogy between men and women and culture and nature, the role of women as mediators, and the contradictory, polarized values associated with women are analyzed in Rosaldo and Lamphere 1974, especially "Is Female to Male as Nature is to Culture?" by Sherry B. Ortner, 67–88.
14. Wolfram Eberhard points out that when Chinese society was transformed from feudal states to an empire with an ongoing civil service about A.D. 100, the gods were like wise transformed from mythological characters with nonhuman origins to men of exemplary virtue and loyalty (Eberhard 1958: 23).

References

Ahern, Emily M. 1973. *The cult of the dead in a Chinese village.* Stanford: Stanford Univ. Press.

———. 1974. Affines and the rituals of kinship. In *Religion and ritual in Chinese society.* Ed. Arthur P. Wolf. Stanford: Stanford Univ. Press.

———. 1975. The power and pollution of Chinese women. In *Women in Chinese society.* Ed. Margery Wolf and Roxane Witke. Stanford: Stanford Univ. Press.

Bloch, Maurice, and Jonathan Perry 1982. *Death and the regeneration of life.* Cambridge: Cambridge Univ. Press.

De Groot, J. J. M. [1892–1910] 1972. *The religious system of China* 4. Taipei: Ch'eng Wen Publishing.

Doolittle, Rev. Justus. [1865] 1966. *Social life of the Chinese* 1. Taipei: Ch'eng Wen Publishing.

Dore, Henry, S. J. [1917] 1966. *Researches into Chinese superstitions* 1. Trans. M. Kennelly, S. J. Taipei: Ch'eng Wen Publishing.

Douglas, Mary 1966. *Purity and danger: An analysis of concepts of pollution and taboo.* Harmondsworth: Penguin Books.

Eberhard, Wolfram 1965. *Folktales of China.* London: Routledge and Kegan Paul.

Elliott, Alan J. A. 1955. *Chinese spirit medium cults in Singapore.* Monographs on Social Anthropology, no. 14 (n.s.), London School of Economics. London: Univ. of London Press.

Freedman, Maurice, ed. 1967. *Social organization: Essays presented to Raymond Firth.* Chicago: Univ. of Chicago Press.

Huntington, Richard, and Peter Metcalf. 1979. *Celebrations of death: The anthropology of mortuary ritual.* Cambridge: Cambridge Univ. Press.

Jordan, David K. 1972. *Gods, ghosts, and ancestors: Folk religion in a Taiwanese village.* Berkeley: Univ. of California Press.

Levi-Strauss, Claude. 1967. *Structural anthropology.* New York: Anchor Books.

Needham, Joseph. 1956. *Science and civilization in China* 2, *History of scientific thought.* Cambridge: Cambridge Univ. Press.

Rosaldo, Michelle Zimbalist, and Louise Lamphere, eds. 1974. *Woman, culture and society.* Stanford: Stanford Univ. Press.

Werner, E. T. C. [1932] 1969. *A dictionary of Chinese mythology.* New York: Julian Press.

Wolf, Arthur P. 1974. Gods, ghosts and ancestors. In *Religion and Ritual in Chinese Society.* Ed. Arthur P. Wolf. Stanford: Stanford Univ. Press.

Wolf, Margery 1972. *Women and family in rural Taiwan.* Stanford: Stanford Univ. Press.

Grotesque/Ethereal

Grotesque realism emphasizes the brute, physical, physiological, sexual, scatological properties of the body as opposed to the pure, metaphysical, spiritual, continent, proper presentation of the body in an etherealized discourse. Mikhail Bakhtin locates in the grotesque "the material and bodily roots of the world." The grotesque body is a transgressive body, a body of parts, of slits and bumps, inverted, invaded, dismembered, and degraded. The dissected corpse in an autopsy is a grotesque body but one that is overwritten by the etherealized discourse of medicine. Transgressions carnivalize the proper body; purifications etherealize the grotesque body.

Discourses of the grotesque and the ethereal appear in the figures of dwarves and giants, of mule-dragons and devils, of eagles and nobles, in the Patum festival of Berga. Antithetical discourses that vein Catalan society are typified, empowered, constrained, and loosed in a festival that condenses a cosmology in an art form.

5. *Still Life with Corpse:* Management of the Grotesque Body in Medicine

Katharine Young

. . . the grotesque ignores the impenetrable surface that closes and limits the body as a separate and completed phenomenon. The grotesque body image displays not only the outward but also the inner features of the body: blood, bowels, heart and other organs. The outward and inward features are often merged into one.

—Mikhail Bakhtin (1984: 318)

Dr. Mercurio, the chief pathologist, escorts me through a labyrinth of corridors in the basement of the University Hospital to the morgue. We enter an antechamber, and there, through an open archway, are four figures in aquamarine scrub suits, masked, capped, and gloved, and the corpse, waxy yellow, laid out on the examination table. The face is tipped toward me, eyes closed, the corners of the lips tilted up in a slight triangular smile. A tendril of black hair clings to the far shoulder. The arms are bent at the elbows so that the hands rest curled against the chest. The abdomen has been opened in a square flap, folded down like an apron covering, as it were modestly, the genitals. Viscera spill out over the rim. The body is utterly im-

This chapter was first presented as a paper at the 1989 American Folklore Society meetings in Philadelphia. Subsequent versions were given as a lecture for the Annenberg School of Communication, University of Pennsylvania, 1990, and as a plenary paper for the Twelfth Annual Conference on Discourse Analysis, Temple University, 1991. The present version profited from a few laconic remarks from Liz Wickett and Herb Simons, specific suggestions from Janet Langlois, and an intelligent reading by Pat Mullen and the outside readers for the University of Tennessee Press and the Publications of the American Folklore Society—as well as advice on sausages from Barbara Kirshenblatt-Gimblett.

mobile, impossibly still, a wax figure. From its abdominal cavity effuse lush glossy inner organs in bruised purples, fatty yellows, membranous whites.

One figure, the technician or pathologist's assistant who performs most of the autopsy, stands behind the corpse, lifting out lengths of intestine, holding them aloft, clipping away their adhesions of fat. These internal tissues have a gray bloom. The other three figures approach us, two men and a woman. Dr. Mercurio introduces me to them and we explain my research. The three stand before us in a semicircle, nodding and speaking through their masks, their eyes flicking and glowing. "What did she die of?" I ask, although, in fact, despite her nakedness, her gender is almost erased. The body is swollen, the thighs huge, belly mounded up, breasts flattened down. Except for the face, it is without particularity. But on the face, her particular personhood is exquisitely inscribed. She died of liver disease; that is why she is so yellow. She has a lacy spray of blood across her lower cheek, fanning out from the mouth. The disease causes internal bleeding. With death, the rosy flush of the organs, the transparency of the skin, turn opaque. They won't ordinarily be so yellow, they say—meaning the other corpses I will see. Dr. Mercurio and I withdraw. "Her expression is so sweet," I say." Perhaps," he says, "it was a sweet release." Sometimes, after death, a rictus of the facial muscles draws up the corners of the mouth giving the face the semblance of a smile.[1]

The Grotesque Body: Bakhtin

The medieval body is held by Mikhail Bakhtin to be "coarse, hawking, farting, yawning, spitting, hiccupping, noisily nose-blowing, endlessly chewing and drinking" (1981: 177). So the body is expulsed by ascetic medieval ideology as "licentious, crude, dirty and self-destructive" (1981: 171), thus inventing an opposition between the spiritual, aristocratic, or ethereal central discourse and the bodily, vulgar, or grotesque peripheral one. The central ascetic discourse is then raised, in literal as well as symbolic space, toward heaven, and the peripheral bodily discourse lowered to earth, or even into hell,

Fig. 5.1. The Grotesque Body: Women making Sausages. From a Flemish Psalter, first quarter of the fourteenth century, MS. Douce 5, fol. 7r. Reproduced with the permission of the Bodleian Library, Oxford University.

rendering the opposition hierarchical. The hierarchy is then reinscribed on the body, whose topography is appropriately oriented so that the face and head are opposed to the genitals, belly, and buttocks (1984: 21), the region of the body Bakhtin describes as the "material lower bodily stratum" (1984: 368). The body in general, or its lower parts in particular, come to represent the tabooed discourse in the form of what Bakhtin calls "grotesque realism" (1984: 18). Peter Stallybrass and Allon White write:

> Grotesque realism images the human body as multiple, bulging, over- or under-sized, protuberant and incomplete. The openings and orifices of this carnival body are emphasized, not its closure and finish. It is an image of impure corporeal bulk with its orifices (mouth, flared nostrils, anus) yawning wide and its lower regions (belly, legs, feet, buttocks and genitals) given priority over its upper regions (head, "spirit," reason). (1986: 8–9)

The grotesque body is contrasted to the classical body, modeled, Bakhtin argues, on Greek statues. "The classical statue," as Stallybrass and White note, "has no openings or orifices whereas grotesque costumes and masks emphasize the gaping mouth, the protuberant belly and buttocks, the feet and the genitals" (1986: 22). By contrast to the classical body, Bakhtin writes, in the grotesque body

> the stress is laid on those parts of the body that are open to the outside world, that is, the parts through which the world enters the body or emerges from it, or through which the body itself goes out to meet the world. This means that the emphasis is on the apertures or the convexities, on various ramifications and offshoots: the open mouth, the genital organs, the breasts, the phallus, the potbelly, the nose. (1984: 26)

Orifices and protuberances are sites where the boundaries between the body and the world are blurred: bodily substances are spilt out, stuff from the world taken in. Dissection incises fresh cuts, slits, apertures into the body. Like those regions Jacques Lacan regards as erogenous—"lips, . . . the rim of the anus, the tip of the penis, the vagina, the slit formed by the eyelids, even the horn-shaped aperture of the ear" (1977: 314–15)—such cuts are loci where desire condenses at the margin or border of the body. Lips are apertures into the act of devouring. These incisions do not articulate the surface of the body; they expose its interior. "Because," as Susan Stewart, following Jacques Lacan, writes, "these cuts or apertures are described on the very surface of the subject, they have no specular image, no outside that they represent" (1984: 104). "It is what enables them to be the 'stuff,' or rather the lining . . . of the very subject one takes to be the subject of consciousness" (Lacan 1977: 314–15). This ambiguity of the lining persists even in the corpse. The extrusion of the lining, the disgorging of entrails over the edge of the incision, the plunging of hands and instruments into its recesses, the interchange of substances, confuses the distinction between inside and outside. When, in the course of the dissection, organs are cut loose, pulled free, and plucked out, the conventional order of the body is destroyed. As Susan Stewart notes, "The grotesque presents a jumbling of this order, a dismantling and re-presentation of the body" (1984: 105), so that the body becomes, in Bakhtin's conception, a body of parts (Stewart 1984: 105). The dissected body is a grotesque body.

> A portly old man with fresh skin and white hair is laid out face up on the autopsy table. His body is dappled with purplish blotches on the underside of the head, back, and legs. The lips are drawn upward and outward, slightly curled, giving the face a sweetness of expression. The chest is lifted up onto a curved block so that the head drops back. The technician sharpens a broad-bladed knife on a steel file. He cuts into the corpse at the upper inner hollow of the shoulder, runs the belly of the knife across the ribs, around the breast, along the lower edge of the rib cage, and up across the ribs to the other shoulder in a single stroke. He makes a second cut from the middle of the first down the abdomen to the pubis, skirting the navel to create a Y-shaped incision. The upper flap of tissue is detached from the ribs and draped over the chin. The two lower flaps are folded outward and clipped to the skin. Blood wells up in the abdominal cavity. He dabs it up, in an incongruously homely fashion, with paper towels.
>
> The technician saws out sides of ribs in triangular sections, lifts them off the chest, and piles them on the autopsy table. He ties off the intestines at the top, twice, close together, and cuts between the ties. He lifts loops of bowel, trimmed loose, out of the abdomen into a pan on the corpse's lap. He dissects out structures in the throat and disconnects organs in the pelvis, detaching them from the sides of the cavity and then from the top. He scoops the heart, lungs, and viscera out onto a board, leaving the clean hollow trough of the abdominal cavity—its lining gray, thick, smooth, and undifferentiated like the skin of a dolphin. The procedure is called abdominal evisceration.

A Discursis on Sausages

Now a brief discursis on sausages, and on feces, intestines, pigs, food, and phalluses. Consider first feces, "conceived as something *intermediate between earth and body*" (Bakhtin 1984: 175), what Bakhtin calls "gay matter" (1984: 335), which constitutes "part of man's awareness of his materiality, his bodily nature, closely related to the life of the earth" (1984: 224). "Dung and urine lend a bodily character to matter," he writes. "If dung is a link between body and earth . . ., urine is a link between body and sea" (Bakhtin 1984: 335).

Consider, then, intestines: that thin, tough, translucent tube that contains feces within the belly. Consider this same tubing, taken from the pig and stuffed with finely minced offal from the pig's belly (see fig. 5.2). Tripe, consisting of both stomach and bowels, Bakhtin describes as "the bowels, the belly, the very life of man" (1984: 162). And the pig, ambivalent animal (Stallybrass and White 1986: 44), is itself intermediate between categories, wild and tame, country and city, animal and man.[2] As Stallybrass and White point out, "The pink pigmentation and apparent nakedness of the pig disturbingly resemble the flesh of European babies" (1986: 47). It is the animal that eats feces and makes food (Stallybrass and White 1986: 45).

Thus the mixture of ingredients according to Bakhtin:

> The bowels are related to defecation and excrement. Further, the belly does not only eat and swallow, it is also eaten as tripe . . . Further, tripe is linked with death, with slaughter, murder . . . Finally, it is linked with birth, for the belly generates.
>
> Thus, in the image of tripe life and death, birth, excrement, and food are all drawn together and tied in one grotesque knot; this is the center of the bodily topography in which the upper and lower stratum penetrate each other. (1984: 163)[3]

Hence, Bakhtin continues, "the carnival role of butchers and cooks, of the carving knife, and of the minced meat for . . . sausages" (1984: 193). Its source is the dismembered body, minced flesh, "based on the grotesque image of the dissected body" (1984: 194). "Carne levare (the roasting and taking up of meat which probably gave carnival its name)," according to Stallybrass and White (1986: 184), in which "the pleasures of food were represented in the sausage and the rites of inversion in the pig's bladder of the fool," the source, as they so sagely point out, of the balloon (1986: 53).

And the sausage, enfolded in a bun whose dough is called *virgin* until it is inseminated by the leaven (Conrad 1986: 52), obtrudes its final carnivalesque transformation. Carnival, ritual of contradiction, "commingling of categories" (Stallybrass and White 1986: 27), site of what Stallybrass and White call "demonization, inversion, hybridization" (1986: 56), presented by Bakhtin as "a world of topsy-turvy, of heteroglot exuberance, of ceaseless overrunning and excess where all is mixed, hybrid, ritually degraded and defiled" (1985: 8). "Eating and drinking", writes Bakhtin, "are one of the most significant manifestations of the grotesque body. The distinctive character of this body is its open unfinished nature, its interaction with the world" (1984: 281). The nexus in which sausages, feces, intestines, pigs, food, and phalluses are entangled is the belly of the dissected body. The corpse, being eviscerated, is carnivalesque.

The carnivalesque move is to turn upside down or inside out, to invert or reverse, to transgress the boundaries between discourses or to switch their content, just as dissection does the corpse. Autopsy thus evinces an affinity with other inversionary gestures, such as "the cartwheel, which by the continual rotation of the upper and lower parts suggests the rotation of earth and sky. This is manifested in other movements of the clown: the buttocks persistently trying to take the place of the head and the head of the buttocks" (Bakhtin 1984: 353). "Down, inside out, vice versa, upside down, such is the direction of all these movements. All of them thrust down, turn over, push headfirst, transfer top to bottom, and bottom to top, bottom in the literal sense of space and in the metaphorical meaning of the image" (Bakhtin 1984: 370). The spatial displacements of dismemberment disturb the conceptual proprieties of the body.

The grotesque body becomes a repository for degradations made flesh. Curses and abuses, obscenities and sacrileges, assault a high discourse and transform it into the low by materializing the discourse bodily, especially in the nether regions of the body. "To degrade by the grotesque method," writes Bakhtin, "they send it down to the absolute lower bodily stratum, to the zone of the genital organs, the bodily grave, in order to be destroyed" (1984: 38). Hence the association of grotesque realism with death, the underworld, and the demonic (Bakhtin 1984: 301). One curious indication of the corpse as carnivalesque: the morgue is always located in the basement, geographically low, constituting itself an underworld, a realm of the dead. The material lower bodily stratum is, according to Bakhtin, a carnivalized underworld (1984: 395).

To cast down a discourse, then, is not only to carnivalize it but also to materialize it, to render it matter—not inert matter but fecund, teeming, productive matter. "All that is sacred or exalted," Bakhtin notes, "is rethought on the level of the material lower bodily stratum" (1984: 370). Hence the connection, rooted in the old agricultural cycle, between death and fertility. "To degrade is to bury, to sow, and to kill simultaneously . . ., to concern oneself with the lower stratum of the body, the life of the belly and the reproductive organs; it therefore relates to acts of defecation and copulation, conception, pregnancy and birth" (Bakhtin 1984: 21). The slit belly of the corpse, exuding and engulfing matter, undergoing transformations, retains this material vitality. Death is "made out of the same stuff as life itself" (Bakhtin 1981: 195). This carnivalesque conception of death is contrasted with the conventional view of the corpse as absence, barrenness, stillness.

Death in the carnivalesque is approached in terms of "food, drink, ritual (cultic) indecency, ritual parody and laughter" (Bakhtin 1981: 218–19), which form the basis of comedy. Death becomes a "gay monster" (Bakhtin 1984: 151 n.6) in which fear of death is defeated by laughter (Bakhtin 1984: 91). This laughter, this assault on the sacred, the aristocratic, the pure discourse, prevents it from becoming authoritative. "Laughter purifies from dogmatism, . . . the single meaning, the single level, from sentimentality" (Bakhtin 1984: 123). The corpse, split and eviscerated in the morgue, remains the site of an inversionary, fertile, grotesque discourse.

Medicine as an Aristocratic Discourse

Suppose, in the face of the grotesque body, you are in the business of constructing an aristocratic discourse?[4] How do you go about it? You press the discourse through an etherealization cycle: on the one hand, raise the discourse hierarchically, purify it, sacralize its language, and, on the other hand, exclude or suppress the low, the grotesque, the material lower bodily stratum. This is difficult in the case of medicine as it is so ineluctably a discourse of the body, and in the case of surgery and pathology especially, a carnivalesque body: one split, severed, dismembered, eviscerated, turned inside out. Its material aspect appears inexpungeable.

> The body of a delicately made woman lies flayed open on the autopsy table. The chest is lifted up on a block, arching the back and tilting the head back so that the top of it rests on the table, chin pointed upward, vessels prominent in the forehead. The abdominal evisceration has included dissecting out the throat structures, leaving the abdomen void and the neck a hollow stem. The technician lifts the head onto a second block, giving the macabre suggestion of a pillow. He incises the scalp from just above the right ear through the furze of gray hair to just above the left. He lifts the head and tugs

> the scalp down over the forehead, holding it by the hair. It folds down, inside out, over the brown face, which crumples underneath like an old leather mask. He continues to cut away scalp along both edges of the incision with a scalpel. The face is now covered with tissue, hair inside, forming a ball of whitish integument, its protruding chin rimmed with gray furze.
>
> The technician peels the scalp off the skull, exposing its sutures. He saws around the skull from the base of the neck to the forehead and back to the base. Bone chips fly, accompanied by the whir and grind of metal on bone and a sawdusty smell. He takes a chisel, taps into the crevice, inserts a great hook into the widened aperture and pulls off the skull cap. The brain, in its transparent sack, droops at the back, jiggling. The technician works his fingers up between the brain and the skull at the forehead, clips it loose, then lifts the brain from underneath and scissors its deeper connections. He lowers the head and rests the brain in the bowl of the skull. Then he reaches around through the chest cavity into the hollow neck and pushes out the brain with his fingers. He removes the block under the neck quickly so that the head drops back, emptying its contents like a goblet into the bowl of the skull. He sets the bowl on the table. The head, hollowed and decapitated, hangs down, the handles of its ears curving just above the rim. In the bowl sits the brain, whorled and ridged like a large walnut.

As an aristocratic discourse, medicine becomes authoritative: monologic, monoglossic, univocal, and sacred. Authoritative discourse, according to Bakhtin, has three properties: it binds participants independently of its power of persuasion; it is both distant and high, an already acknowledged authority—what he calls a prior discourse; and "its language is a special (as it were, hieratic) language. It can be profaned. It is akin to taboo, i.e., a name that must not be taken in vain" (1981: 342). As physicians were transformed toward the end of the nineteenth century from servants who attended upon their patients into masters who were themselves attended upon, their discourse shifted toward the aristocratic. Consider Francis Delafield's 1872 description of a brain autopsy:

> The scalp is divided by an incision across the vertex from ear to ear. The flaps are directed forward and backward, taking up the temporal muscles with the skin and leaving the pericardium attached to the bone. The internal surface of the scalp and the pericardium are to be examined for ecchymoses and inflammatory lesions. A circular incision is then made with the saw and the roof of the cranium removed. The incision in front should pass through a point three and a half inches above the root of the nose, behind through the occipital protuberance (1872: 9).

Here the body appears to disarticulate by itself: "The scalp is divided by an incision"; "the flaps are directed forward and backward." The agent of this disarticulation, the pathologist with the scalpel, has dematerialized. Its perceiver describes the events from a locus outside or above them. We, the readers, take up the same perspective. From it, the detached perceiver appears to have unlimited knowledge of that realm of events. Hence the affinity of the external perceiver with the omniscient narrator. Speaking in the present tense de-realizes the event by purporting to transact it right before our eyes and at the same time not doing so. The description is not of any one particular autopsy but of the course of such autopsies in general, rendering it generic rather than idiosyncratic. The particularity, the possible personhood, of the corpse is elided by the passive voice, which not only banishes agent and perceiver but also objectifies the object of perception.[5] What appears is not the act of one person on the dead body of another but a self-disclosing object (Harcourt 1987: 49–50). The dissected body reveals its affinity with sixteenth-century anatomical drawings in which the corpse is represented as holding open its own body cavities, uplifting its muscle flaps or supporting its eviscerated organs (see figs. 5.2 and 5.3). In a sense, no one is there; the corpse dissects itself.

The dissected corpse is never fully embodied. It divides itself into already intelligible categories, not chunks of blood, bone, and flesh, but ecchymoses and inflammatory lesions; the vertex, the pericranium, and the occipital protuberance; the temporal muscles. These Latinate terms are associated with the scientific, the academic, the intellectual, the mental. This hierarchy of Latin over Anglo-Saxon in the root languages of English arises, like all linguistic hierarchies, from a quirk of history, in this instance the Norman conquest of the Angles and Saxons. As part of the aristocracy of language, Latinate terms are held to be pure as well as high, free from the vulgarity and coarseness of rude speech. And, of course, Latin is a sacred language whose contemporary context of use is a religious one. Latinate terms are tinged with ritual authority.

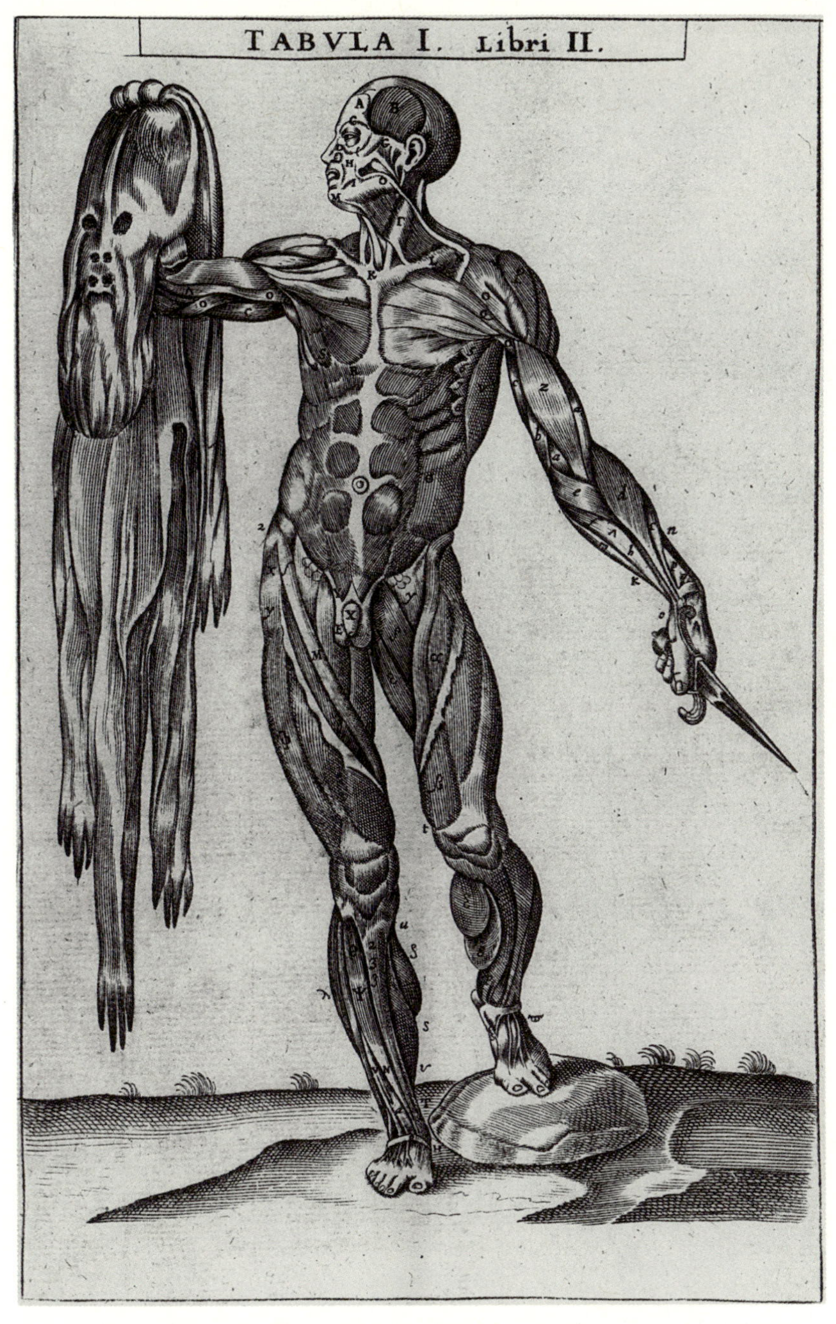

Fig. 5.2. The Self-disclosing Body I: Medieval anatomical drawing taken by Juan Valverde di Hamusco from Andreas Vesalius. In A. Vesalii en Valuerda, *Anatomie* (Amsterdam: Cornelis Denckertz, 1647), Libri II, Tabvla I, page 16a. Reproduced with the permission of the Department of Special Collections, Van Pelt-Dietrich Library Center, University of Pennsylvania.

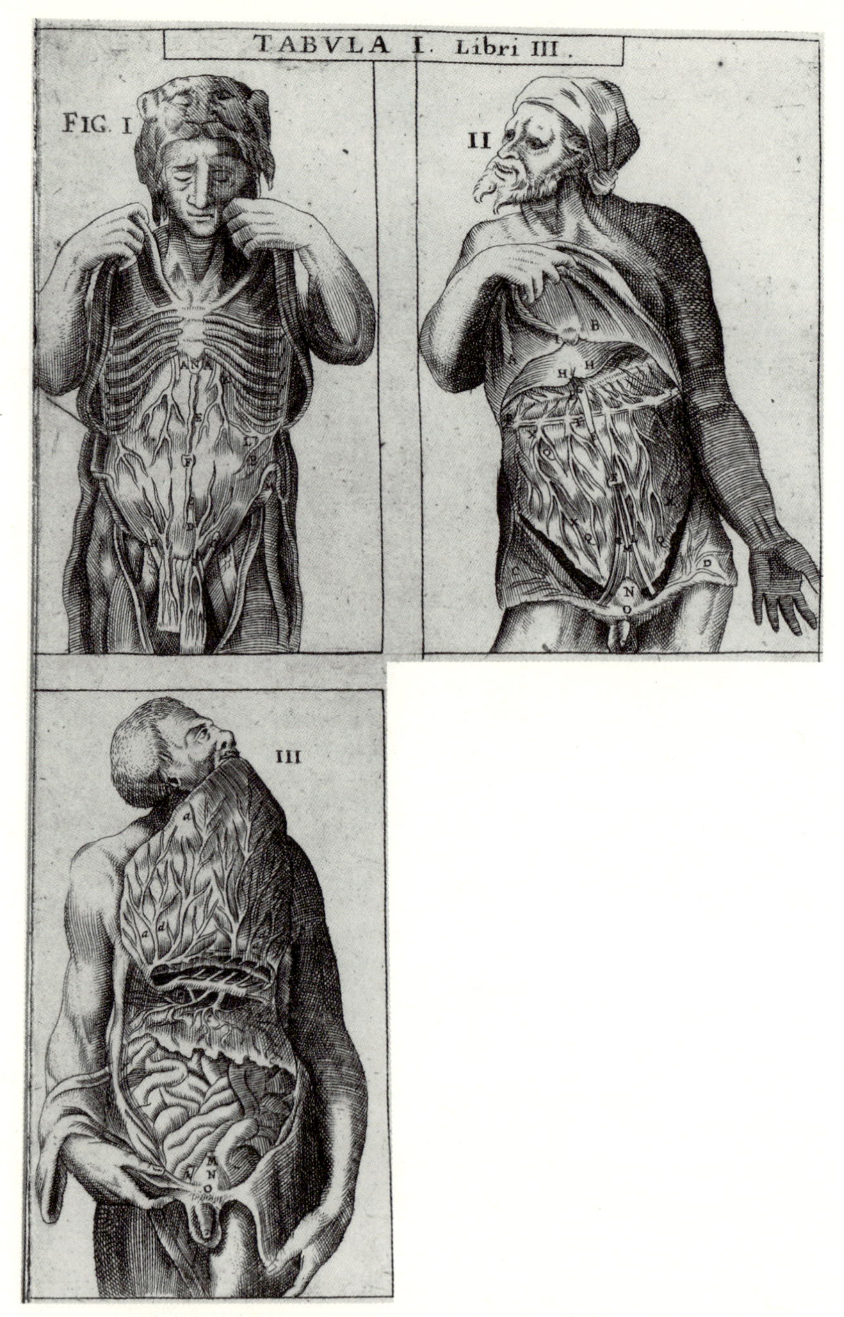

Fig. 5.3. The Self-disclosing Body II: Medieval anatomical drawings taken by Juan Valverde di Hamusco from Andreas Vesalius. In A. Vesalii en Valuerda, *Anatomie,* Tabvla I, Libri III, page 56a (Amsterdam: Cornelis Denckertz, 1647). Reproduced with the permission of the Department of Special Collections, Van Pelt-Dietrich Library Center, University of Pennsylvania.

Some contemporary texts retain the passive construction so that the body still appears to disarticulate itself, but they shift toward a slightly less Latinate vocabulary and reassert the voice of the pathologist in the form of authoritative remarks, advice, or evaluation. There are occasional parenthetical remarks in the first person (for instance, pages 7 and 96 of Ludwig 1979):

> The head is elevated slightly with a wooden block or a metal headrest attached to the autopsy table. The hair is parted with a comb along the line of the primary incision. The latter is made through an imaginary coronal plane connecting one mastoid with the other over the convexity . . . A sharp scalpel blade can then be used to cut through the whole thickness of the scalp from the outside . . .
>
> The anterior and posterior halves of the scalp are then reflected forward and backward, respectively, after short undercutting of the scalp with a sharp knife which permits grasping of the edges with the hands. The use of a dry towel draped over the scalp edges facilitates further reflection, usually without the aid of cutting instruments. If the reflection is difficult, a scalpel blade can be used to cut the loose connective tissue that lags behind the reflecting edge as the left hand continues to peel the scalp. The knife edge should be directed toward the skull and not toward the scalp. The anterior flap is reflected to a level 1 or 2 cm above the supraorbital ridge. The posterior flap is reflected down to a level just above the occipital protuberance. (Ludwig 1979: 95–96)

The pathologist with the scalpel has reappeared, if only to take instruction from the narrator as mentor. The perspective on the autopsy is now internal to that realm of events but still not embodied in its perceiver. The act of instruction is represented here. We oversee the gestures of the pathologist and overhear the instructions of the mentor but remain, as perceivers, omnipresent but disembodied, an intelligent effluvium hovering about the autopsy.

In the current autopsy manual of an Eastern university hospital (anonymous here to protect the identity of research subjects), the authoritative voice of the pathologist is rendered in the imperative mode:

> Separate the hair, undoing any braids or coiffure present, to mark out the line of incision . . . Use a fresh bladed scalpel to make a single clean incision with the belly of the blade cutting down through the galea aponeurotica. With the initial incision in place, use the

> scalpel to cut the fascia binding the undersurface of the galea to the pericranium. With a dry towel, grasp the anterior edge of the incision and roll it forward, simultaneously cutting the strips of fascia. Turn the anterior flap down over the face to about the mid part of the forehead. In a similar fashion, turn the posterior flap to about the external occipital protuberance. (Autopsy Manual 1989–90: 45–46)

Here the pathologist appears without the scalpel to issue instructions for what might materialize as an autopsy. In the instructive mode, the act remains implicit, intentional. Just as well, for here it is we who take the part of the perpetrator, who hesitate on the edge of incising the corpse. We perceive this possibility from close up. Although voice remains objective, omniscient, and authoritative, perspective has shifted from the disembodied external perspective in which the perceiver, like the speaker, is both immaterial and remote to an embodied internal perspective in which the perceiver is materialized in the morgue. It is we, the perceivers, who are embodied as subjects; the corpse takes the inscription of its objectivity from the discourse of medicine.[6]

Dissection, shifting in the mid-seventeenth century from public spectacle to private event (Barker 1984: 13), eschewed its old association with the grotesque, freakish, and carnivalesque in order to present itself as refined, rarefied, pure, priestly, and aristocratic. It was only at the end of the eighteenth century that chirurgeons, who severed the body, were permitted to switch their affiliation from barber to physician. The sacralization of medicine entails the banishment or concealment of the grotesque body in the interest of producing a pure discourse. This discourse is exclusive and hierarchical with respect to ordinary discourse. The hierarchy is reinscribed within the discourse so that apprentices are themselves etherealized as they rise through the discourse of medicine to become masters. An anomaly remains: The grotesque body of pathology is a threat to the aristocratic discourse of medicine.

The Privatization of the Body: Barker

From the Renaissance to the modern period, the spectacular medieval body is reinvented in a series of moves exquisitely illuminated by Francis Barker. Initially the body is privatized, withdrawn from public view underneath clothes, inside rooms, behind institutions, into writing. This privatization depends on the invention of "the public and private as strong, mutually defining, mutually exclusive categories, each describing separate terrains with distinct contents, practices and discourses" (1984: 34). Banishment dematerializes the body. It becomes, in the first instance, invisible, for, as Barker points out, "the body has certainly been among those objects which have been effectively hidden from history" (1984: 12), and in the second instance, unmentionable, for etiquette excludes not only the body but also its verbal tokens from discourse. But this "decorporealized etherealism," as Barker calls it (1984: 94), is only one aspect of the strategy. The other, and at the same time antithetical aspect, is the reinscription of the body as an object of representation (Barker 1984: 80, 97). No longer the representing subject, the body becomes other, even to itself. Finally, the body is materialized as an object. By contrast, the self, retaining the ascetic medieval imagery, is etherealized as subject. This ether, this essence, this absence is encoded, writes Barker, as "an individual, privatized and largely passive consciousness: systematically detached from a world which is thus beyond its grasp" (1984: 36). This ethereal subject is then interiorized in the body object. The spectacular inscription of the self on the surface of the body is erased and rewritten, inscrutably, within.

So the materiality, the objectivity, the objecthood of the body is not a natural disposition but a cultural accomplishment. The critique of materialism as idealism suggests that to see the body as material is itself an idealization (Bataille 1985: 15). The consequent incommensurability between the material substance of the body and the ethereal substance of the self constructs the mind/body problem. How is the person hitched to the body, the mind to the brain, the ethereal to the grotesque? Are mentality and physicality different orders of event? If so, as Hegel suggests, the corpse can be regarded as the ultimate presentation of body as object (1977: 114).

So we arrive, via the Barker moves, at a discourse, medicine, and its object of representation, a reconstituted body. "Neither wholly present, nor wholly absent, the body," writes Barker, "is confined, ignored, exscribed from discourse, and yet remains at the edge of visibility, troubling the space from which it has been banished" (1984: 63). Consider now medical discourse and the unreconstituted body that haunts its edges.

The Spectacular, the Speculative, and the Specular: Foucault

The medieval body is constituted of the same four elements as the cosmos: earth, air, fire, and water, transmuted in the body into the four humors: melancholy, blood, choler, and phlegm (Tillyard 69). As they transmute in the body, the humors rise and rarefy so that the upper regions of the body are infused by the finest humors and the lower regions by the most base. The tempering of these elements composes both constitution and temperament so that health, like personhood, is inscribed on the skin. A person's humor is manifest on the body. Disease is the dis-ease of body with cosmos. Medicine is designed to re-balance the bodily humors so that they correspond with the cosmic order. Dissection, carried out before its audience of philosophers, physicians, anatomists, artists, aficionados, and onlookers as a performance, a sideshow, a carnival turn, is merely an extension of the surfacing of meaning on the body. The medieval practice of dissection as spectacle is a subset of the body as spectacular.

Splitting self from body also splits off body from cosmos. The material body and the ethereal self become different orders of event: the body becomes pure substance and the self the absence of substance, insubstantiality, pure absence. The admixture of materiality and ethereality in the medieval body is uncompounded and redistributed into incommensurable substances. Body is no longer cosmos. Disease, separated in the same gesture from its elemental cosmology, becomes a metaphysical idea with a locus in what Michel Foucault calls classificatory space (1975: 9). Its course is only disturbed by its passage through the body (Foucault 1975: 14; also see 8). Symptoms are clues to a reality that subsists elsewhere. Medicine, from being spectacular, becomes speculative (Foucault 1975: xii). Diagnosis is detection. Disease has become an etherealized essence that can be interiorized in the patient so that it is, as Foucault puts it, "concealed within him like a cryptogram" (1975: 59).

With the reinvention of the body as an object, disease is precisely re-inscribed on the tissues (Foucault 1975: 127). "The space of the configuration of the disease and the space of the *localization* of the illness in the body have been superimposed . . ." (Foucault 1975: 3). No pathological essence exists beyond the symptoms; the symptoms become the disease (Foucault 1975: 91). "By acquiring the status of object, [the body's] particular quality, its impalpable color, its unique transitory form took on weight and solidity" (Foucault 1975: xiv). Disease is now entirely inscribed on its surfaces. "Medical rationality plunges into the marvelous density of perception, offering the grain of things as the first face of truth, with their colours, their spots, their hardness, their adherence" (Foucault 1975: xiii). Autopsy, which has the property of rendering the body nothing but surface, of surfacing the interior, of dismantling interiority, makes the grain of things perceptible throughout its layers. As a consequence, medical knowledge is "redistributed in the space in which bodies and eyes meet" (Foucault 1975: xi). Medicine is now merely specular, a reflection of and upon the visible. But "the forms of visibility have changed" (Foucault 1975: 195). Medical looking is not naïve, but, as Foucault puts it, an "intellectual eye" (1975: 120), one that reads "the deep structures of visibility in which field and gaze are bound together by *codes of knowledge*" (1975: 90). Autopsy is the attempt to scrutinize these inscriptions on the flesh.

The Corpse as Still Life

Hence, the corpse as still life. When my mother first introduced me to still lifes, I thought they were paintings of things that just happened to be still: cut flowers, bowls of fruit, objects on a table. It did not occur to me till years later, introducing my daughter to still lifes, that the things painted were themselves forms of life but severed at the root, lives stilled, what we came to call "small murders." (The French term, *nature morte,* perhaps captures this possibility more clearly.) Just so with the corpse as with the pear, the wedge of cheese, the haunch of venison, the hung pheasant, the smoked fish: the subjects are arrested in the course of transmuting. They have not altogether lost their character as life forms but have begun nonetheless to take on the character of things, substances, material objects.

The Mind/Body Problem

Susan Ritchie locates the dead body as a site of slippage in our ideology of persons and hence an interesting place to look at subjectivity (1988). The corpse is given as static, spatially extended, specular. The body becomes the terrain of a disease, which it surfaces, literalizes, materializes. The move to traverse that terrain, ambiguously alluded to by its practitioners not as an autopsy but as a pathological examination, is a move to preserve its objecthood by reiterating its ontology as superficial, visible, phenomenal, that which does not hide anything else, which is not transparent to anything else, which cannot be opened to anything else. In the course of this traversal of its anatomy, the corpse nonetheless intimates its subjectivity.

> A corpse arrives wrapped and tied. When the technicians unwrap it, her the face and genitals have been draped in a white cloth. Her toenails have been recently manicured and painted blood red.

> An identification tag is tied round her big toe.
>
> On another occasion the pathologist pats the corpse of an old man on his bald rosy head and then dissects out his brain. After the dissection, the technician stuffs the hollowed skull with crushed paper toweling, remounts the skull cap, unfolds the scalp and stitches it back together. The abdominal cavity is similarly split, stuffed, and stitched. The body rests on slats mounted over a corrugated metal surface like a washboard. Tiny faucets above the head pour water underneath to a drain below the feet. The technician hoses off the body, spraying the face lightly and sponging it down. Water squirts out of the ears. He dries off the corpse with paper towels from head to toe; lays a white cloth over the face; ties the wrists, ankles, and chin with strips of cloth; and rewraps the corpse in its huge paper sheet, tying the bundle round the neck, middle, and ankles. The shrouded body is lifted onto a cart and rolled back into the refrigerator.
>
> While the husk of another body is thus being reassembled, one pathologist runs loops of intestine through his fingers at the sink. Another is examining the brain on the autopsy table. The technician has the heart out. Two pathologists inspect lungs and kidneys on another table. Viscera, severed, split, sectioned, and sliced are scrutinized, mounted on slides, slipped into test tubes, dropped into jars. Dr. Wood comes in, looks at the lung on the table and says, "Does she have a pneumonia there?" They speak of her condition, her disease, her death, as if she were impersoned in these slivers of tissue. This is so even after the container for these body parts has been closed up and taken away.
>
> After the pathologists finish with the brain, the technician ties one end of a piece of string to it, suspends it in a jar of clear fluid, and winds the other end around the jar's neck, tucking in the loose end of string to which her name tag is attached.

These irruptions of subjectivity through the discourse of objectivity attest to the fragility of the framing of the body-as-object. The toe, that particular gnarled and wrinkled toe with its modest indulgence of feminine vanity, is a locus of personhood. This allusion of the corpse to its own personhood, this insistence on its presence, is attested to by the curious gentleness of the pathologist's pat on the head of the old man, administered with the kind of cheerful absentminded tenderness with which one pats a child, without any particular expectation of response. The tenderness is reiterated in the way the technician washes the corpse's face, not squirting it directly but spraying it and sponging it gently off. The pang of unease we experience when water, sprayed in through the mouth or the nose, comes out the ears of the corpse, likewise signals its not-quite-objecthood. The drapes over the face and genitals, shielding the corpse's most public and particular as well as its most private and generic parts, also describes personhood on the body. The pathologists find personhood in the woman's parts even discorporated, dissevered, and dispersed about the room. Thus the brain, incongruously name-tagged like the toe, bears in its jar an eerie presentiment of the person. Attempts to reach through the frame to the person, or to break out of the frame by the person, trouble the distinction we are culturally concerned to maintain between subject and object, self and body, life and death.

Death, which suggests itself as the moment in time and the locus in space in which the body-as-object is definitively broken off from the body-as-self, is in reality spatially and temporally ramifying. Bodily tissues are affected differentially: vital processes continue to transpire in some tissues while others become inert and still others begin to undergo processes of decay. As Foucault remarks, "Death is therefore multiple, and dispersed in time: it is not that absolute, privileged point at which time stops . . ." (1975: 142). It encroaches on us. It exscribes the edges of our universe of discourse. The corpse portends a presence that is also an absence. Hence, Julia Kristeva's claim for the corpse as *abject*:

> In that compelling, raw, insolent thing in the morgue's full sunlight, . . . I behold the breaking down of a world that has erased its borders: fainting away [from *cadere,* to fall, and so akin, according to Kristeva (1982: 3), to *cadaver*]. The corpse . . . is the utmost of abjection. It is death infecting life. Abject. It is something rejected from which one does not part, from which one does not protect oneself as from an object. Imaginary uncanniness and real threat, it beckons us and ends up engulfing us (1982: 4).[7]

It is this ambiguity with which we feel uncomfortable. Hence the attempt of pathology to reinscribe the space of death on the body as precise, to rearticulate the time of death as instantaneous. These are attempts to make clear the ontological status of the corpse as subject-turned-object by conjuring up crisp, clear, clean boundaries in space and time. We would be more comfortable with an unambiguous shift, like a magical transformation into elemental particles, ash for instance, which accounts, perhaps, for the popularity of cremation. The tenuousness of the reinscription dictates the concealment of the death, the corpse, the autopsy. Fear of death is fear of ambiguity. The corpse remains incorrigibly carnivalesque.

Death and the Carnivalesque

When the chief pathologist escorted me through the underworld to the morgue, he warned me against giving way to unseemly merriment, cracking jokes, mocking the corpse. Nothing was further from my mind. The autopsy seemed to me entirely unfunny, awesome if anything, and I was not tempted at any time in the course of it to make a joke. I realized on reflection, however, that if under the tension of suppressing the shock of my first encounter with a corpse, someone else had offered up a bit of black humor, I might well have burst out laughing.

Washing down the table after an autopsy, the technician said, "As far as I'm concerned, once the"—he hesitates—"soul leaves the body, that's it." The view participants in the discourse of pathology put forward is that nobody is there, just an arrangement of tissues. Yet this reading is threatened by the way the body makes allusion to the person: the mystery of embodiment. The nerve end of this allusion, this threat, appears in black humor, which comes off only under the eerie assumption that somebody is still there to be insulted, profaned, abused, mocked. Insults can only be offered the self, not the object. Evidence of this metaphysical unease about the ontological status of the corpse appears in the prohibition against black humor.

The content of black humor is carnivalesque, and what it threatens is not so much the dignity of the corpse as the aristocracy of the discourse that inscribes it, the discourse of medicine. The threat of the carnivalesque must be vanquished by the discourse of medicine in order to assure its aristocracy. Medical apprenticeships entail learning to overwrite the corpse with the new discourse. The pathologist describes the evisceration of the old man in the autopsy report:

> The usual "Y" shaped incision is made disclosing musculature with increased hydration and a panniculus measuring 4 cm. The organs of the thoracic and abdominal cavity are in

> their normal anatomical position. There is a large amount of straw colored fluid in the chest cavity bilaterally. There are adhesions noted in the apex of the left lung and a 150 cc. of fluid are noted in that thoracic cavity. On the right side there are adhesions all over the lateral surface of the right lung which are fairly dense and the 300 cc. of straw colored fluid is noted in that side. There is dependent stasis on both lungs. (Autopsy Reports 1987)

And with respect to his brain autopsy:

> The scalp is reflected in the usual manner and the bony cover appears intact. The pachymeninges are thin, fibrous and glistening. There is no evidence of previous laceration, contusion or healed fracture. The cerebral hemispheres are rounded and reveal normal convolutions and sulci. The venous tributaries are markedly congested. The brain weighs 1360 gm. The brain parenchyma is soft, smooth and glistening with no evidence of hemorrhage or petechiae. The vessels at the base of the brain are unremarkable. (Autopsy Reports 1987)

The brain of the African-American woman is described thus:

> Both external and internal surfaces of the dural leaflets are patent. There is no evidence of herniation of the cingulate gyri, unci or cerebellar tonsils. The leptomeninges are thin, translucent and free from exudate. Examination of the arteries of the circle of Willis and their major branches reveals they are patent and free from atherosclerosis. The superficial veins of the brain and the cranial nerves are unremarkable. (Autopsy Reports 1987)

For initiates, the carnivalesque body is not there, only its anatomical reinscription as the proper body. Concealment of the corpse is a recourse against the uninitiated, who might catch its carnivalesque qualities. The discourse's very establishment of itself as aristocratic sets it up for assault by the carnivalesque, an assault that translates the high, refined, and pure into the pompous, stuffy, and snobbish. Like all aristocratic discourses, medicine is dependent on what it excludes (Hegel 1977: 111–19; Stallybrass and White 1986: 5). The low, the profane, the grotesque stand as the discourse against which it defines itself. At the same time they constitute the discourse to which it is vulnerable. Autopsy is threatened by the breakthrough of grotesque realism, by the thought, the hint, the whiff of sausages.

Notes

1. The site of these events is real, but the hospital and its inhabitants, living and dead, as well as the documents pertaining to them, have been given fictitious names in order to protect the privacy of the research subjects. My research on the body in medicine was partially supported by a Wenner-Gren grant.
2. The pig taboo in Jewish tradition was enhanced by the animal's reputation for eating refuse, but it is rooted, according to Mary Douglas, in the pig's categorical transgressions: "Cloven-hoofed, cud-chewing ungulates are the model of the proper kind of food for a pastoralist" (1970: 69). "The dietary rules," she writes, "should be taken as a whole and related to the totality of symbolic structures organizing the universe. In this way the abominations are seen as anomalies within a particular logical scheme" (1973: 60). Within this order, an analogy is proposed between the altar and the table, the meal taking the form of a slightly attenuated but still pure version of ritual sacrifice. Just as the blemished or impure cannot enter the temple, so the anomalous cannot be eaten. Clearly "the purity in question is the purity of the categories . . . The sanctity of cognitive boundaries is made known by valuing the integrity of physical forms. The perfect physical specimens point to the perfectly bounded temple, altar and sanctuary" (1984: 269).
3. Mary Douglas, too, notes the affinity between pigs and death. The boundaries between categories are preserved to maintain the intellectual coherence of a system of thought and, by extension, a body of people. Both pigs and death transgress the boundaries between the sacred and the profane, the proper and the taboo, the pure and the blemished. "Much of Leviticus is taken up with stating the physical perfection that is required of things presented in the temple and of persons approaching it. The animals offered in sacrifice must be without blemish, women must be purified after childbirth, lepers should be separated and ritually cleansed before being allowed to approach it once they are cured. All bodily discharges are defiling and disqualify from approach to the temple. Priests may only come into contact with death when their own close kin die. But the high priest must never have contact with death" (1970: 64).
4. The term *discourse* as it has come into use in the social sciences does not mean texts, writings, or utterances, *particularly. Discourse,* I take it, alludes to *universe of discourse,* the realm of events, the world, of which texts, writings, utterances, and also gestures, acts, thoughts, spaces, times, objects, and so on, are a part. Physicians' way of writing within their own discourse embodies its ontological characteristics. Such writings are not to be regarded as descriptions of a reality but as something more like manifestations, instances, of it.
5. For technical aspects of perspective and voice, I am indebted to Shlomith Rimmon-Kenan's work (1984).
6. For an illuminating investigation of the textualization of the body in medical discourse, see Susan Ritchie's chapter in this volume, "A Body of Texts: The Role of the Humanities in Medical Discourse."
7. This line of thought from Kristeva was suggested by Janet Langlois.

References

Bakhtin, Mikhail. 1981. *The dialogic imagination.* Ed. Michael Holquist. Trans. Caryl Emerson and Michael Holquist. Austin: Univ. of Texas Press.

———. 1984. *Rabelais and his world.* Trans. Hélène Iswolsky. Bloomington: Indiana Univ. Press.

Barker, Francis. 1984. *The tremulous private body.* London: Methuen.

Bataille, Georges. 1985. *Visions of excess: Selected writings, 1927–1939.* Ed. and trans. Allan Stoekl with Carl R. Lovitt and Donald M. Leslie, Jr. Minneapolis: Univ. of Minnesota Press.

Conrad, Barnaby III. 1986. Let them eat bread. *Connoisseur,* Feb., 49–53.

Delafield, Francis, M.D. 1872. *A handbook of post-mortem examinations and of morbid anatomy.* New York: Wood.

Department of Pathology. 1989–90. *Autopsy manual.* An Anonymous Univ. Hospital.

Douglas, Mary. 1970. *Purity and danger: An analysis of concepts of pollution and taboo.* Middlesex, England: Penguin.

———. 1973. *Natural symbols: Explorations in cosmology.* New York: Random House.

———. 1984. Deciphering a meal. In *Implicit meanings,* 249–75. London: Routledge and Kegan-Paul.

Foucault, Michel. 1975. *The birth of a clinic.* Trans. A. M. Sheridan Smith. New York: Vintage.

Harcourt, Glenn. 1987. Andreas Vesalius and the anatomy of antique sculpture. *Representations* 17: 28–61.

Hegel, Georg W. F. [1807] 1977. *Phenomenology of spirit.* Oxford: Clarendon Press.

Kristeva, Julia. 1982. *Powers of horror: An essay on abjection.* Trans. Leon S. Roudiez. New York: Columbia Univ. Press.

Laboratory of Pathology. 1987. *Autopsy reports.* An Anonymous Univ. Hospital.

Lacan, Jacques. 1977. *Ecrits: A selection.* Trans. Alan Sheridan. New York: W. W. Norton.

Ludwig, Jurgen, M.D. 1979. *Current methods of autopsy practice.* Philadelphia: W. B. Saunders.

Rimmon-Kenan, Shlomith. 1984. *Narrative poetics: Contemporary fiction.* London: Methuen.

Ritchie, Susan. 1988. Reanimating the corpus: Points of slippage in the ideological creation of subjecthood. Paper presented at the American Folklore Society meetings. Cambridge, MA.

———. 1993. A body of texts: The fiction of humanization in medical discourse. In *Bodylore.* Ed. Katharine Young. Knoxville: Univ. of Tennessee Press and Publications of the American Folklore Society.

Stallybrass, Peter, and Allon White. 1986. *The politics and poetics of transgression.* Ithaca, NY: Cornell Univ. Press.

Stewart, Susan. 1984. *On longing: Narratives of the miniature, the gigantic, the souvenir, the collection.* Baltimore: Johns Hopkins Press.

Tillyard, E. M. W. N.d. *The Elizabethan world picture.* New York: Vintage Books.

6. Contesting the Body Politic: The Patum of Berga

DOROTHY NOYES

T'hi ficaràs o no? they demanded. Are you going in there or not? I was surprised at the insistence on this question in the weeks before the feast of Corpus Christi and my first experience of the Patum of Berga.[1] I had been given lots of advice about how to protect myself. Watch from a balcony until you know what it's about, always move counterclockwise, get some heavy shoes, tie up your hair under a good hat, wear cotton instead of inflammable synthetics. I am not brave, and they convinced me of the necessity of being careful. "If you lose your wallet, if you lose your shoes, if you lose your pants, don't stop for anything!" an old man warned me. "Once the *plens* have started, not even God enters!"

But suddenly my willingness to get burned appeared to be the fundamental test of my seriousness as an ethnographer. If I really wanted to know what people in Berga were like, I had to enter the crush of the Plaça Sant Pere during the *salt de plens,* the final unleashing of devils that is the culmination of the Patum. I had come to this city of fifteen thousand in the Catalan Pyrenees[2] to live for six months, of which I had been there three. I had earnestly sat in the library and combed the municipal archives; I had talked to old people and solemnly requested interviews of *patumaires*—until I realized that the Patum comes up in half the conversations in Berga anyway, and the interviews just made people nervous. My welcome had been enthusiastic, and so far most people in Berga seemed to approve of me, interpreting my speaking Catalan, singing with the Easter carolers, and dining in the "popular" bars as marks of my willingness to see things from their point of view. As the festival approached, however, it became apparent that seeing was not enough.

La Patum s'ha de viure, they said over and over as I asked for analyses, anecdotes, personal histories. It's no use my trying to put it in words, the Patum has to be lived. And when the Patum came, I found that Berguedan goodwill was intent on making me live it properly. "I saw you up on that balcony!" said one woman after I'd retreated for a better view and to rest my unaccustomed feet. "This isn't theater, you know. You can't understand the Patum by looking at it." During the evening *passacarrers,* the night-long processions of the Old Giants, the maces, and the guites, they made sure I did more than look. A bar owner I knew was jumping the *maça,* a club with firecrackers affixed to the top. As it burned lower, she thrust it into my hands, and I had no choice but to start skipping, bouncing the pebble-filled mace up and down to keep it lit, showering myself with sparks until my turn was over. The Guita Xica, the smaller and more mobile of the two firebreathing mules, chased me into a corner every time it set eyes on me: I cowered with my hands over my head until it tired of shaking the flame over me and went after someone else (see fig. 6.1). Agustí, the guide at the head of the beast, was unabashed when I later taxed him with his pursuit. "Daughter," he said, "this is the baptism by fire we all have to suffer." Through the five days of the festival, I opened my mouth to fierce alcoholic mixtures in leather flasks and glass *porrons;* I let children take up my arms and dance me across the plaça; I ducked inside the Eagle and the Black Giant; I rode on the back of the Guita Grossa, exulting over the black wave of the crowd beneath me; I put a shoulder under the Guita Xica when the *guitaires*' girlfriends carried it up the Carrer Major and shouted savage delight with the rest of them as we lowered the neck to charge; I went out to eat supper every night at five in the morning, drank champagne and sang until eight, and rose three hours later in an unsuccessful effort to get myself to mass—so as properly to document the complete event. My much-ridiculed little notebook became more and more illegible. I began to lose sight of the symbolic oppositions that had seemed so obvious in book and video and at last attained a glimmering of what they'd been trying to tell me: the Patum is not a mere spectacle of traditional dances, but a force that runs through you.

Having taken in this lesson, I dislike representing the Patum in list form or as a neatly bounded object. If my readers will forego a formal description-definition of the event in favor of a little of the bewilderment I myself encountered, I will compromise so far as to enumerate for their convenience the *comparses* (effigies) that come out in sequence in the plaça[3] on Corpus Christi and the following Sunday. Note that the turns of the guites and the two sets of devils are distinguished as *salts,* "jumpings," rather than the more structured *balls,* "dances," of the other Patum personages. The salts are marked by the beating of the *tabal,* and, until the end of the last century, by the absence of music:

1. The *tabal,* or "drum," wielded by a young man in a seventeenth-century suit and hat of red velvet. Its pa-tum, pa-tum punctuates the entire festival and is assumed to be the origin of the festival's name (Armengou 1968: 27).
2. *Turcs i cavallets,* "Turks and horsemen": a combat dance in which the Turks are defeated. The Turks are in costume; the horsemen wear papier-mâché skirts in the form of a horse.
3. *Maces,* "maces." Four devils dance with clubs until the firecrackers in these explode; they are then dispatched by St. Michael and an angel.
4. *Guites,* "kicking mules." Two long-necked mule-dragons in green canvas with firecrackers in their mouths chase the public in the plaça to the beat of the tabal (fig. 6.1).
5. *Aliga,* or "eagle." A papier-mâché eagle does a slow and elegant dance that speeds up to a final spin (fig. 6.3).
6. *Nans vells,* the "old dwarves." Four papier-mâché heads with tricorns and pigtails representing eighteenth-century municipal councillors. They waltz; then a faster second section ends with a spin. This is the form of the dance for the next two comparses as well (fig. 6.6).
7. *Gegants,* "giants." Four tall figures with sculpted heads and hands and long robes, dressed as medieval kings and queens. The older pair are Moorish; the New, or Black, Giants are dressed as Christians, but darker-skinned than the others (fig. 6.2).
8. *Nans nous,* "new dwarves." Two couples, one old and one young, whose dress is generally assumed to mimic the shopkeeper class in its Sunday best at the end of the nineteenth century (fig. 6.4).
9. *Plens,* "full ones"—that is, devils full of fire. Devils with the same masks and heavy red and green costumes as the maces, but wrapped in damp clematis vines as protection from burns. Three firecrackers are affixed to each horn and two to the tail. Seventy or eighty plens dance among the crowd and fill the plaça with smoke and sparks (fig. 6.5).
10. *Tirabols.* At the end of the midday Patum briefly, and at great length after the passacarrers and the final salt de plens of the night Patum, the crowd links arms in round dances. The tirabol is typified as a spiral in graphic representations and described as this in the past, but is now too big to have any recognizable shape. The demasked plens, the guites, and the two Old Giants also dance.

Et surt de dintre, ran the third refrain. It comes up from inside you. The Patum, with all its antiquity, all its complexity, is not fundamentally a part of the external world: it lives in the body of each Berguedan, who has heard the beat of the tabal since infancy, danced

Fig. 6.1. ***Guites:*** The *guita,* or "kicking mule" runs its head along the *barana* of the plaça, showering spectators with sparks. Foto Luigi, Berga.

along with the giants since learning to walk—"sucked in the Patum with the mother's milk," as more than one person told me. The Patum bursts out of Berguedan bodies on joyous occasions—an out-of-town reunion of Berguedans, a victory of the Barcelona Football Club—and is simply bottled up the rest of the time. Agustí Ferrer, the present mayor of Berga, writes: "At Corpus, the Patum which beats inside you throughout the year explodes all at once" (Ferrer 1989: 2).[4]

The Patum is considered by Berguedans to lie deeper than the accidents of social structure within the community; this is why it has survived so little changed through the endless political restructurings suffered by Catalonia since its loss of independence in 1714. The Patum must be lived, *s'ha de viure,* and this bodily experience is an epistemological mode distinguished by the Berguedans from the apprehension of everyday sociopolitical realities.

Ordinary social life, especially for the middle class, is controlled by the tyranny of the eye. The eye works on the body to discipline it into conformity with the norms of respectability and to classify it according to the town's moral and social hierarchies. "In

Berga you always have to follow the fashion," explains Queralt, a university student. "People are always watching to see what you come out with on Sunday, and they make commentaries—if it's old, if it's always the same. It's only for the Patum that I can relax and dress to be comfortable." "Just imagine if I were drunk in the street on a normal evening," says Ramon, a manager in an insurance company. "The next day in the office everyone would know about it, everybody would be whispering behind their hands. It's only during the Patum that nobody watches you—of course, they're all drunk themselves." Lluís, an office worker, says, "I sit at a desk all year long," "I never do anything. I go to work and I come home again. The Patum is the only time I do anything physical, I can unleash."

The Patum is a time of personal liberation, all agree; and the liberation is primarily from the fear of being *mal vist,* "badly seen," which gives rise to *males llengües,* the "evil tongues of gossip." Sight is the seat of judgment, which inherently tends toward the negative: I have rarely heard the phrase *ben vist* and never *bones llengües* in Berga. However, even praise is divisive, repressive. The gaze of the community isolates the individual, making her conscious of the body as a casing, a mask over the true self and a boundary separating her from her fellows. She learns to monitor herself, her eyes on the mirror standing in for the eyes of others. She begins to evaluate others so as to rank herself, thus reinforcing the very mechanism that controls her.

But the experience of the body radiates through these surface distinctions and attains a different kind of knowledge. Communal action creates a shared reality, and over time, a fund of common experience: it makes mutual understanding at some level possible. Consensus, as James Fernandez has noted, is etymologically con-sensus, feeling together (1988: 1–2). The Patum's intensity of performance brings the individual's senses into concert to receive strong impressions. Near-universal Patum participation in Berga guides the senses of the entire community in the same direction, obliges them to feel together in a way that their divided everyday experience can never foster.[5]

A range of techniques of the body work together to disempower the judgmental eye and to dissolve the surface inscriptions of social structure into the felt shared purpose of communitas.[6] *A Berga, Patum i mam,* "in Berga, Patum and booze," is a saying endlessly repeated during the time of Corpus, and associated with more than mere drinking: it describes the general sensual intoxication of the festival.[7] The consciousness-altering procedures of heavy drinking, sleep deprivation, vertigo, pushing the body to the limits of its strength (in carrying and dancing the heavy effigies, or simply in constant dancing for nonmembers of the Patum *comparses*),[8] all force the body's attention to its own sensations, rob the eye of its ability to focus. Darkness, fire, and smoke deter even the most determined gaze, as does the uniformity of dress—jeans, heavy shirts, kerchiefs, and cotton hats—intended to protect the individual from sparks but equally protecting him or her from the curious. Contact between people is forced by the sheer density of the crowd: the boundaries of the self cannot be monitored, nor can those of others.[9] Food and drink are freely passed between people during the Patum; arms are linked and bodies collide in the dancing. The common focus on a central image—the waltzing giants, the leaping maces—also assists in the relaxation of self-consciousness.

These bodily dispositions, of course, are reinforced ideologically. The Patum is generally understood to recapitulate the history of Berga's struggles as a community against a succession of invaders, beginning with the Moors. Subsequent enemies have been redefined according to the period and the political stripe of the interpreter, but their precise identity matters little. Still less precision has been required since the period of democracy, when both scholars and locals have referred the Patum back to the primordial time whence the historical community emerged. The event works as a reminder of a unity imagined as older and more basic than the divisions of structure.

Some people in Berga explicitly articulate the Patum experience as a leveling of classes. "For the Patum, el senyor Doctor and el senyor Lawyer come down to the plaça and become like anyone else," explains Gustau, a ceramist. Lluís, who has carried the giants for fifty years, says, "You'll see, for the Patum everyone is equal. But on Monday, everyone goes back to being what they are." "For the Patum," says Sílvia, a schoolteacher, "suddenly people who haven't talked to you all year will come up and embrace you—'Oh, how have you been? How nice to see you!' The very day after, it goes back to, 'Oh, hello.'" "We don't stick to our usual cliques for the Patum, everybody associates with everybody."[10] "There's a feeling of brotherhood—how can I describe it to you? It's a beautiful thing." I found that before as well as during the Patum social barriers—represented in spatial barriers—do indeed relax. In spring, as the festival approaches and the weather warms up, the more respectable people, the ones who mostly stay in their houses except for Mass and the Sunday afternoon stroll down the Carrer Major, begin to show up at the bars, eat in the restaurants, and assemble in groups chatting along the streets and squares.

Everyday and Patum ways of knowing have been shaped by opposing class positions. It is primarily the middle class that lives by the eye, and it is their values that define people in everyday life. For the Patum it is widely recognized that the tables turn: "Twenty men who have no kind of protagonism the rest of the year give the orders."

The fundamental social distinction in Berga today is between the *popular* and the *respectable. Popular* is partly a euphemism for *working-class,* but it really refers to a life-style, and many middle-class people have chosen to affiliate themselves with it. It entails informality, egalitarianism, public sociability, and active participation in local tradition. Respectability is not usually given a name, but it is also a recognizable congeries of traits, including Catholicism and concern for reputation and privacy. "You make yourself too popular," complained a judge I know to his son, specifying that he should spend less time in the bars and be charier with his company. Bodily distance makes for respectability; sharing and closeness without discrimination of ranks are popular habits.

Until the 1960s this distinction was clear-cut in Patum participation. Respectable people looked on from the balconies while the Patum was danced in the plaça by the working class. Evaluations were made on the balcony, communitas achieved on the plaça, often with little understanding passing in between. A story is told of a mayor during Primo de Rivera's dictatorship in the 1920s, serenaded for a Carnival celebration. "It's like Africa down there!" he cried, and is said to have thrown a wardrobe off the balcony to get rid of his unwelcome guests.

The comparses had always been recruited from the male working class. From the earliest document of the Patum in 1632 (Farrás 1979: 77), we know that the municipal corporation paid local people in money and sometimes in drink and new shoes to dance the festival effigies. The role of patumaire could be dangerous: the early *fuets* (slow-burning firecrackers with a long fuse and a charge at the bottom) exploded more strongly and less predictably than today's factory-made imitations. Even today there are accidents; in earlier times there was a risk of disfigurement. The people who "lived" the Patum before the 1960s were people who could not afford to place much importance on their looks. Laborers, they were accustomed to living in the body: they had no time or resources for making a good showing. Their sociability, like their work, was based in bodily sharing.

The balconies of the Plaça Sant Pere belonged to the finest houses in the city until the suburban-style expansion of the twentieth century. These balconies sheltered those bodies that needed to be protected from contamination,[11] made visible those bodies that relied on being seen for their status. A special dignity belonged to the balcony of City Hall, where the municipal authorities and their distinguished guests presided. Red velvet drapes and heraldic banners signaled the seat of social power: the municipal corporation and its distinguished visitors. In the balconies, too, sat the early authors on the Patum, who from this transcendent view perceived a symbolic contest of good and evil, not an experience of undifferentiated community (Vilardaga 1890; Sansalvador 1916; Huch 1955).

It was to the balconies that the upper classes of southern Europe retreated in the early modern period during all kinds of civic rituals and public festivals (Burke 1978: 270–81; Amelang 1986: 191–210). The growth of cities made the upper classes fearful of the disorder of the mob; the norms of bodily decorum developing during this period led them to distance themselves from the touch of the plebeian. But the aristocratic function of display, of embodying social power, caused them to create a stage for themselves rather than retreat entirely. Raised physically above the common people as they were symbolically, the upper class isolated itself among its peers. From this position they could control the plebs with their gaze and conveniently evaluate each other. For young upper-class women, whose market value depended on being untouched but who had to be seen to find a buyer, as it were, the balcony was of particular importance.[12]

An intermediary position was the *barana,* a long railing dividing the rising Carrer Buxadé from the plaça. Behind this stood working-class women and children and, most prominently, the peasant families visiting for the Patum and the Corpus Christi fair. "Patum and booze and the peasants at the barana," goes another variant of Berga's famous saying, and photographs from the late nineteenth century through the 1950s show families with picnic baskets leaning over the barana to see the show without getting hurt. These outsiders were not above the urban working class, but were, like the upper class, removed from participation with it.

This bodily comportment of the classes was, of course, not unique to the Patum, but reflected more general early modern European norms. Norbert Elias (1978) has written about the growth of *homo clausus:* the gradual formation of a bounded body and a private self among the court society and the bourgeoisie. Such a body was intrinsically hierarchical, relying on physical distance to maintain conceptual distinctness.

The plebeian alternative has been described by Mikhail Bakhtin (1984: 18–30) in his work on Carnival culture. Here the orifices of the body become channels of communication between man and nature, self and other. The urban festival body attains wholeness through a loss of boundaries, a massing with its fellows, and an unabashed indulgence in the senses. This body's recognition of temporal and physical process mock the pretensions of the finished classical body delineated by the early modern bourgeoisie.

The two bodies are balanced and mutually defining in the structure of the Patum: its effigies and dances recapitulate the dialogue of balcony and plaça. One pole is the beauty, distance, and definition of the giants and Eagle. The other is the grotesquery, unboundedness, and ambiguity of guites and devils. In the middle are the dwarves and Turks and horsemen, orderly but humble bodies regarded with affection and without awe for their humor and homely charm.

On Wednesday noon, the day the tabal and the giants come out of City Hall and process through the streets to announce the beginning of the festival, I was following along with Ritxi, the director of the municipal music school, and Pep, his second-in-command. When the *geganters* stopped at Cal Tonillo to take a drinking break before turning back toward the Plaça Sant Pere, Ritxi waved a finger at the four giants lined up under the eaves outside. "There's a pretty picture for you," he said. "Go ahead, take it: you'll never get a chance again to catch them all together in profile" (see fig. 6.2). So I took the photograph and we went into another bar to wait. Ritxi became melancholy, as is sometimes his way in between bursts of festival boisterousness. "You can't understand what we feel today, of course," he said to me. "Not even you, Pep, who are younger, feel it the same way—for you it's just a time to have fun. But we—Look at the giants!" He waved his glass toward the door. "Aren't they beautiful? You know, I've seen them come out every year of my life. And they're always the same, always beautiful. You and I grow old, I'm getting bald"—he patted his head ruefully. "Those never change."

He gazed into the bottom of his glass while Pep and I gulped ours down to return to the street and the tabal. Outside we met Pep's brother Màrius, who jerked his chin at the giants: "Fan respecte, eh?" They make you respect them.

Beauty can intimidate, and I saw the hairdressers who fix the giants' coiffures each year go about their task almost with trepidation. We should remember that beauty has social meaning. The norms of classical beauty, as Bakhtin pointed out, are a bourgeois invention. And they are exclusionary. In a community like Berga, which is still poor by Catalan standards and knew hunger until the 1960s, only the well-off had money for adequate food and for doctors, not to mention clothes, jewels, and cosmetics. They did not perform punishing physical labor. They were far more likely than the poor to keep

Fig. 6.2. ***Gegants:*** The four giants stand in front of City Hall when they are not dancing. Above on the balcony, the municipal corporation and visiting dignitaries preside over the Patum. Foto Luigi, Berga.

all their teeth, clear skin, and straight backs after the age of twenty. The classical body does not exhibit the invasions of experience. In Berga, only the wealthy could so insulate themselves.

The giants, aligned with the upper classes by their height and royal dress, are the epitome of incorruptible beauty in Berga. The two New, or Black, Giants of 1891 are considered by Berguedans to be the most beautiful of Catalonia, the best made, and best but most challenging to carry: the once ninety-kilo Black Giant is a real test of manhood. People often comment on the fineness of the faces, the majesty of the figures, the elegance of the dresses. The dress and coiffure of the Black Giantess, indeed, used to set feminine styles for the summer at the turn of the century.

Where the giants embody upper-class beauty, the Eagle reinforces the claims of the social structure dividing balcony from plaça. Prized as a symbol of the city, the Eagle too wears a crown (see fig. 6.3). The loudspeakers request silence for its dance, universally qualified as "majestic." Before dancing it salutes the embodiments of ecclesiastical

Fig. 6.3. ***Aliga:*** The eagle, considered a symbol of the city, stands in profile against the parish church. This photograph, a Patum icon, is displayed in many houses in Berga. Foto Luigi, Berga.

and civic power with a bow each to the parish church and City Hall. For the past three years, the municipal corporation has returned the acknowledgment by rising for the Eagle's dance. Nowadays the Eagle carries carnations or laurel branches in its beak, but it was known to have carried a live dove in the last century, a nice image of the ambiguities of power. Is the tender bird in the hard curved beak protected or entrapped?

Boundaries between comparsa and public are carefully maintained by *geganters* and *aligots,* those who carry the giants and Eagle. The giants are always encircled by their red-shirted guardians, protected from flames during the plens by sparklers waving the crowd away (the dresses are expensive, the geganters explain). The Eagle, with only three dancers, is given space by a common effort of the patumaires and Berguedan taboo ("watch out for the tail—it killed a soldier once"). An outsider resentful of Berga's haughtiness during Patum told me that a friend who once ventured to caress the Eagle was actually struck by the aligot and told, "L'Aliga no es toca!" (Nobody touches the eagle!). The Eagle does not participate in the structure-dissolving tirabols (the giants dance in a corner with a little circle protecting them from the crowd), nor in the processions of Wednesday and Saturday. It never leaves the protected space of the Plaça Sant Pere, under the watchful eyes of church and state. Like women and the upper classes, former denizens of the balconies, giants and the Eagle have bodies susceptible to pollution from contact: they must be removed from flames, from spectators.

Bodies accessible only to the gaze, protected by continual vigilance from the depredations of time and contact almost cease to be bodies. Stallybrass and White note the connection of the classical body with a raised and isolated position: they are thinking of the statue on a plinth, but it applies equally to the aristocrat on the balcony, the giants standing above the crowd, the Eagle inside its circle. "The classical statue is always the radiant centre of a transcendent individualism, 'put on a pedestal,' raised above the viewer and the commonality and anticipating passive admiration from below. We *gaze up* at the figure and wonder . . . In a sense, it is disembodied" (Stallybrass and White 1986: 21–22).

The guites, on the other hand, are very much present in the flesh. The more cumbersome Guita Grossa runs its neck along the barana on the side of the plaça, forcing the crowd to shrink down. It raises its fuets to the balconies, rattling them on the railings and driving well-dressed spectators inside. And it lowers its head and spins in the plaça, sending everyone to earth. The Guita Xica, or Boja ("Mad One"), has more flexibility. In addition to spinning and chasing, this smaller guita climbs up into the musicians' balcony and rides on the back of dump trucks. It pushes its way inside bars, the more elegant the better, until all its carriers are supplied with free drinks. Its invasions of inappropriate spaces often have distinct political implications. It regularly tries to get inside City Hall, its success depending on the particular political epoch. During the Franco period, it was once chased out of the barracks of the Guardia Civil with pistols, and in subsequent years those hated representatives of Spanish power prudently shut up their balconies and locked their doors for the duration of the festival.

The guites are the most obvious transgressors of the boundaries of inside and outside, high and low, spectator and participant. The maces also let down the barriers by the openness of their participation: except during the midday Patum, anyone who lines up may take a turn with the raised flame. The plens, by their numbers, have the greatest participation of any comparsa, and they force still wider participation, scattering through the crowd so that the entire plaça is engulfed in the smoke, nobody knows who is who, and everyone has to dance or be trampled. All of these *coses de foc* (things of fire) not only penetrate other spaces and bodies but also share the substance of their own, exploding in paper and powder to burn whomever they touch.

The eroticism of the encounter of public and comparsa is most visible with the guitz. People chase after it, drawing back when the guitz turns to caress them. The guitz advances to the provocations of children offering their hats to be burned or to outsiders cowering in a corner; it engages in a coquettish play of advance and retreat with umbrella-bearing tempters. Drawing back just before the climax, it celebrates the explosion with a humping tremor across its green frame.

The comportment of the comparses, obviously, is mirrored by the conduct of the public. Giants and Eagle must be known by the gaze; devils and guites are experienced through touch, desired or not. The principal exception to this rule is notable precisely as an exception, and has taken on a ceremonial quality. The four giants have moments of accessibility on Thursday and Sunday morning before the midday Patum. They are set out in a row under City Hall, a giant for each of the four tall columns, and left within public reach, the geganters nowhere to be seen. This is the great annual occasion for family photographs. All in their best clothes, they line up before the giants, and the photographer makes a group portrait of the family with Berga's "family." Parents bring their children, especially newborns, and hold them up to touch the hand of the Old Giantess or the Black Giant; the parents themselves caress the heavy velvet of their dresses, gaze up into the faces. They line up to approach the giants much as the faithful line up to approach the image and kiss the hand of the Madonna of Queralt on feast days.

Even here the eye's dominance is apparent: proximity to the prestige of the giants is recorded in photographic testimony. The photograph captures knowledge, freezes the gaze. Conventional images have developed in Berga, such as the photo Ritxi told me to take of the four giants in profile under Cal Tonillo. Another is the Eagle in profile against the façade of the church, a picture I've seen in more houses than I can remember. "Look, there you've got a beautiful photograph!" someone said to me, pointing out the Eagle as it lined up with the church. Dutifully, I snapped it, reproducing yet again one of Berga's favorite icons.

If the orderly bodies of the Patum are captured in icons, one might say that the disorderly bodies are captured in stigmata. The guites and the devils do not separate themselves but mix with the crowd and share their substance with it. The sign of contact that remains with the receiver is the burn. After my first Patum, my hands and arms were repeatedly seized and examined, my hat surveyed for holes. Then they shook their heads and derided my cowardice. People like to show you their Patum scars: one man tried to show me his permanently reddened buttocks from the days when the fireworks were of artisanal manufacture and exploded harder. Only in his fifties, he had gone mostly deaf from thirty-five years of doing four salts de plens per Patum, but it was clearly the world well lost so far as he was concerned. Old hats and sweaters—"more holes than sweater"—are brought out and worn every year, testimonials to participation. Several people recommended that I muddy up my new Patum hat, perhaps even burn it a bit with a cigarette so as not to look like an outsider. And burns when not given are sought: I saw lots of little boys holding their heads under the guita's flame. People standing along the barana nowadays are clearly asking for it: "If they're at the barana they know they're going to get burned." One guitaire, observing my intact kerchief on Saturday night, gave me a pitying look. "Give it to me," he said. "I'll bring it back well burned for you."

The analogies to icons and stigmata are perhaps not farfetched. The Patum clearly has a kind of sacrality that goes beyond its recent civil-religious status as "the baptism of Berguedan citizenship," "the ancestral rite," and the official occasion for invocations to unity. This civil religion would not enjoy its undoubted efficacy if it were not based in folk devotion. The customary practices surrounding the Patum effigies, collective and traditional, recall the "folk sacramentals" described by David Hufford at pilgrimage shrines (1985: 198). Both gaze and touch are ways to open channels of communication with Patum personages. But they reflect differing views of the nature of the sacred. The Patum had its origins precisely in an "argument of images" (Fernandez 1986: viii) between disciplined aristocratic bodies and open plebeian ones, between gaze and touch as ways of knowing. The terms of this argument were religious.

Corpus Christi is, of course, the feast of the Body of Christ. Instituted in the thirteenth century and diffused throughout Catalonia in the fourteenth, it was intended as a triumphal occasion to show the unity of the church militant against various heretical movements denying the reality of transubstantiation.[13] The church militant was also conceived as a body, Christ's mystical body. Hierarchically ordered, its head was Christ himself, and members were ranked according to their degree, from Pope and royalty down to the humblest believer. By this time this ecclesiastical metaphor had been borrowed by political theory, in the conception of society later known as the *body politic* (Kantorowicz 1957: 194–206).

Catalan Corpus Christi processions were laid out as literal representations of the social order following this hierarchical model. All the smaller corporations of the early modern city walked in order of their importance: the secular bodies, from guilds up to municipal corporations and the nobility; and the religious bodies, from lay confraternities, convents, and monasteries to the inquisitors and bishops. The climax of the procession was the Host under a canopy, the privilege of carrying which was annually disputed by the most illustrious men of the community. Preceded by clerical string players, the consecrated wafer was enthroned in a jeweled monstrance of precious metal that took the form of a blazing sun. No longer the humble Christ of our daily bread, this Host was a thing surrounded by shining gold, removed from reach, protected by mediators. It had almost ceased to be a body.

The mystical body and the body politic were thoroughly interpenetrated in these processions. The Corpus Christi procession, indeed, was identical in form to the entrée of visiting royalty, who took the place of the Host under the canopy. It is not clear whether royalty or divinity first made use of these forms: their lexicons of homage had clearly been shaping each other since the early days of Christianity (Kantorowicz 1957: 193). But this conflation made for many disputes between ecclesiastical and municipal authorities about control and precedence. The ranking implicit in proximity to the Host was also a source of disputes between corporations on the same level: rival guilds sometimes came to blows, and rival religious orders very nearly. The procession that attempted to represent the unity of the Christian community through a hierarchy of every man in his place led to a fierce struggle of the social body's members.

And we find a remarkable thing in the account of the Barcelona procession of 1424. After a lengthy and painstaking enumeration of the entities participating, we are told that there followed "two wild men carrying a bar to hold back the crowd. Behind, all the people" (Milà i Fontanals 1895: 379). In short, the urban plebs could not be fitted into this orderly conception. Headless, undifferentiated, the mob was cut off from the procession by that exemplary boundary symbol, the wild man.[14] Were the people also part of Christ's mystical body? Did they belong to the body politic?

The plebs soon appears in the historical record. Some of the common people participated in the procession as actors in allegorical scenes of the Old Testament and the lives of Christ and the saints. The clergy frequently complained of their lack of decorum in these roles: the Virgin Mary pinched the baby Jesus to make him cry affectingly, St.

Margaret's dragon snapped at pretty women, and so forth. From these scenes, apparently, originated the popular comparses of Catalan festivals—the giant from Goliath, the mule from the Nativity, and so on. It does not much matter whether this was indeed the case or whether the comparses are survivals from pre-Christian ritual, as many recent scholars would like to claim (Fàbregas 1979: 241–50; Farràs 1986: 36). It seems clear that the impetus of folk Corpus Christi observances in Berga and the rest of Catalonia, whatever their origins may have been, was popular exclusion from the body of the procession.[15] And the noisy, violent character of these celebrations suggests a rejection of the harmonious and differentiated social body that the procession described.

The Patum first appears in Berga's municipal records in the early seventeenth century as *les Bullícies*, the "racket" or "uproar." It was an adjunct to the ecclesiastical acts of the feast of Corpus Christi, performed inside the church a little before or after the procession (Farràs 1979: 70). Until 1695 the festival had only Turks and horsemen, devils, and mules. It was accompanied not by the band of today but by the tabal alone. It opposed the imagery of combat to the surface order of the procession, the noise of drum and explosions to the procession's stringed instruments. The mule, then a recognized symbol of lower-class intractability (Amelang 1986: 150), forced its way into the church in a refusal of exclusion. The devils mocked the church's claim to universality. But all these messages were sent in the safely coded language of the body. When the Bishop of Solsona complained in the early eighteenth century about the blackening of the church with smoke and the improprieties between devils and women in the side chapels, the locals defended the Bullícies as an allegory of Satan, infidels, and brute beasts rendering homage to the sacrament (Armengou 1968: 13–14, 23–24).

The local elite now had good reasons to defend the Patum. When City Hall took up the responsibilities of paying the performers and maintaining the effigies in decent repair, it turned the event into an occasion for civic display as well as a lure drawing the peasantry of the surrounding *comarca* to Berga's markets. The corporation thus disentangled itself from the church, leaving the clergy with the rule of the procession and easing friction.

Municipal sponsorship infused the Patum with the vocabulary of local patriotism and gradually brought about a domestication of its forms into a rather tidy dance-drama, smartened up with new clothes and music. As of the eighteenth century, the Patum was understood as a contest of good and evil, and embodiments of social order were gradually

Fig. 6.4. ***Nans Nous:*** The New Dwarves, shopkeepers in their Sunday best, are on a level with the crowd. Foto Luigi, Berga.

added to balance, we may guess, the threatening symbolism of guites and devils. The increasingly elegant giants, the Eagle symbolizing the city, the neat bourgeois dwarves added in the nineteenth century (see figs. 6.4 and 6.6) encapsulated the closed and hierarchical bodies of the procession; the music regulating their movements opposed the infernal drum of the uncontrolled salts. Sponsored by the forces of order, but still danced by the lower classes, the Patum came to synthesize and abstract the symbolism of both the procession and the Bullícies that contested it.

This balanced Patum of the nineteenth century persisted substantially unchanged until the early 1960s, unaffected by the political permutations that regularly gave new names to the heroes in the closed bodies, the enemies in the open ones. Then something happened to Patum practice and the norms of the social body. Participation became respectable. In Berga, the divisions of the Spanish Civil War were beginning to heal. Former Republicans and the Catholics who had reluctantly sided with the Nationalists to defend the church were united in their resentment of the Franco regime's brutal repression of Catalan culture. The Patum, tolerated because of its religious interpretation and as a safety valve for popular energies, was one of the few available channels of protest. Its symbolic violence could safely be directed at the balconies of power without fear of reprisal.

But something was stirring on the balconies as well. Mossèn Josep Armengou i Feliu, a Berguedan priest influential in the clandestine revival of Catalan nationalism, gained enormous local importance as an interpreter of Berguedan tradition in Catalanist terms. As he gave covert Catalan lessons to the children of the middle class, he instilled them with enthusiasm for the "baptism of Berguedan citizenship," the "school of Berguedan patriotism," and "the festival of Berguedan unanimity." The Patum, he wrote, was not "like any vulgar Festa Major": it was "the crucible of our race" (Armengou 1968). Armengou's preaching helped to legitimize the participation of women and the upper class in the festival, for whom it had hitherto been mal vist.

Other changes encouraged the descent from the balcony. This was a time of new prosperity for the factory workers and thus for the shopkeepers; it was also the period when the regime opened up to international influences. Berga began to see televisions, automobiles, washing machines, Coca-Cola, and "Frankfurt"-style modern bars. Media images of modernity entered the country, and Berguedans could now travel over the French border to see X-rated movies. The children of the upper and, eventually, middle classes began to go to university in Barcelona. These changes contributed to the relaxation of upper-class notions of decorum as well as the restrictions on women in public life.

The crowd increased further with outsiders from the surrounding region—always a presence, but now an invasion—and with enthusiasts from all over Catalonia. The Patum was one of the few festivals "of the street" that had been permitted to survive the dictatorship without heavy controls, Carnival having been everywhere suppressed, so both Catalanist fervor and a desire to let loose not elsewhere attainable found their outlet in the Patum. The Berguedans have not welcomed this "massification," which has diminished their "civic intimacy" and created significant problems of public order, but their own motives for intensified participation in no way differed from those of the visitors. The changes some attribute to outside influences were Berguedan initiatives.

Since the 1960s, the twelve or sixteen plens have increased to seventy or eighty per salt and sometimes more, well beyond the comfortable capacity of the plaça (see fig. 6.5). The three *tandes* of the Thursday and Sunday evening Patums (repetitions of the whole sequence of dances) have increased to four, with two salts de plens each night. The

Fig. 6.5. *Plens:* The infernal *plens* are the climax of the Patum in the plaça. Foto Luigi, Berga.

passacarrers, which successive mayors have tried to control by curtailing the route, have never ended before four in the morning, and have been followed by a "Patum of the Drunks" or "Patum of the Poor," done in the plaça without benefit of effigies or musical instruments. The tirabols, the final fusion of comparses and public into a single body whose beating heart is the tabal, have gone from three to about thirty at once, ending only when the musicians are exhausted.

The meaning of Patum communitas depends on the contrast with structure. But the internal opposition of the festival forms became all but invisible in the intensification of the Dionysian aspects of the festival. Rather, structure was in the forms of the dictatorship, the pressures of daily life.

Fig. 6.6. ***Nans Vells:*** The Old Dwarves waltz in the plaça. A nineteenth-century addition, the dwarves have been considered the entry of the middle class into the symbolism of the *Patum.* Foto Luigi, Berga.

The early dictatorship saw an obsession with social order and a full revival of the tyranny of the eye. No one knew who might denounce them for political indiscretions past or for present illegalities necessary for economic survival. Private sentiments and identity had to be masked in a public show of uniform submission: speaking Spanish, attending Mass, raising the arm in the Falangist salute. The gaze of the regime enforced hypocrisy and encouraged the self-policing of the community in mutual gazing.

At the same time, it revitalized the old hierarchical image of the body politic. The first action of Berga's Catholic elite after the end of the war, in what one must assume was intended as a gesture of community reintegration, was the construction of a new monstrance for the Corpus Christi procession. Finished in 1943, this monstrance was made of solid silver in a period of hunger and hardship. It depicted the sun of the Host sustained by Santa Eulàlia, patroness of the city, in turn supported by the Baroque columns of the high altar of the parish church (burned in 1936). Figures of Berga's churches adorned the sides. On the base were arrayed the comparses of the Patum, Eagle and giants occupying pride of place, and the devils, of course, trodden underfoot as supports to the whole construction. The Patum was thus admitted to the official symbolism, but subordinate and internally differentiated. On the back of the monstrance, the secular hierarchy was made equally clear with the engraved names of the Caudillo, the civil governor of Catalonia, and the mayor of Berga, their authority forever inscribed on this embodiment of the community (Serra 1944).

Like the plebeian crowd who danced les Bullícies in a rejection of the Corpus Christi procession, the crowd in the Patum of late Francoism reasserted the right of the people to resist the structure imposed on them. Like their ancestors they resorted to the indigenous lexicon of the open body: darkness, violence, primitivism. A teacher born in 1950 writes of the change he observed: "The Patum transformed itself into one of the few dances in Europe that's tribal, warlike, frenetic, primitive, and heartening. The ecstasy of abandonment to the night and the fire . . . the exaltation of hell and being an outlaw (the law of the inquisitorial church and the humiliating dictatorship), the perception of absolute freedom in the pain of the fire and the conquest of fear . . . made the culminating moment" (letter to author, Mar. 9, 1990).

Catalanist longings began to make participation respectable. The restoration of democracy in 1979 set the seal on this process. Now the balcony and the plaça are voluntary locations, but the plaça is normative. The balcony is the refuge of small children and the old. Tidy-minded persons who prefer not to disarrange themselves make the excuse that the Patum has gotten out of control since so many outsiders started coming. The municipal corporation and their visitors make the ritual lament that their official role forbids them to descend to the plaça: a lament sometimes feigned and sometimes genuine, but in either case obligatory.

The structure of the festival has begun to reframe the distinction of order and disorder. Occasion rather than class position has become the general guide to conduct. The noonday Patum *de Lluïment,* Patum of "show" or "splendor") is for dressing up and looking on; the Patum at night is for dancing in your old clothes. The relative focus of the Patum in the plaça contrasts with the spatial disarray and improvisatory quality of the passacarrers. The Friday Children's Patum puts the dancing of the less well-regulated adult Patum to shame: to see the shape of things before the crowd got in the way, they told me, you have to see the kids do it.

The dialectic of division and integration in the social body thus persists in democratic Berga, but detached from its moorings in social class. We have seen that popular and respectable lifestyles have become a matter of choice as well as of economics. Similarly, social divisions are much remarked upon, but as a split of equals owing to competition and quarrelsomeness. "In Berga everything is double" has attained the status of a proverb. There are in Berga, they endlessly point out, two music schools, two theaters, two ski clubs, two political parties, ideologically identical but personally opposed. In Berga, as in Catalonia generally, the great disillusionment of democracy has been the squandering of opportunities for progress in petty factional fighting. "If you put three Catalans on a desert island, you get two political parties and a secessionist," a Barcelonan familiar with Berga told me. "It's Turks and horsemen," remarked a Berguedan about Barcelona's politics. Divisiveness is the bitterest evil of daily life, but the denunciations of partisanship are still made by partisans.

But the Patum is an occasion of unity, and Berguedans have repeatedly advised me not to make so much of social conflict in my analysis of it. I record their objection and hope they will forgive me for persisting. The insistence on a dance-drama of combat as an avenue to social harmony certainly sums up some of the paradoxes of Berga's body politic. It is notable that the discourse currently surrounding the Patum resolves the same paradox in a metaphor of the open body. Unity in division is expressed through reproductive symbolism.[16]

I was walking down the Carrer Major on Friday night of the Patum with my friends Ramon and Benigne. It was early—only 2:00 A.M., perhaps—but we were all tired and heading homeward, this being the one night when such early retirement is possible. But a voice hailed Ramon, and we turned into the bar it came from: one more glass. They were a middle-aged couple of some social prominence; they were leaning against the bar for support, and they were in the highest of spirits. Ramon introduced me, and, as was inevitable, we began to talk Patum.

"The Patum is unique," said the woman. "For example, what exactly *is* the guita? Is it male or female? Have you ever thought about it? How does the guita reproduce? There are two of them! Where did they come from?"

"It's obvious," murmured her husband. "The guita is hermaphroditic."

"Just think!" she went on. "Just think, if one day you were walking through a desert somewhere and you saw little guites running around. The daughters of the guita! If you were from Berga, your eyes would fill up with tears this big!" Her eyes glisten and she begins to reflect. "You know what I'd like to see, I'd like to see the guita stripped."

"What are you saying now?" said the husband.

"Yes, just once, to see it come out completely naked. Aren't you curious at all?"

Her husband protested, "Poor beast, what do you want to do to it? It would be too sad!"

But she was obstinate. "Stripped! Hey! What if we did a *Patum pornogràfica!* Everything without anything. The guites stripped, the giants nude, everything!"

Benigne, who was not quite as drunk as the rest of us, observed, "Casserres [a local giant-sculptor] would have to make some new pieces . . ."

Now the husband warmed to the idea, his opened eyes like saucers. "Imagine the balls of the Black Giant! And when they're dancing!"

This astonishing conversation was my introduction to the wealth of erotic fantasy revolving around guites and giants. As it suggests, their sexuality is not divorced from procreation. More decorously, the giants are conceived as a family among themselves, ancestors to the people of Berga. Mossèn Armengou wrote, "Let tradition say what it will [about the supposed Moorish identity of the giants], the fact is that after so many centuries of living together, today we Berguedans look at our Giants with the love and veneration with which we would look at our great-grandparents" (1968: 59).

The Patum itself is a mother. "They suck their mother's breast and they suck the Patum," said Rossendo of the plens about the children of Berga. The word for suckling, *mamar,* also creates the noun *mam,* used for Patum drinking—as in "Patum i mam." A young printer told me as we followed the drum down the street with an army of children, "Do you know why little kids like the tabal so much? They say it's the rhythm of the mother's heart in the womb." I never heard this again, but I saw souvenirs for a baby's baptism made in the form of a tiny tabal.

The salt de plens is commonly referred to as "baptism" or "initiation." To be dressed, the devil-to-be goes down below City Hall, through dark narrow corridors, and into a small room, where she is wound about with vines and bandages, masked, and costumed into blindness. She is led back up to the plaça, where the lamps have been put out, by a guide. When the music starts, the guide sets her alight and she begins to dance for her life, the crowd pressing, the sparks falling on her hands and inside her mask. When I did my first salt, I had no idea which of the explosions above my head were mine, or who or what was around me: helpless, I did what my *acompanyant* told me until it was over and he lifted my mask and the lights came up. I gasped for air and gaped at the plaça: it was truly emergence from a place I hadn't been before.

As they kept telling me, I cannot expect to feel what the people of Berga feel, and the placidity of the academic life has ill prepared me for such experiences. But insofar as anyone can speak of the plens, the referents are orgasm and rebirth. A salt de plens has a well-known double meaning in Berga. And birth is in the violence of the process, the struggle to get through it and out. In a single moment, the plens condense the beginning and the end of generation.

The mother is credited with decisive creative powers in Berga. Bad temper is known as *mala llet,* "bad milk," and a vile person is *malparit,* "badly born" or "aborted." *Ben parit,* in popular speech, is a term of the most tender praise. And the mother-child relationship is an intimacy like no other. Once I heard a woman make a declaration to her lover in the company of people unaware of the relationship. "*Nen* (little boy)," she said, "I know you as well as if I'd given you birth."

We might remember Freud's concept of the "oceanic feeling," the religious sense of boundlessness or unity of the ego and its surroundings that he explains as a memory of the child's bodily union with its mother (1961: 11–20). Without seeking to create such an explanatory link, we may recognize the appropriateness of the maternal as metaphor. The mother-child relationship of close contact and sharing of substance describes the sensation of undifferentiated well-being many experience during the Patum. This is in contradistinction to the comparatively distant, abstract relations with the father, more proper to the judgment of the eye than the communion of the body.

And it is in contradistinction to the masculine sacred, the fragile white Host surrounded by its priestly guardians. The mother and child, united in a single image as black as the earth it was buried in, are the focus of Catalan folk devotion. Believed to have been found by shepherds in coves or by streams of the native mountains, the images of the Mother of God[17] around Catalonia (Camós 1949) provided an autochthonous version of the sacred to those excluded from the self-declared universal church. The power of the Mother of God was open to the individual believer. Her divinity was immanent, whereas the male power of God was not directly knowable and required a hierarchy of access. She could be touched; she was known to accept favors and to return them. She sympathized with the humble, as her well-known miracles made clear, but God the Father and God the Son seemed to demand much of the poor for an uncertain recompense.

The Mother of God of Queralt has a devotion that goes well beyond practicing Catholics in Berga: her image was saved from the flames in 1936 by the town's own revolutionary committee. The Patum, sharing her traits, but also polymorphous and open to redefinition, is still more beloved. Its ability to make one body of many, to reproduce itself over the centuries, and to incarnate simultaneously contradictory Berguedan self-images is a kind of divinity. By calling the Patum a mother, Berguedans celebrate its transformative power. Participating, living the Patum, they drink in its regenerative force. The bounded body ultimately denies its own reality: the Corpus Christi procession is dead. It is the ambivalent body open to history that takes on immortality.

Notes

1. Fieldwork was done from March through June 1989 and June and July 1990. I owe an enormous debt to the people of Berga for their unfailing generosity and insight. Roger Abrahams and James Fernandez have provided guidance from the inception of this project; many other teachers, colleagues, and friends have endured my obsession with good humor and useful suggestions. The University of Pennsylvania gave me a Mellon Dissertation Fellowship for 1989–90 and 1990–91.
2. Catalonia is a triangle of land on the Iberian Peninsula stretching from the Eastern Pyrenees to the delta of the Ebre River on the Mediterranean, with Barcelona as its center and capital. It is a nation incorporated by force into the Spanish state in 1714 and again in 1939. Although the definition of nationhood is contested, Catalonia fits the usual criteria: a strong medieval polity, a long history of autonomous institutions, a distinctive language and culture, and a nineteenth-century nationalist movement. But I call it a nation because my Berguedan informants consider it one—an experiential unity felt as "home."
3. In English, of course, it is natural to write this word as "plaza." But the Catalans have so long and so inappropriately been viewed through a Spanish lens that I would rather not use the familiar spelling: the Patum is not a familiar reality.
4. All translations are mine.
5. Fernandez notes that in Catholic societies, of course, the great occasion of consensus building was once the ritual of the Eucharist (1988: 12–13). In Berga the Eucharist does not unite the community, because much of the traditionally anticlerical working class and a certain proportion of the middle-class intelligentsia are not practicing Catholics. First Communion, indeed, is many children's introduction to the tyranny of the eye: "It's all for the sake of the long dress," complained one freethinking mother whose daughter had insisted on going through the ceremony with her friends. However, Catholic habits of thought persist, and commensality is an important symbol of community in Berga. Restaurants in the "popular" bars have long tables to be shared by all comers; working-class people in particular frequently eat out in groups rather than at home en famille, as do the more status- and privacy-conscious middle class. This habit is formalized in the frequent *apats de germanor,* "meals of brotherhood," of voluntary organizations and festival occasions.

6. Victor Turner first distinguished structure and communitas as modes of social relatedness. Structure depends on evaluation and the assignation of social roles; communitas emerges in ritual as the equality of community members before a deeper reality (1969: 96–97).
7. Conservative voices in more repressive periods have denounced this phrase as the slanderous *blason populaire* of outsiders who do not understand the contemplative character of the festival (Armengou 1968: 71). However, such contemplation as may occur is aided by wine, and the old man who counsels you to drink with good sense will simultaneously force a dozenth glass on you. *Patum i mam* is painted on the blue jeans and shirts of teenagers, and I heard an immigrant mother instilling spirit in her three-year old son as he practiced for the Children's Patum with the cry of "Patum i mam, boy!"
8. The word *comparsa* refers to the people dancing the festival effigies as well as to the effigies themselves.
9. Angel, the bookseller on the Carrer Major, likes to explain that the erotic delight of his adolescence in the Franco period was rubbing up against the relatively few women then in the plaça. He claims that he was occasionally slapped for transgressions not of his committing, given the difficulty of determining the offender in the crush of people. I was also told (by a priest) of an old widow who used to say, "I love the Patum. There's always some shameless fellow who gooses you."
10. This is not strictly true, as far as I can tell. People do the Patum with their everyday friends. However, the usual group is augmented by returnees and visitors; group boundaries are perhaps more flexible and more recognition is exchanged between groups. The force of the crowd makes a stronger impression, perhaps, than the company of one's usual group.
11. On the isomorphy of the body and the social group, and the dangers of pollution through bodily contact, see Douglas 1982.
12. It is important to note that women made uses for the balcony subversive of their enforced spatial isolation. The balcony allowed a woman to communicate with the other sex, and to control the communication: it lay in her power to show herself or withdraw, to drop a message or make a sign. Several Catalan proverbs report that a girl who lingers on the balcony will come to no good, and the image of a woman on a balcony in Catalan folk song is almost always a prelude to an illicit sexual act (corpora examined include Blasco 1989; Ferré et al. 1988; Serra i Vilaró 1989). In these songs, as in so many other contexts, the house, to which the woman was confined and for which she was largely responsible becomes isomorphic with her own body. The balcony, as an orifice of the house, is a ready metaphor for her sexual availability.
13. For the history of Corpus Christi in Catalonia, see Very 1962, Duran i Sanpere 1973, and Milà i Fontanals 1895. A good analysis of bodily symbolism in the English celebration is James 1986.
14. A reminiscence of whom we may possible see in the vine-covered Plens of the Patum.
15. The best discussion of the procession-people dynamic for a city in the Catalan linguistic area is Ariño 1988: 363–496.

16. An energetic Freudian could easily discover images of digestion and defecation instead of copulation and birth in the Patum. But my concern is with local understanding. Although the Berguedans are not at all squeamish about the scatological, I have yet to hear such metaphors applied to the Patum.
17. Popular usage in Catalonia refers to Mary as *la Mare de Déu,* the Mother of God: she is rarely spoken of as the Virgin.

References

Amelang, James S. 1986. *Honored citizens of Barcelona: Patrician culture and class relations, 1490–1714.* Princeton, NJ: Princeton Univ. Press.

Ariño, Antoni. 1988. *Temes d'etnografia valenciana.* Vol. 4. *Festes, rituals, i creences.* València: Edicions Alfons el Magnànim.

Armengou i Feliu, Josep. 1968. *La Patum de Berga.* Berga: Edicions del Museu Municipal.

Bakhtin, Mikhail. [1968] 1984. *Rabelais and his world.* Trans. Hélène Iswolsky. Bloomington: Indiana Univ. Press.

Blasco, Artur. 1989. *Rosa vermella, rosa galant. Parles, cançons i cantarelles.* Barcelona: Audiovisuals de Sarrià, S.A.

Burke, Peter. 1978. *Popular culture in early modern Europe.* New York: Harper and Row.

Camós, Narciso. [1657] 1949. *Jardín de Maria Planteado en el principado de Cataluña.* Barcelona: Editorial Orbis.

Douglas, Mary, 1982. *Natural symbols: Explorations in cosmology.* New York: Pantheon.

Duran i Sanpere, Agustí. 1973. Les festes de corpus. In *Barcelona i la seva història* 3: 529-571. Barcelona: Curial.

Elias, Norbert. [1939] 1978. *The history of manners.* Trans. Edmund Jephcott. New York: Pantheon.

Fàbregas, Xavier. 1979. *Tradicions, mites i creences dels catalans: la pervivència de la Catalunya ancestral.* Barcelona: Edicions 62.

Farràs, Jaume. 1979. Textos i comentaris sobre les Bullícies de Berga al segle XVII, segons les actes i comptes municipals. In *XXIII Assemblea intercomarcal d'estudiosos celebrada el Juny de 1979 a Berga,* 69–77. *Revista del Centre d'Estudis Berguedans,* 1 Berga: Ajuntament de Berga.

———. 1986. *La Patum de Berga.* Barcelona: Nou Art Thor.

Fernandez, James W. 1986. *Persuasions and performances: The play of tropes in culture.* Bloomington: Indiana Univ. Press.

———. 1988. Isn't there anything out there we can all believe in? The quest for cultural consensus in anthropology and history. Paper read at the Institute for Advanced Study School of Social Science, Princeton.

Ferré, Gabriel, Salvador Rebés, and Isabel Ruiz, eds. 1988. *Cançoner tradicional del Baix Camp i el Montsant.* Barcelona: Editorial Alta Fulla.

Ferrer i Gàsol, Agustí. 1989. Script for audiovisual, La Patum: Foc i fantasia. Berga: Ambit de Recerques del Berguedà.

Freud, Sigmund, 1962. *Civilization and its discontents.* Trans. James Strachey. New York: W. W. Norton.

Huch i Guixer, Jaume. 1955. *Notes històriques de la ciutat de Berga.* Berga: Privately published.

Hufford, David, 1985. Ste. Anne de Beaupré: Roman Catholic pilgrimage and healing. *Western Folklore* 44 (3): 194–207.

James, Mervyn, 1986. Ritual, drama, and the social body in the late medieval English town. In *Society, politics, and culture: Studies in early modern England,* 16–47. Cambridge: Cambridge Univ. Press.

Kantorowicz, Ernst H. 1957. *The king's two bodies: A study in medieval political theology.* Princeton: Princeton Univ. Press.

Milà i Fontanals, Manuel. 1895. Orígenes del teatro Catalán. In *Obras completas* 6. Barcelona. N.p.

Sansalvador, Antoni. 1916. *La Patum.* Barcelona: Llibreria Antonio Pérez.

Serra, José. 1944. *La custodia monumental de Berga.* Berga: Impremta Huch.

Serra i Vilaró, Joan, ed. [1913] 1989. *El cançoner del Calic.* Bagà: Ajuntament de Bagà.

Stallybrass, Peter, and Allon White. 1986. *The politics and poetics of transgression.* Ithaca: Cornell Univ. Press.

Turner, Victor. 1977. *The ritual process: Structure and anti-structure.* Ithaca: Cornell Univ. Press.

Very, F. G. 1962. *The Spanish Corpus Christi procession: A literary and folkloristic study.* Valencia. N.p.

Vilardaga, Jacinto. 1890. *Historia de Berga.* Barcelona: Privately published.

Embodiment/Disembodiment

The body as a locus of self is impugned by the lodgement of discourses of the self off the body. Quilts elaborate a gendered discourse, an *écriture feminine,* in Hélène Cixous's words, by which a self is embodied elsewhere. The material properties of the quilt can encode the corporeal properties of the self. What the quilter fabricates turns out to be her own body.

Manifestations of saintliness are directed against the materiality, the solidity, of the body. The capacity of the Muslim Sheikh Mūsa to vanish, to reappear in two places at once, or to levitate attest to a rarefication of bodily substance, further evidenced in the frothy effluvium that issues from his mouth. This attenuation of substance eventuates in an emanation of the spirit out of the body. The disembodied spirit, in turn, substantially affects the material world. The contingency of the lodgement of the spirit in the body—the mind/body problem—becomes the central problematic of these inquiries.

7. *Quilts and Women's Bodies:* Dis-eased and Desiring

JANE PRZYBYSZ

I wonder if I am dead.

—Anonymous quilter. Words appearing on a Victorian crazy quilt, stitched on a "simple black velvet patch, in the midst of the most incredible profusion of textures, colors, embroidered animals, plants, and countless 'show' stitches." (Holstein 1973: 62)

[Making quilted and embellished clothing] is what I do to keep from going into a room and screaming, Here I am! Notice me!

—Elinor Peace Bailey, contemporary doll and quilt artist

By writing her self, woman will return to the body which has been more than confiscated from her, which has been turned into the uncanny stranger on display—the ailing or dead figure, which so often turns out to be the nasty companion, the cause and location of inhibitions. Censor the body and you censor breath and speech at the same time.

—Hélène Cixous, "Laugh of the Medusa"

In the February 1988 issue of *Quilter's Newsletter Magazine* there appeared a fictional short story by Paula Kay Martin entitled "The Quilt Addict." The piece began as follows:

> My hands were sweating; my heart was pounding. A sea of faces stared up at me, waiting for words to emerge from my mouth. My knees wanted to fold up and go home. I rallied my courage, "I'm . . . uh . . . I'm . . . uh . . ."

Fig. 7.1. The Quilted Body: "I loved the idea that I contained more than one person within me. That made me a crowd and talking to myself became a great deal more like talking to an audience, and there is nothing I like better than an audience." Elinor Peace Bailey, *Mother Plays with Dolls* (1990). Photograph by Jane Przybysz.

> I tried again, a little louder this time. "I'm a quilting addict." There, I'd said it. The audience applauded. My heartbeat slowed. Before me sat fifty poor, suffering souls that were in the same boat.
>
> "It's a disease," they said. "Probably not curable, but controllable." There was hope. I went back to my seat, elated by my confession. I was subdued by the thought of never quilting again. As I sat down, I thought back to how it had all started . . . (Martin 22)

The author then goes on to chronicle the development of her addiction. She describes the symptoms of the disease:

> I found my hand running over and over the curved surface. I sat and stared at the colored prints while tracing the quilt thread streams with my finger . . . I would sneak back downstairs before going to bed each night (usually closer to early morning) to get one more look [at the quilt] . . . I had trouble sleeping . . . My life revolved around fabrics. I would go into my sewing room and not emerge for days. My husband threatened to leave me. My kids refused to wear any more quilted clothing. They said they wanted clothes like the other kids wore.

At the end of the piece, the narrator, whose visit to a meeting of Quilters Anonymous is coming to an end, decides she will always be a quilter. "But," she says, "I must control my disease or my husband will leave me for sure. I will try not to quilt through dinner. Yes, that would help. Maybe I could limit myself to three quilt projects at a time; that would also help. I could leave my quilting projects at home when we go to the beach . . . I could even give up quilting from 2 to 4 A.M." Yet as she leaves the meeting, she feels her fingers itch from quilting withdrawal. She races out the door, her heart pounding and hands sweating in anticipation of quilting once again.

Initially this story seemed simply an expanded version of the tongue-in-cheek slogans slapped on bumper stickers, mugs, and T-shirts that quilters buy and sell at quilt festivals: Warning: Quilt Fever; Warning: Quilting is Contagious; Old Quilters Never Die, They Just Go to Pieces; My Wife is a Quilter and Our House is in Pieces; Quilting Forever, Housework Whenever. Yet subsequent fieldwork conducted at the first international quilt festival in Europe sponsored by the Houston-based American/International Quilting Association and in preparation for an exhibit about quilt-making groups in Delaware County, New York, made it seem otherwise. Increasingly "The Quilt Addict" seemed to provide a kind of narrative coherence to the ways quilters consciously and unconsciously use metaphors of illness, madness, and desire—not only in the stories they share with one another at quilt events but also in the names they give the quilts and quilted garments they make. Stories about how they got "hooked" on quilting, about how "crazy" they are to have a closet full of unfinished quilt projects, and about "bouts" of fabric buying abound wherever quilters gather. The viewers' choice award at Quilt Expo Europa went to a quilt entitled "Crazy Quilt for a New World." A glance at the quilted garment fashion show program revealed names such as "I'd Rather Be . . .," "Fantasy in Flame," "Saw Grass Fire," "My Heart's Desire," "The Gypsy in My Soul," "Spacial Palatial Dancin': The Black Hole Strut," and "Rumba, Samba, Cha-Cha-Cha!"

In addition to offering a narrative framework that might be used to interpret all the talk of illness, madness, and desire that goes on among contemporary quilters, "The Quilt Addict" resonated in a very curious way with a mid–nineteenth-century fictional story by George Washington Harris entitled "Mrs. Yardley's Quilting." Set in rural Tennessee, the story is narrated by Sut Lovingood, an illiterate and shameless country fella. Describing Mrs. Yardley, he says,

> Yu see quilts wer wun of her speshul gifts; she run strong on the bed-kiver question. Irish chain, star ove' Texas, sun-flower, nine dimunt, saw teeth, checker board, an' shell quilts; blue, an' white, an' yaller an' black coverlids, an' callicker-cumfurts reigned triumphan' 'bout her hous'. They wer packed in drawers, laying in shelfs full, wer hung four dubbil on lines in the lof, packed in chists, piled on cheers, an' wer everywhar, even ontu the beds, an' wer changed every bed-makin. She told everybody she cud git tu listen to hit that she ment to give every durn'd one ove them tu Sal when she got married. Oh, lordy! what es fat a gal as Sal Yardley cud ever du wif half ove em, an' sleepin wif a husbun at that, is more nor I ever cud see through. Jis' think ove her onder twenty layer ove quilts in July, an' yu in thar too. (1973: 135)

As Sut approaches the Yardley house the day of the quilting, he marvels:

> All the plow-lines an' clothes-lines wer straiched tu every post an' tree. Quilts purvailed. Durn my gizzard ef two acres roun that ar house warn't jis' one solid quilt, all out a-sunnin, an' tu be seed. They dazzled the eyes, skeered the hosses, gin wimen the heart-burn and perdominated. (1973: 136)

Both "The Quilt Addict" and "Mrs. Yardley's Quilting" seem to describe a similar phenomenon: quilters who threaten the "health" of both the physical and social body. The quilt addict "suffers" a heart-pounding and palm-sweating sort of excitement and disrupts family life to the extent that her children revolt and her husband threatens to leave. Mrs. Yardley scares animals, gives women heartburn, and problematizes male-female relations. Her daughter Sally's potential suitor imagines himself suffocating beneath the layers of quilts Mrs. Yardley has promised to bequeath to Sal when she marries. This seems to seriously dampens his inclination to wed Sal.

Both stories similarly locate the dis-ease that quilters represent in the female desire to materially and symbolically amplify and extend the self, and in the excited bodily states quilts and/or quilt making inspire in women; yet they propose very different cures. The cure for the quilt addict is to physically move outside the domestic sphere into spaces organized and controlled by like-minded women where she experiences her body sweating and palpitating in anticipation of *speaking* in the same way she experiences her body sweating and palpitating in anticipation of *quilting*. Her cure comes not from ridding her body of disease but from allowing it to inhabit her body more fully so that it spreads to other realms of expression, other realms of experience. In effect, the cure for the quilt addict's disease is a refusal to be cured.

The way "Mrs. Yardley's Quilting" is constructed, Mrs. Yardley becomes the accidental victim of a practical joke Sut plays on a town fella who has also been invited to the quilting. But I guess I wonder just how accidental a victim she is. Disturbed by the fact that Mrs. Yardley has invited a person outside the immediate, rural community—a "town fella"—to the quilting party, Sut ties the end of a clothesline filled with Mrs. Yardley's quilts to the stirrups of the town fella's horse and then scares the horse so that it runs away. The horse runs over Mrs. Yardley and, with its leg poked through one of her prized quilts, drags it along after him. At the moment she is struck down, Mrs. Yardley is standing beside one of her quilts, basking in the admiration being showered upon it—upon her—by another woman. Uttering the words, "Oh, my preshus nine dimunt quilt," Mrs. Yardley dies. It's not clear, however, whether she dies of wounds inflicted by the horse; or of wounds inflicted on her quilt, which she experiences mimetically as wounds to her body; or because Sut finds her desire for self-extension, to invite that which is "other" (in this case, urban) into her community and home, and the pleasure she derives from quilts and from "intercourse" with women a threat to his masculine identity and privilege.

Literary critic Milton Rickels accounts for the deadly ending of this supposedly comic tale by noting that it is Harris's "satire on literary sentimentalism" (1965: 77). A feminist reading of Mrs. Yardley's demise, however, yields an interpretation more consistent with Sut's view of women as wanting "tu be a man; and es they cant, they fixes up thar case by being devils" (Rickels 1965: 54).

In *The Newly Born Woman,* French feminists Hélène Cixous and Catherine Clément analyze the feminine role as it has historically been constructed by white, male-dominant, Western cultures. They attempt to formulate, to dream their way out of this role, to give birth to their selves as "newly born women." In the first half of the book, Cixous suggests the need to recognize the hysteric and the sorceress as rebellious signs of women's excess desire, excess rage, and excess creativity. She argues that "these women, to escape the misfortune of their economic and familial exploitation, chose to suffer spectacularly before an audience of men: it is an attack of spectacle, a crisis of suffering. And the attack is also a festival, a celebration of their guilt used as a weapon . . ." (1986: 10).

The hysteric stages this attack on her own body as visible signs of psychic distress, which have the effect of "introduc[ing] disorder into the well-regulated unfolding of every day life." The sorceress attacks the establishment by healing against the church's canon, performing abortions, and hosting the sabbat—a celebration of endogamous, nonconjugal love marked by an absence of the exchange of women and by sexual unions that do not result in procreation. The sabbat celebrates what most marriage contracts—based as they are on the exogamous exchange of women between men for the purpose of (re)producing children and, hence, the social order—are designed to discourage. To the extent that quilt addicts use quilts to visually and materially disrupt what might be called, borrowing Bourdieu's term, the *habitus* of family life, and to the extent that quilters regularly gather with other women at quilt events–cum–sabbats to celebrate their dis-ease with the given social order, they appear to embody the roles of both the hysteric and the sorceress.[1]

According to Cixous and Clément (1986: 36), the attacks staged by the sorceress also take the form of mixing together partial objects and transforming them into useful objects that she then puts back into circulation. These partial objects, "especially powerful . . . [as] where the object of desire settles," consist mostly of wastes—"nail clippings, menstrual blood, excrement, a lock of hair; scraps of the body are what will act as a charm" (Cixous and Clément 1986: 35). That many quilts are useful objects made from partial objects, scraps of fabric and scraps of clothing that might be understood metonymically as scraps of skin or scraps of bodies, suggests that quilts are to quilters what charms are to the sorceress—objects of desire made and circulated to disrupt dominant cultural economies of pleasure.

Embracing the hysteric and sorceress as role models is not, however, unproblematic, as Cixous is well aware. For although they are both anti-establishment in their ability to stage attacks of spectacle, spectacles of suffering that "shake up the public, the group, the men," they are also conservative, because, like Mrs. Yardley, "every sorceress ends up being destroyed" and the family closes around the hysteric so that she, too, effectively disappears.

Clément devotes the second half of *The Newly Born Woman* to re-viewing Freud's narrative of the development of female sexuality. She underscores the difficulties women in patriarchal configurations of necessity experience in shifting their allegiance away from the female (or mother) to the male as the primary love object. Clément posits that these "difficulties" are in fact an advantage for women in so far as women seem to be capable of experiencing a polymorphous sexuality. Whereas male notions of sexual pleasure appear to be highly dependent on narratives that picture men reaching orgasm inside a woman, Clément suggests that female sexuality is experienced more diffusely, often in ways that do not depend on stereotypical male sexual narratives. To resist the feminine role prescribed by white, male-dominant discourses, Clément recommends that women need only explore their more polymorphous sexuality.

Although quilt making is a cultural activity that historically has been used to deform, reform, and transform female children into complacent, obedient, and self-sacrificing wives and mothers (an effective way of "killing" women off), it seems to me that quilt making also has functioned as what Cixous has termed *écriture feminine*—a term I translate as "female writing" and interpret to mean a cultural practice that is a body praxis some women use to alter patterns of female and male body use in the domestic sphere, thereby disrupting "the environment of everyday practical activities that generate and reinforce both stereotypical ideas and body habits" (Jackson 1983: 334). Although quilt making as a cultural activity can certainly be practiced to accommodate gender-, sex-, race-, and class-specific body habits that maintain the status quo, I would suggest that when pursued with a "passion"—a term that appears again and again in both popular and academic writing about the role of quilt making in women's lives—as an erotic and healing practice, it plays havoc with body habits that are "the ground of what is thought and said" (Jackson 1983: 337). Destabilizing the ground of what is thought and said, quilt making as practiced by some women in specific sociocultural and historical contexts, seems to make possible new ways of experiencing, thinking and speaking about the self.

Women's relation to space and time is central to the narratives quilters formally and informally exchange about their dis-ease. Quilt addicts describe how their first quilt project generally began on a small scale, confined to a table in a seldom-used domestic space. But in a relatively brief span of time, the number of quilt projects undertaken multiplied, the projects became larger in size, and soon no room was without a piece of a quilt-in-progress or at least traces of some quilt in the form of loose threads clinging to clothes, furniture upholstery, and rugs. According to what might be termed "how-I-began-quilting" origin stories, women eventually begin taking handwork with them outside the home, often in the context of family outings, thus moving into public view what is generally perceived as a domestic activity.

Just as the space women take up with the making of quilts expands within and beyond their homes, so the space the quilts themselves come to occupy increases exponentially. Soon there is no room in the house that does not have a quilt on a bed, on a wall, or draped over a chair. In no time, family members moving between the domestic and public spheres are awash in quilted and embellished clothing, the surface of their bodies functioning as theatrical space in/on which quilters display their desire and dis-ease.

Women's efforts to appropriate space—a (sewing) room of their own—for their quilt making activities seem very much linked to a desire for an experience of time that is uninterrupted, and an experience of self as sensuous, desiring, and whole. For the many women whose bodily and social energies are constantly at the service of children, husbands, and/or employers, and hence fragmented, the experience of working in a concentrated manner on anything is something they crave. In addition, each of the activities involved with quilt making—designing, ironing, cutting, machine sewing, and hand sewing—induces various body experiences. Working with color, texture, and pattern at the design and the quilting phase is exhilarating to the touch and to the eye. Ironing and hand sewing for extended periods of time can induce trancelike, meditative states of calm. Using a sewing machine requires exacting hand-eye-foot coordination. Many women derive great pleasure from the speed with which increased body mastery allows them to sew by machine. Engaging in any of these activities in the presence of other women who are likewise dis-eased generates a performative space in which this new relation to time, to body, and to self might be spoken.

Providing coherence and continuity to a fragmented and fragmenting experience of reality and self, and reclaiming/reframing the female body as a self-sufficient, sensuous, and desiring source of pleasure, quilt making potentially brings women to conceive of their "selves" as speaking subjects and marks their entrance into history as social and political agents. Quilt making as *écriture feminine*—not an essentialist, eternally "feminine" form of writing, but one that developed historically as a "feminizing" cultural activity in western patriarchal cultures—has been sustained and periodically revived by some women as a body praxis to cure their dis-ease with social relations under patriarchy. Creating literal and metaphorical space and time for experiencing their bodies as sources of pleasure and constructing their "selves" as multiple (as capable of incorporating that which is "other"), yet coherent, speaking subjects, some quilters have used and continue to use quilts to stage an attack of spectacle, a crisis of suffering for an audience of men; to implicitly, if not explicitly, resist cultural constructions of "woman" as the eternal comforter, wife, mother, and America; to make visible and sharable the enormous, invisible, and undervalued work of caring for and (re)producing human beings and social relations; and to disrupt the economy of desire and pleasure organized primarily around the organ of sight—the eye. It is an attack of spectacle that is simultaneously a celebration of narcissistic and homosocial pleasures, of touch, of multiple selves momentarily made to cohere, and of a female speaking and acting subject.

The Boise Peace Quilters are perhaps the best example of a group of women whose quilt making activities have brought them "to language" as social and political actors. Since 1982 these women have made quilts they have presented to the Leningrad Peace Committee; to the people of Hiroshima; and to peace activists Pete Seeger, Marjorie Tuite, Dr. Helen Caldicott, and Norman Cousins. In 1984 they made what they called a National Peace Quilt, under which they asked each U.S. senator to sleep and subsequently record his or her dreams for peace in a diary that was to circulate with the quilt.

More recently the Boise Peace Quilters collaborated with women from the Soviet Women's Committee to make a quilt depicting both American and Russian children, a quilt they aimed to install in the negotiating chamber in Geneva during U.S.-Soviet arms talks. In *A Stitch for Time*—a film documenting the quilters' efforts to realize their goal—we follow a small, but determined, group of the Boise women to Geneva where they press U.S. and Soviet officials for permission to display the quilt in the arms negotiating chamber. (Earlier written requests had apparently gone unanswered.) The film informs us that part of the reason for the quilters' trip to Geneva was their plan to meet a Soviet woman with whom they'd collaborated on the project. In the end, however, the women are disappointed on both counts. For reasons that are never made clear, the quilt was hung not in the negotiating chamber but out in an adjacent hallway. And the Soviet woman who was to arrive in time to also meet with Soviet and American officials, showed up the day after the scheduled meetings. In addition to being late, this Soviet woman was not the woman the Boise women had previously met or who had previously participated in the quilt project.

Considering that the quilt made by the Soviet and American women depicts the cheerful faces of Soviet and American children, and in no overt way attempts to convey a political message, one has to wonder why it was not permitted to accompany the arms talks. One would think that the presence of a documentary film crew would have encouraged Soviet and U.S. administrators to comply with the quilters' wishes. Certainly one could attribute the administrators' refusal to display the quilt in the negotiating chamber to a disregard or simple lack of enthusiasm for the quilters' project. It seems to me, however, from having watched the film several times, and from having attended closely to the body language of the Soviet and U.S. officials (all of whom were male), that the physical presence of women from Idaho in Geneva with a quilt upon which they had painstakingly embroidered and quilted the faces of real children disarmed or, at least, discomforted them. I would suggest that the quilt—a celebration of endogamous love that knows no nationality—represented an attack of sentiment and suffering to which these men found it difficult to respond affirmatively. With their very pathos, the "private" and "personal" bodies of women and children physicalized by the quilt potentially threatened the "public" and "political" space in which men's dis-embodied talk presides. The quilt threatened to collapse the kinds of binary oppositions—private/public, personal/political—upon which patriarchal Western cultures have come to rely. To the extent that the quilt successfully materialized Soviet and American arms (and hands) negotiating to create a quilt between them, its presence perhaps suggested the abstract and unsubstantiated/insubstantial nature of speech as a form of political action. In some sense, the Soviet and American quilters preempted and materially accomplished what Soviet and American men were still only talking about.

Although it is, of course, important to recognize and applaud the efforts of women like the Boise Peace Quilters to use quilts to become culturally visible as political actors, what interests me most about the contemporary quilt revival is not projects like that of the Boise women, the needleworkers who created a ribbon to "package" the Pentagon, or makers of the Names Project AIDS quilt. I am concerned with the more subtle, more pervasive, and perhaps more subversive ways women who might be characterized as quilt addicts are using quilts and quilt making to "write the body," to engage in a body praxis that provides a venue for them to "proceed through bodily awareness to verbal skills and ethical views" that constitute a critique of the social relations of the domestic sphere (Jackson 1983: 336).

The quilt making practices of quilt addicts and of the women and men involved in the Boise, ribbon, and Names projects differ considerably both in the degree to which they locate and politicize the domestic sphere as perhaps the primary site at which unequal and exploitative social, economic, gender, and sexual relations are (re)produced and in the extent to which they constitute "woman" as a desiring subject and hence challenge dominant cultural notions of her as the eternal comforter, self-sacrificing wife, mother, and America. In none of the needlework projects consciously framed as "political" is quilt making promoted as a cultural practice that is a body practice integral to an ongoing way of life aimed at disorganizing and reorganizing power relations in domestic sphere.

In *A Stitch for Time,* the quilt making activities of the Boise Peace Quilters are represented not as disruptive to, but as congruent with, and an extension of their domestic roles as caretakers of their families. The quilters' desire for world peace is what appears to motivate their making quilts, not a dis-ease with the way the work of caring or the giving and getting of pleasure is organized in their own homes.[2]

Discussing her own experience of making a ribbon panel in the introduction to *The Ribbon,* project director Justine Merritt does allude to sewing as a body praxis, even as a way of life, but not one that seems in any sense disruptive to the gender or sexual ideologies that support the status quo: "I found that as I would thread my needle, I was confronting the fear, confronting the grief and terror [of living in a nuclear age]. As I drew the needle up through the cloth, I was praying for peace, and the prayer became an affirmation of life. The very task of creating my panel helped empower me to face the reality of living in a nuclear age . . . I felt less grief-stricken, less afraid, less angry, and more committed than ever to working for peace . . . I felt a great sense of healing" (Merritt 1985: 11). Focusing on the therapeutic effects of hand sewing and invoking a comforting image of quilts and of "woman," Merritt hoped the ribbon would serve as "a gentle reminder to the nation that we love the earth and all its people." Ultimately the ribbon that was tied around the Pentagon to memorialize the fortieth anniversary of the bombing of Hiroshima and Nagasaki aimed to draw attention to a symbol of national violence, not to the violence of social relations in most people's homes.

Also capitalizing on a comforting image of quilts and of "woman" in an effort to redeem AIDS and its mostly male victims of their association with (homo)sexuality, the Names Project has effectively staged a spectacle of mostly male suffering that the national "body" has recognized, embraced, and successfully incorporated. Unlike the quilt of the Boise Peace Quilters, which was marginalized in the hallway outside the American-Soviet arms negotiating chamber, and unlike the ribbon, about which most Americans have never learned because of the negligible media coverage it received, panels from the Names Project have occupied center stage on the White House lawn and achieved a degree of legitimizing visibility that the other projects have failed to garner.

There seems no little irony in the fact that organizers of the Names Project successfully appropriated an art tradition invented and perpetuated by American women to—among other reasons—exorcise the fear that sex in marriage would lead to physical and/

or metaphysical death in childbirth and to combat the psychosocial "death" experienced by many women whose marriages separated them from mothers and female support networks. That an art tradition developed by women, at least in part, to cushion themselves against the loss of female life and to ease female suffering in (hetero)sexual relations has been used to focus the national gaze on the loss of mostly male lives and mostly male suffering in (homo)sexual relations suggests that the almost uniformly celebratory critical response to the Names Project bears reexamination, a task that is outside the scope of this essay.[3]

In 1976 Karey Bresenhan opened a quilt shop in Houson and—together with her mother, her mother's sister, and a cousin—founded the Greater Houston Quilt Guild. That same year Bresenhan managed to organize Quilt Fair, an exhibition of some two hundred quilts that drew a crowd of about twenty-five hundred. By 1986 the Greater Houston Quilt Guild had become the American/International Quilt Association, and Quilt Fair had become the annual Houston International Quilt Festival, a four-day event that featured five hundred quilts from twenty-five countries, more than one hundred lectures and workshops, two quilted-garment fashion shows, a festival banquet, a show-and-tell session, and a vendor's mall with 210 booths. Approximately twenty thousand visitors attended the 1986 festival, most of them women.

In the summer of 1988 the American/International Quilt Association worked with the national quilt guilds of England, Ireland, Denmark, France, West Germany, and Switzerland to sponsor Quilt Expo Europa, a three-day quilt festival in Salzburg, Austria. Limited by budget and the need for a space equipped to make simultaneous translations of lectures from English into French and German, Bresenhan organized an event considerably smaller than the Houston festival, but one that nonetheless retained most of its key features: an opening and closing ceremony, quilt exhibits, a quilt contest, lectures, workshops, a quilted-garment fashion show, and a show-and-tell session. Most of Quilt Expo Europa took place in a conference center next to the Sheraton Hotel in Salzburg's business district. There just over a thousand women from twenty-six countries gathered to see, touch, and talk about quilts that clamored for attention everywhere.

In the lobby, contemporary quilts hung from free-standing frames as well as from a second-floor balcony. In the main, one-thousand-seat auditorium, quilts suspended above the proscenium stage provided the backdrop for all festival programs, excepting the workshops, and still more quilts—like flags of nations that exist nowhere—fluttered down from the balcony that wrapped around the audience. On the second floor, some seventy contemporary and antique quilts decorated rooms and hallways alike.

The contemporary quilts were noticeably different from most of antique ones in their overwhelming lack of adherence to a grid or block structure; in their use of curved seams, fabrics of multiple textures, and finely graduated colors; and in their asymmetrical arrangement of irregularly shaped and different-sized pieces of fabric. Whereas the antique quilts were striking in the degree to which color, shape, and texture appeared controlled in mostly symmetrical block arrangements, the contemporary quilts presented a more disorderly kind of visual and textural ordering.

More often than not, festival participants arrived clutching a bag—often a quilted bag—out of which they eventually produced some kind of quilt. And if they hadn't brought a quilt to show, they were frequently wearing one—a quilted vest, a patchwork skirt, a dress with a Seminole Indian pieced-style bodice, or an embroidered and embellished denim jacket. The many different approaches to the presentation of self through clothing used by quilters again suggested the multiplicity of pleasures women experience and enact at quilting events.

As it turned out, the quilted and embellished garments many women wore at the festival were mere ghosts of those that would be modeled at the fashion show. "God Save the Queen" turned out to be a floor-length, black velvet coat upon which Kim Masopust had meticulously stitched—in thread, sequins, and beads—the images of King Henry VIII and all his dead wives. "That Cotton Pickin' Garment" by Georgia Bonesteel consisted of a one-size-fits-all cotton tunic worn over a pair of pants. On the tunic, Bonesteel had appliquéed a bold, highly exaggerated image of a cotton bole in yellow, blue, green, black and white. "Jewels of India" by Bonnie Benson was likewise an outfit consisting of a tunic worn over pants. But Benson chose to use turquoise and fuchsia silks to create an embellished tabard and a luxuriously draping sash to go on top of the tunic.

These garments were remarkable in a number of ways. They made use of patterns that were interpolations of Western and "other" cultural modes of dress, and that did not prescribe an ideal female body type. They refused to fetishize parts of the female body for the viewing pleasure of "the male gaze." They constructed ideas of "woman" that did not easily fit with white, male-dominant cultural narratives that position her as the passive object of male desires. And these garments were visually striking from a distance, yet invited close inspection and almost begged to be touched. One might even say they were, in this sense, "bisexual"—designed to provide visual pleasure, stereotypically associated with men, and tactile pleasure, stereotypically associated with women. Together with the titles the quilt artists gave them, the garments did not present an image of "woman" that was especially comforting; they laughed, they seduced, and seemed as potentially disruptive as Mrs. Yardley's quilts.

From 8:00 A.M. to 8:00 P.M., the conference buzzed continually with the sound of women's voices in all different languages, punctuated by peals of laughter and admiring sighs. Amidst all the talk, hugs, and smiles, acquaintances were renewed and friendships made firmer. Trading news of recent quilt shows and of their families, women would run their fingers along the surfaces of each other's quilts, quilted garments, or photos of quilts left behind. Saturday afternoon the lecturer on quilting in New Zealand announced that crates of New Zealand apples had just arrived and apples were in the lobby for the taking, for the tasting. A workshop participant who had visited Switzerland before coming to Austria shared her stash of Swiss chocolate bars with class members who had been unable to get lunch during the scheduled break. One morning I found two women—both wives of American military men stationed in West Germany—giggling about the fact that they had just been served a sumptuous breakfast at the Sheraton free of charge because the hotel staff had wrongly assumed they were guests of the hotel. The final day of the festival, a woman passed through the lobby handing out the remainder of small, ribbon-tied packets of fabric she had brought to the festival as gifts for quilters from other countries she was sure to meet. One of the women I'd interviewed in the course of the festival found me as I was about to leave and presented me with a quilted paperback book-cover.

Women's voices laughing, sighing. Women's bodies close together, touching, holding, caressing quilts, and quilted garments on women's bodies. Women feeding each other, trading talk, trading fabric, giving gifts. This is the homosocial festival atmosphere in which the talk of illness, madness, and desire insinuated itself.

Kathie Furlong of New Zealand, in a formal lecture on the state of quilt making in her country said,

> Surely only a quilter would be *crazy* enough to travel half way around the world for a one-hour slide lecture—but then people think we are *mad*—cutting up fabric, only to sew it back together again. But we know better don't we? . . . When I quit work to have my third child, I decided I'd use all that free time I was going to have at home to make a quilt. Needless to say, I'd forgotten how much time little babies take. Finally, I joined a class in order to have two hours a week to myself. Initially this *satisfied* me. But when I

> spent the whole weekend making an American, pieced-style potholder, I knew I was *hooked.* My husband thought I was *mad* . . . While attending the Continental Quilting Congress in the United States with a small group of quilters from New Zealand, I asked where one member of our party had disappeared to and was told she was upstairs *stroking* her fabrics. And Polly, our traveling psychologist, diagnosed the problem as *quilters' bulimia,* caused by *bingeing* on fabric. Immediately after attending the Congress, I met my husband in San Francisco. I was repacking the suitcase on one occasion and he said, "How many pieces of fabric have you got there?" So he began counting. He stopped at over 100. Reports of 150 pieces of fabric arriving home with one quilter were not unusual. I wasn't the only one.

Not unlike the fictional narrator of "The Quilt Addict," Kathie Furlong, standing before an audience of quilters, confesses her illness. In effect she parodies what Foucault has pointed to as two primary social dramas—that of the church confessional and that of psychoanalysis—in which sexuality is "spoken" so that it might be organized and directed for ideological purposes by the priest and psychoanalyst. The difference, in Furlong's case—as well as in the story of "The Quilt Addict"—is that desires are confessed not before an audience of men but for an audience of women whose presence ultimately fails to organized and redirect the desires that threaten the social body.[4]

The symptoms of Furlong's illness? She finds time away from her family "satisfying." She has an all-consuming weekend affair with a potholder. One suspects that, like her friend, she secretly strokes her fabric and suffers from "quilters' bulimia." Bingeing on fabric, she purges herself through narratives that appropriate and parody the medical discourse evolved to describe women's psychosocial disease/dis-ease. Gorging herself on color, pattern, and texture, Furlong redeems herself with tales of a disease that manifests itself in the desire for time for herself, for narcissistic pleasures derived from working with fabric, and in bouts of international travel to quilt events. Not surprisingly, it is the spectacle of bingeing—the presence of piles of fabric purchased with funds diverted from family use—that makes her husband take notice and show concern.

In the spring of 1986, I conducted fieldwork at the Great American Quilt Festival in New York City. When I was interviewing Ione Bissonette, Vermont state winner of the Great American Quilt Festival Contest, she described quilt making as "both my sanity and my insanity." It seems to me that in the text just quoted, Kathie Furlong is saying much the same thing. Becoming involved with quilts and quilt making seems to have been the way Furlong cured herself of her dis-ease with a living arrangement that had become somehow too close, too self-enclosed. Unlike the late–nineteenth-century hysteric (or the present-day anorexic) who in response to family situations that were similarly too close, too self-enclosed, attacked her own body as a bid for independence and autonomy, Kathie Furlong started making quilts.

In *Studies on Hysteria,* Breuer and Freud expressed an awareness of the disruptive potential of needlework. In their clinical studies, they found a correlation between an extremely monotonous existence in a puritanically minded family, needlework, and hysteria. The problem, as Freud and Breuer saw it, was that needlework made women prone to an addressee-less daydreaming. Needlework made women prone to excess, to a nonutility that fed the narcissistic self-sufficiency to which—in their view—women were always prey (Doane 1985). In other words, needlework as a body praxis was potentially dangerous to a woman's health and to the health of the family because it led to states of mind where women experienced their "selves" creating and enacting narratives in a private theater to which men had no access. Without the regulating presence of dominant cultural narratives that position "woman" as the passive object of male desires, without the regulating presence of the male gaze, Freud and Breuer believed that women were susceptible to disease.

It seems to me that many contemporary women are engaging in quilt making as a body praxis and participating in quilt-related activities as a way of creating literal and psychic space for their selves to dream their way out of culturally constructed and constricting feminine roles. In her essay "On Conceiving Motherhood and Sexuality," Ann Ferguson offers the conceptual category sex/affective production as "a way of understanding the social organization of labor and the exchange of services that occur between men and women in the production of children, affection, and sexuality" (1982: 156). Ferguson conceives of both sexuality and affection as "*bodily* as well as *social* energies" that are "each specific manifestations of a general type of physical/social energy we can call 'sex/affective' energy" (156). Of the many different modes of sex/affective production Ferguson surveys in the different historical periods of different patriarchal cultures, "they all have in common an unequal and exploitative production and exchange of sexuality, affection, and parenting between men and women; that is, women have less control over the process of production (e.g., control of human reproductive decisions) and the services exchanged; and men characteristically get more than they give in the exchange of these services" (156).

Making a quilt and/or participating in quilt-related activities affords women the opportunity to challenge this unequal and exploitative production and exchange of sexuality, affection, and parenting. Passionate involvement with the quilt revival potentially disrupts the family, whose smooth operation has depended on an unequal exchange of sex/affective energy. Variations on the "how I began quilting" stories women recount at quilt events specifically mention changes in the behavior of household members precipitated by participation in the quilt revival. In the context of yet another formal presentation at Quilt Expo Europa, one speaker noted that the first time she attended a weekend-long quilt event away from home coincided with the first time her husband had ever changed a diaper.

All the talk about "not being able to keep my hands off of fabric" and about women secretly "stroking" their fabric that goes on at quilt festivals seems to indicate some women find working with fabric an autoerotic activity. And the feeding, touching, and sharing so characteristic of quilt-related activities undeniably contribute to a kind of homosocial bonding that has flourished with the contemporary quilt revival. In other words, it seems that—without knowing it—some quilters have taken up Clément's challenge that women explore their more polymorphous sexuality. Quilt festivals are a veritable quilters' "sabbat," which promote an economy of desire organized around the "female touch" as much as the "male gaze."

It also seems that many contemporary quilters have, likewise, unknowingly responded to Cixous's call for women to embrace the hysteric and sorceress as rebellious signs of women's excess desire, rage, and creativity. Along with the quilts and quilted garments these women are making, metaphors of illness, madness, and desire circulate at quilt events as rebellious signs of a disruptive "excess" that, unlike that of the sorceress or hysteric, has yet to be contained.[5]

The madness some quilters have embraced closely resembles what Bakhtin has described as a "festive" madness that makes people "look at the world with different eyes, not dimmed by 'normal,' that is by commonplace ideas and judgements" (1984: 39). It is a madness that far from leading to isolation, silence, and, ultimately, death is bringing women together to critique the sex/affective economy of the domestic sphere and to model a different sex/affective economy that is manifest most clearly in the secular ritual exchanges women stage at quilt events. There is a sense among quilters that people who quilt understand, value, and practice the ethic of sharing that underpins the numerous gift exchanges at quilt events. Many women make quilts and attend quilt events because unlike much of the work they do as wives, mothers, and/or employees, these are activities from which they derive as much sex/affective energy as they give. To participate in the madness that is the contemporary quilt revival is to embrace a body practice that is also a regenerative and utopian ethical and political practice.

Notes

1. Bourdieu defines *habitus* as "systems of durable, transposable *dispositions,* structured structures predisposed to function as structuring structures, that is, as principles of the generation and structuring of practices and representations which can be objectively 'regulated' and 'regular' without in any way being the product of an obedience to rules, objectively adapted to their goals without presupposing a conscious aiming at ends or an express mastery of the operations necessary to attain them and, being all this, collectively orchestrated without being the product of the orchestrating action of a conductor" (1977: 72).
2. I do not want to suggest that the quilt-making activities of the Boise Peace quilters have not in fact altered power relations in the homes of project participants. But at this point, disrupting female and male body habits in the domestic sphere is not represented as a primary, or even secondary, aim of the project. There is no indication in *A Stitch for Time* or in the organization's promotional brochure that the Boise quilters make any connection between what is wrong in the world "out there"—that is, the proliferation of nuclear weapons—and what is wrong "at home."
3. Although AIDS and persons who have died of AIDS certainly deserve the public acknowledgment they have received, most critical writing about the Names Project sidesteps issues of class and gender that arise when one considers the success of this project relative to those organized and produced by women. That the Names Project could have, but did not, use quilts to focus on the way that sex and death have recently become linked for some men in the way that it historically has been linked for most women suggests that the success of the project has been, on some level, at women's expense. Much to the Smithsonian's credit, administrators of its Political History Department are in the process of acquiring not only panels of the Names Project but also the Boise Peace Quilt and panels from the Ribbon Project. Quilts from the Boise Quilters and Ribbon Project will remain in the Political History Department; panels from the Names Project will be housed in the Medical Sciences Department in conjunction with other AIDS documentation.
4. Although the all-female audience does ultimately fail to get a sister addict to control her disease, there is a very real sense in which quilters—as individuals and in groups—embody and enact the very dominant cultural discourses they attempt to resist by making quilts and attending quilt events. There is a genuine uneasiness vented in narratives at quilt festivals about the extent to which participating in the revival disrupts gender- and sex-specific body habits and power relations in the home that is not always resolved in favor of the quilt addict continuing to pursue her passion with abandon.

5. Government, corporate, and cultural institutions have made great strides toward containing and focusing the disruptive potential of quilt making as a cultural and body practice by: (1) sponsoring quilt contests with themes that reify a notion of "woman" as the eternal comforter, wife, mother, and America; (2) sponsoring contests with rules that privilege particular quilt-making practices (i.e., requiring that quilts be the work of individuals and be hand-quilted); (3) organizing and mobilizing the volunteer labor of quilters in the service of quilt documentation projects of dubious scholarly merit; and (4) focusing on quilts as art in a manner that deflects attention away from the material circumstances that give rise to women making quilts, and from quilts' historical association with beds as primary sites of sex, birth, and death.

References

Bailey, Elinor Peace. 1989. Telephone interview with author on Oct. 7.

———. 1990. *Mother plays with dolls.* McLean, VA: EPM Publications.

Bakhtin, Mikhail. 1984. *Rabelais and his world.* Trans. Hélène Iswolsky. Bloomington: Indiana Univ. Press.

Bernheimer, Charles, and Claire Kahane, eds. 1985. In *Dora's case: Freud-hysteria-feminism.* New York: Columbia Univ. Press.

Bourdieu, Pierre. 1977. *Outline of a theory of practice.* Trans. Richard Nice. Cambridge: Cambridge Univ. Press.

Breuer, Joseph, and Sigmund Freud. 1895. Rpt. 1982. *Studies on hysteria.* Translated from the German and ed. James Strachey. New York: Basic Books.

Cixous, Hélène. 1983. The laugh of the Medusa. In *The signs reader: Women, gender & scholarship.* Ed. Elizabeth Abel and Emily K. Abel, 279–97. Chicago: Univ. of Chicago Press.

Cixous, Hélène, and Catherine Clément. 1986. *The newly born woman.* Trans. Besty Wing. Minneapolis: Univ. of Minnesota Press.

Doane, Mary Ann. 1985. The clinical eye: Medical discourses in the "woman's film" of the 1940s. In *The female body in Western culture.* Ed. Susan Rubin Suleiman, 152–82. Cambridge, MA: Harvard Univ. Press.

Ferguson, Ann. 1983. On conceiving motherhood and sexuality: A feminist materialist approach. In *Mothering.* Ed. Joyce Trebilcot, 153–82. Totowa, NJ: Towman and Allanheld.

———. 1989. *Blood at the root: Motherhood, sexuality and male dominance.* London: Pandora.

———. 1991. *Sexual democracy: Women, oppression, and revolution.* San Francisco: Westview Press.

Foucault, Michel. 1980. *The history of sexuality* 1, *An introduction.* New York: Vintage Books.

Harris, George Washington. 1867. Mrs. Yardley's quilting. Rpt. 1973 in *Sut Lovingood's yarns and American literature: The maker and the Making* 1. Ed. Cleanth Brooks, R. W. B. Lewis, and Robert Penn Warren. New York: St. Martin's Press.

Harriss, Joseph. 1987. The newest quilt fad seems to be going like crazy. *Smithsonian* 18 (May): 114–24.

Holstein, Jonathan. 1973. *The pieced quilt: An American design tradition.* New York: Galahad Books.

Jackson, Michael. 1983. Knowledge of the body. *MAN* 18 (2): 327–45.

Martin, Paula Kay. 1988. The quilt addict. *Quilter's Newsletter Magazine* 19 (Feb.), no. 2: 22–23.

Merritt, Justine. 1985. Introduction. In *The ribbon.* Ed. Lark Books staff and Marianne Philbin, 11–13. Asheville, NC: Lark Books.

Rickels, Milton. 1965. George *Washington Harris.* New York: Twayne Publishers.

Scarry, Elaine. 1985. *The body in pain: The making and unmaking of the world.* New York: Oxford Univ. Press.

Schneider, Jane, and Annette B. Weiner. 1986. Cloth and the organization of human experience. *Current Anthropology* 27 (Apr.): 178–84.

———. 1989. *Cloth and human experience.* Washington: Smithsonian Institution Press.

8. *The Spirit in the Body*

ELIZABETH WICKETT

Say to my brethren when they see me dead and weep for me,
lamenting me in sadness,
Think ye I am this corpse ye are to bury?
I swear by God, this dead one is not I
When I had formal shape, then this my body served as my
garment
I wore it for a while

—Ghazali (twelfth-century Sufi poet)

Introduction

A phenomenology of the body entails a mapping of its metaphysical as well as physical properties. In the folk religious tradition of Luxor in Upper Egypt, the soul of a living sheikh šeēẖ) may become disconnected from the body and peregrinate in space. The disconnected soul may also be re-incorporated in a second image (or manifestation) of the body so that the sheikh may appear in two places at the same time. This incarnated vision of the sheikh may be seen as an etherealized form of his self and a sign of his innate ability to transmute and dematerialize his worldly substance into more spiritlike form. The boundaries between the divine power inherent in him and the outside world are also permeable. A sheikh is endowed with a divine energy or life-force known as *baraka,* which may radiate from him in life and in death and be absorbed and ingested by others at feasts after his death.

In the context of modern Luxor (the site of ancient Thebes) and its rural surround,[1] the word *sheikh* commonly denotes a holy man (*walī*) to whom divine powers have been miraculously granted, though the term may also designate an orthodox and educated religious leader incapable of metaphysical feats or a secular village headman in whom judicial power and authority is vested.

In analyzing the phenomenology of sheikhs (pl., *missāyih*), I shall examine Sufi models of the soul and its relation to the divine within the transcendental and ecstatic tradition of Islam, in addition to ideas about embodiment and spirituality found in other genres of Upper Egyptian (*Ṣaʿīdī*) expressive culture. Furthermore, to evolve a comparative framework for analysis, I will counterpose ancient Egyptian cosmological notions of the eternity of "soul" and body with modern conceptions of the relationship.

In the ancient Egyptian cosmological system, both the physical body and its skeleton, or "husk," were understood to comprise the complete person in life. The personalized soul (*ba*) and life-force (*ka*) would become separated from these corporeal forms at death, however, though they would still remain symbiotically linked. The husk and corporeal body preserved after death would provide a housing for the peripatetic soul bird and the life-force that would guarantee the perpetuity of the person throughout eternity.

Sheikh Mūsa, who came from Karnak, near Luxor, was renowned for his metaphysical abilities during his lifetime. Before he died in 1988, he decreed the date of his own *mūlid,* or "birth feast" while still alive (a celebration customarily only performed after death) and thus affords a unique paradigm of a living sheikh. Like all divinely empowered beings, he was believed to inhabit an atemporal frame that would enable him to overcome the constraints of mortality. In philosophical discussions of the mind/body problem, *mind* and *body* are considered different substances, possessed of antithetical attributes. The Luxor sheikhs are capable of performing feats with the physical body, usually associated with the metaphysical soul, especially with a soul that has been detached from the body in death.

The veneration of sheikhs is not unique to Egypt, for the tradition of the *awlīyā' allah* (holy ones of God), complemented by the celebration of annual festivals of these holy men and women, variously known as *mušāyiḫ* (sheikhs), *āsīyād* (masters), or among the Awlad ʿAli tribe of the Mediterranean coast, *murabiṭīn* (those tied to God), thrives throughout North Africa, either within the Sufi tradition or independent of it. Festivals to venerate regional holy men and women flourish in Morocco (where they are known as *mūsim*, pl. *muwāsim*), as they do in Egypt and, to a lesser degree, Tunisia and Libya. The aim of this chapter, however, is to examine the traits of a Luxor sheikh, venerated during his lifetime, in relation to the history of Luxor and the distinctive features of his divinely inspired *karamāt* (miracles). This focus will permit us to analyze the particular cosmological features of mind and body, inherent in the person of a living sheikh, within Egyptian tradition.

Sheikh Mūsa

After his death, the sister of Sheikh Mūsa described him as "one of those who have become 'aware of' or who have 'reached' the desert valley" (*min mudarakīn ilwadī*), where the desert valley connotes death. This is a traditional epithet ascribed to other *awlīyā' allāh,* including the twelfth-century patron saint of Luxor, Sīdī Abu'l Ḥajjāj ("My master, Abu'l Ḥajjāj"), where it is invoked in a praise song to the sheikh.[2] Such an epithet was also applied to the favored Amenhotep I, son of Hapu, from the early Eighteenth Dynasty in Egypt, a man who was venerated after his lifetime as an intercessor between the living and the deified.[3]

The paradigm of Sheikh Mūsa, whose *baraka* was manifest during his lifetime as well as after his death, affords an insight into the capabilities of these beings who can pass between the realm of the living and the dead while in the body. In a divination scene in the Egyptian oral epic (*sīrat banī hilāl*), the diviner begins the incantations by addressing the lord of "two worlds"(*ʿalamēn*)[4] in order to receive divine guidance. The Egyptian cosmological universe is believed to be divided into two realms, that of the living and that of the dead, and by virtue of their divine empowering, sheikhs are entitled to move between them in order to intercede between God and man after death. Sayyida Zeinab ("Our Lady Zeinab," from *sayyida*, the feminine form of *sayyid,* "master"), the granddaughter of the Prophet Mohamed, venerated every year by millions in her annual *mūlid*) is described as having "two existences in which her aura is fragrant" (*ʿalilkunēn atarīk fāḥ*) (Salih 1971: 331). This attribution attests to her power to penetrate both realms.

Sheikh Mūsa was able to levitate through space and materialize in two places at the same time, oblivious to the laws of gravity and corporality, according to his devotees. This feat attests to his ability to etherealize the body and at the same time, to divide and transmute his ether into two facsimiles of the same "person."

In Western culture, the ability to disassociate soul from body we customarily attribute to disembodied spirits, such as ghosts, who remain in the realm of the living after death. In Luxor cosmology, though, the ability of the soul to leave the body is highly elaborated with respect to extraordinary beings. A prevalent belief that the souls of twins may leave the physical body at night to inhabit the bodies of black cats suggests that there are certain specially endowed souls with the ability to disassociate from the body and transmigrate. The capacity ascribed to twins could be understood as an epi-phenomenon of binary beings who are metaphysically as well as physically split from the moment of conception. It seems that they are accorded the ability to disassociate from their bodies by virtue of the bifurcated nature of their souls. Likewise, the ability of sheikhs to fly and appear in two places simultaneously may indicate their binary nature.

The notion that the soul is transmigratory after death appears also in the folk belief that souls may inhabit the bodies of ordinary insects, especially scarab beetles (Galal 1937: 244). Scarab beetles are never trampled underfoot, perhaps because they are still regarded as symbols of regeneration and rebirth, a vestige of ancient Egyptian belief. Divinely empowered sheikhs may also assume that sacred form after death. In fact, according to a medieval hagiographer, the "patron saint" of Luxor, Sheikh Abu'l Ḥajjāj, a Sufi teacher and ascetic, is believed to have declared, "My sheikh is a scarab beetle,"[5] an epithet which suggests that his divine powers were bequeathed to him from a mentor who assumed the form of a scarab beetle as a symbol of the eternity of his divine soul.

Sheikhs also are believed to manifest other signs of their inherent powers in physical form. According to his sister, at birth Sheikh Mūsa "frothed at the mouth" (*taftaf,* a doubled, ancient Egyptian root that has retained its original meaning of "spitting" or "exuding froth from the mouth" in Arabic).[6] This was taken as a sign (*ᶜalāma*) of his divine nature. In phenomenological terms, this frothy spittle may be seen as ethereal, a fusion of spirit and substance that is therefore divine, like the sheikh himself.

As a symbol of the divine, it also has ancient precursors in Egyptian mythology. In legends of the ancient Egyptian creator god, Atum, the very act of exuding spittle from the mouth was the act performed by God upon the earth in the creation of Adam. In a variant of the creation story of Adam and Eve, recorded in 1988 in Luxor, the Coptic storyteller ᶜAmm Rizq recounts the act: "Fa ṭafil ᶜalil'arḍ wi ṣanᶜ min iṭṭifla ṭīnan" (So he spat on the ground and formed from the shale/spittle earth).[7] Thus frothing at the mouth or spitting is a divinely inspired act, an emanation of divine efflux that can only be performed by a divinely empowered being. It is invoked by sheikhs to transmit healing. At the *zikr,* during which devotees whirl into trance to achieve a state of oneness with God, froth or spittle is the sign that the divine spirit has momentarily possessed the body of a devotee, a state known as *malbus,* literally, "clothed with the spirit." In cases of general spirit possession, other metaphors are deployed. One is possessed (literally, "ridden") by a sheikh (*rākib ᶜalēh šēẖ*), whereas in the case of Sufis or members of religious orders (*ṯuruq ṣufiyya*) known as devotees of the Family of the Prophet (*āl ilbēt*), the loss of mental stability in the physical world is called the state of being "attracted" by God (*magzūb*). This may be broadly interpreted to mean a state of total possession by the divine in which the person becomes filled with the spirit with consequent loss of mental faculties.

Sheikh Mūsa's spiritual and corporeal states were also in harmony with each other. As his soul was peripatetic, so was his body. He roamed the streets as a child and slept in makeshift dwellings. He could not be contained and was said to have lived in a conically shaped mudbrick dwelling (*somᶜ*), which denotes a granary, the traditional habitation of ascetic monks and sheikhs, until captured by his father and incarcerated in a small room at the age of fifteen. From a trap-door window in the door of this room, he would extend an "effeminate,"[8] pure white hand, the manifestation of a spiritual being in the body.

This sexually anomalous identity is not typical. Many living sheikhs are known to be sexually active, even promiscuous, and their sexual desires are regarded as divinely inspired and therefore unassailable. It is the custom for women to venerate sheikhs after their deaths explicitly to acquire *baraka*—in this instance, the ability to conceive a child. In this case the feminized aspect of the sheikh suggests androgyny, which could be interpreted as an idealized presentation of self that complements the sheikh's inherent masculinity. Although not commonplace, this androgynous aspect may attest to his ontologically divine nature. Androgyny was a common feature of many ancient Egyptian gods, who were depicted as having male and female attributes. This aspect may suggest his liminality and divine place between both poles of human sexuality.

Sheikh Mūsa could also attenuate his substance and sail across the Nile "on a handkerchief," a feat reputed to have been performed by another local sheikh, Abu'l Qomsān. Both were motivated by a fit of anger rather than a desire to display superhuman capabilities. Despite the frequency of its occurrence, this ability is not peculiar to Luxor holy men and women but one generally ascribed to medieval Islamic sheikhs.[9]

Sleep is regarded as a time for soul travel in which the dreamer may encounter a sheikh in the spirit world. After death a sheikh may appear in a dream and request a shrine be erected in his honor in a particular place. This was the case with Sheikh Mūsa's contemporaries, Abu'l Qomsān and IlGharīb. In contrast, Sheikh Mūsa was venerated in life as most are venerated after death, in his own house. His small cell was a site of visitation, where he would be given offerings of food in the form of brown biscuits, which he would bite from and divine the owner's thoughts.[10] He would also offer those who came to visit him *muᶜasal* (honey-flavored tobacco for smoking in the *šīšl* ("waterpipe"), which would reputedly never make one cough or choke, so imbued with *baraka* was it claimed to be.

Sheikh Mūsa further exerted his spiritual will by determining the day of his own mūlid, customarily dated to the day of a sheikh's death, in his own lifetime. Through this act, he symbolically marked his rebirth into a new existence, as if he had already traversed the *wādī* ("desert valley"), or metaphysical divide between the living and the dead. As further evidence that he had declared himself to exist in a liminal state between the living and the dead, Sheikh Mūsa's "coffin" called *tabūt*, in actuality a sarcophaguslike frame covered with a *tōb,* or "canopy," had been paraded twenty years before in the mūlid of another Luxor sheikh, Abu'l Ḥajjāj, as if he were already dead. The annual perambulation of this sheikh[11] was believed to renew his latent spiritual energy through the act of "going round." In a similar way, the dormant soul of Sheikh Mūsa would have been revived.

The tradition of venerating a saint or sheikh during his own lifetime has noted precursors from the Pharaonic period in Thebes. The deified Eighteenth Dynasty king, Tutankhamen, for example, was actively venerated during his own lifetime.[12] Similarly, as Sheikh Mūsa supervised the construction of his own mausoleum in Karnak, so the noble Sennemut of Thebes presided over the building of his own tomb, according to ancient Egyptian hieratic texts.[13] Although the construction of a mausoleum cannot be interpreted as evidence of derivation from one religious ideology to another, it can be construed as proof of both men's concern for the repose, protection, and status of the body after death.

Devotees claim that during his funerary procession, Sheikh Mūsa managed to propel himself forcefully backward when pallbearers who had persecuted him in life tried to whisk him away elsewhere. This exertion of will was seen as the sheikh's determination to be buried in the place he had chosen. This particular manifestation of spiritual power is often cited as a mark of divine energy and thus an identifying feature of sheikhs. Sheikh IlGharīb, a deaf and dumb mendicant who lived on alms gained by roaming the streets and playing a broad drum "for God," refused to be buried directly. Instead he propelled himself at his funeral through the streets of Luxor into the cinema, the police station, and every public edifice before, allowing himself to be placed in a tomb for his eternal repose. Though his role as a deaf mute and peripatetic singer would already have marked him as someone "nurtured" by God, this divine sign elevated him above the ordinary and confirmed his empowered status.

The manifestation of spiritual power during funerary processions also suggests correspondences with oracular processions from the Saite period in Thebes. From

Twenty-sixth Dynasty records (c. 600 B.C.), it is clear that movements of shrines during the processionals of the gods were interpreted as revelations of divine will.[14] Requests for intercession would be put to the statue of the god on its barque as it moved through the streets. They would be answered according to the movements forward and backward of the procession: a forward thrust indicating a wish granted, a backward movement a wish refused. As in the funerary procession of Sheikh Mūsa, movement was interpreted as evidence of divine volition.

The same oracular function is attributed now to the "going round" (*dōra*) of Sīdī Abu'l Ḥajjāj, during which the *baraka* of the saint is dispersed. This custom of circumambulating the walls of Luxor was previously performed at ancient Theban feasts such as the annual festival for the funerary god, Sokar, in which the sacred barques of the gods were pulled around the mortuary precinct to define the territory over which the god retained power. The "going round" is also a ritual performed at a *nadr,* or "ex-voto," for a saint or sheikh in gratitude for divine intervention. In this act of veneration, a canopied litter on camel back is pulled around the spiritual dominion of the sheikh to the accompaniment of flutes (*zummāra*) to celebrate and disseminate his *baraka.*

Clearly the fate of the physical body is critical to the sense of well-being of these divinely inspired sheikhs. Equally important is the orientation of their bodies to the forces of the cosmos. Sheikhs are customarily positioned under the sacred sphere or dome (*qubba*)[15] in a canopied sarcophagus marked by capped pillars at four axis points, denoting the four heavenly supports. In this way the physical body of the sheikh is symbolically placed under the "dome" of heaven and centered for eternity within the cosmos between the axes of four opposing, directional points, the cardinal points or the solstice points.[16] In addition, the direction of the head is marked by a *šāhid,* "witness": a turbaned head or canopy over an anthropomorphic, humped protuberance, in shape not unlike the Sphinx.[17] It could be argued that the protection and continued potency of the sheikh after death is contingent on this marking and cosmic orientation.[18] Sheikh Mūsa expressed in a symbolic dimension his placement between the dead and the living by inhabiting first a cone or dome-shaped granary and then a domed sanctuary. By inhabiting in life a model of what he would inhabit in death, he again signaled his dual and liminal nature.

How then can the relationship between the soul and body be defined phenomenologically? The physical body is manipulated by spiritual energy in the manifestations of these sheikhs. Moreover, belief in the capacity of the soul to survive outside the body is clearly critical to an understanding of this relationship. Both ancient and modern Egyptian conceptual systems offer some insight.

As a highly complex and unique historical model, the ancient Egyptian conception of the "integrated" soul focused on the fact that the vitality of the life-force or *ka* that survived after death was dependent on the proximity and well-being of the physical body. In ancient Egyptian theology, the composite soul-person consisted of eight parts:

1. The *ba,* which represented the personification of the ego or individual person. After death, the *ba* was incarnated in the form of a migratory stork or human-headed bird, the embodiment that would enable this aspect of the soul to move between both worlds.
2. The *ka,* the life-force or vital energy that remained by the body after death in the tomb, to be venerated in visitations and fed with offerings of food. The *ka* was represented by the ideogram of outstretched human arms or a miniaturized "soul double" or Doppelganger, construed to be in the image of the person but depicted as following after the life-size human soul. The *ka* symbol was depicted in the earliest inscriptions and seems to have been connected conceptually with life and fertility. Its root means "generative force," and when written with the phallic determinative, it denotes male potency or "the bull," and in its feminine form, the female sexual organ (Mercer 1952: 18).
3. The *akh,* the spiritual essence of the soul. It was a separate entity, analogous to the shining light of the divine spirit, radiated by angels and sometimes by divinely inspired beings such as sheikhs and monks.
4. The *ib,* "heart."
5. The *ren,* "name."
6. The *khaybit,* the shadow that may linger after death to haunt the living.
7. The *khat,* "physical body."
8. The *sahu,* the skeleton and husk.

Each of these was conceived of as a separate entity, yet all constitute parts of the integrated person (Mercer 1952: 18).

In the modern folk conception of the mind-body duality of ordinary mortals, each human being is born with a soul double, which is designated in a variety of ways, *qarīn* (m.)/ *qarīna* (f.), from its etymological root meaning "wedded spirit," *uẖt,* "sister," or *mutābʿ* (m. and f.), "that which follows after."[19] The gender of this double remains ambiguous, however, as some but not all informants claim that this soul double is of the opposite gender. This spirit entity exists in symbiotic union with the mind/soul of the person, though it may occasionally disrupt the harmony of coexistence and cause psychological disorders associated with schizophrenia. On the birth of a new child to her soul mate (in this case, the mother), this same spirit sister who emanates from "under the earth" (*taḥt il'arḍ*), in this case called the *qarīna* (f.), is deemed capable of jealousy and may try to induce cot death. To prevent this, the child is secured within the protective circle of the "sieve" for the tenuous first seven days of life.

At death, the qarīn/a appears to be disassociated from the person but no conception of the qarīn/a lingering after death has been described. It appears to be connected only with the living psyche and remains embedded in the earth. Although such an entity is not commonly discussed, it may be invoked where there has been an infraction against the sanctity of the earth where these spirits dwell by unwitting human beings. On these occasions, it is provident to say, "May the name of God be upon you, you and on your 'sister'[who is] better than you" (*ism'ullah ʿalīk wi ʿala uḫtik aḥsan minnik*)[20] to avoid censure and inexplicable illness.

In relation to the ancient construct of the soul, this soul double is only consonant with the notion of the life-force of the ancient Egyptians in so much as it is conceived of as "following after," It is not an entity that survives after death, though in the case when the qarīna becomes a child-slaying she-devil and is believed to kill a newborn child, a black fowl is slain to appease the jealous soul double and the cleaned carcass placed under the threshold, ostensibly for the qarīna to inhabit. The manifestation of this belief in the appeasement of a voracious qarīna would seem, furthermore, to corroborate the notion that a skeleton is the proper receptacle for a spirit, even a nonhuman one, to inhabit.[21]

In older, written sources, Sufis define the mind-soul conundrum in terms of three organs of spiritual communication: the heart (*qalb*), who knows God; the spirit (*rūḥ*), which loves God; and "the innermost ground of the soul" (*sirr*, literally, "secret").[22] The *sirr* of sheikhs survives after death and is similarly capable of disassociation. It is believed to inhabit the *ṣāri,* or "mast pole," erected for sheikhs at festivals held in their honor.[23] Moreover, at the shrine of Abu'l Ḥajjāj in Luxor, there is an ancient door leading to the crypt of the sheikh, called "the door of the innermost soul" (*bāb issirr*). This is the passageway of the celestial saints in and out of the crypt. The door is a physical entity that acts as a conduit for souls, like the false door of ancient Egyptian tombs that acted as the passageway for the *ka.*

In the ecstatic Sufi tradition within Islam, God's *baraka* is received in various forms by those initiates in the appropriate state of grace. Although it is the *sirr* of sheikhs that survives after death, hovering in or around the tomb, it is the *rūḥ* (life-spirit) of other creatures that is expected to survive. In the folk conception, this potency inhabits anything originating from living creatures. Moreover, it is transferable from that living source. Thus Copts of the Orthodox church in Egypt refrain from eating any food in which there is *rūḥ,* that is, food from any living creature. By adhering to this strict vegetarian diet for extended periods of fasting, Copts eat no meat, no milk and no butter (foods containing life), with the result that those foods associated with the life-force are almost solely consumed at feasts and ritual occasions.

The question of the survival of the soul of ordinary mortals after death is more complex. According to the Egyptian anthropologist Mohamed Galal, who published an ethnographic account of funerary practices in 1937 after fieldwork in the Delta, it was popularly believed that the soul leaves the body immediately after death and then returns to remain with the body for several hours until it is placed in the earth (1937: 204). Belief in the life of the soul after death in Upper Egypt is manifest in the funerary laments addressed to the separated soul of the person on his or her journey to the afterlife.[24] This soul is often represented in the image of a migratory bird, one depiction of the ancient Egyptian *ba,* and addressed as a sentient spirit, still in communication with the living. Belief in the eternity of the soul is also evinced in the custom of placing offerings at the grave on feasts, a custom observed by both Christians and Muslims. The *ṭāliᶜ* (ascension) of the surviving soul is believed to take place on certain defined days: the third, the seventh, the fifteenth, and the fortieth day after death. On those days, visits to the grave are essential. Similarly, on certain Islamic feast days such as *ilᶜaīd ilkibīr* (the Great Feast), the soul is believed to ascend, and on these days also the faithful visit the tombs of their relatives. The most grievous sorrow, though, is for the man who dies in foreign lands, because his body is deposited in alien ground and will not receive offerings or hear the laments for the soul's well-being that are usually performed at funerary rituals.

The *baraka* that sheikhs possess and dispense to the faithful after death survives them. Their confinement in the body is both transient and revocable. Moreover, sheikhs traditionally denigrate the physical body. Sheikh Mūsa, like his contemporaries, Abu'l Qomsān and IlGharīb, wore a coarse shift of burlap as a sign of the primacy of his spiritual aspect over the physical. Ironically, these shifts are preserved now on the walls of his former cell as mementos of his corporeal presence (see fig. 8.1). In death, veneration is centered around the tomb, repository of the body and soul, and also the container (*tabut*) in which the symbolic body is placed at his mūlid. The appellation *mūlid* stems from the Arabic root *w-l-d,* "to give birth." The mulid feast is usually dated to the day of death and therefore is associated with the idea of death as a rebirth into renewed life. For the spiritual powers of the sheikh to be regenerated, the "coffin" must be circumambulated in his annual feast. In other words, the *baraka* is not eternal. It must be revitalized annually in the ritual act of propelling the *tabut,* a symbolic coffin in the form of an empty wooden frame, draped in a canopy and thus a skeletal representation of the sheikh's repository, around his precinct. By engaging in the "going round" (*dōra*), his *baraka* is reenergized. The metaphor of the coffin not only invests the procession with funerary connotations but also suggests that the sheikh's power and spirit are linked to the presence of the physical body. Furthermore, the continual well-being of the sheikh appears to be physically nurtured by offerings called *nudūr* (pl., from *nadr,* "ex-voto"), which may consist of dates, feast cakes (*manūn*) and animals slaughtered "for the sheikh."[25]

In ancient Egypt, the notion of embalming was developed in order to preserve the physical body for the purpose of creating an eternal receptacle for the life-force. Though embalming is no longer practiced in Egypt, the folk practice of venerating the *baraka* of sheikhs by the entombed physical body remains.

At the phenomenological level, the integration of material substance and spiritual essence of all human beings is based on belief in the fusion (or association) of soul and body in life and their fission (or disassociation) but mutual dependency in death. In the case of the metaphysical being of sheikhs, where the spiritual power granted by God dominates and subsumes the constraints of the physical body, there is a greater ability to disassociate spirit from body at a much earlier stage, in life itself. In consequence, the soul becomes associated with pure, divine power, or *baraka,* rather than the particular soul of the sheikh. Sheikh Mūsa was believed to have detached body from spirit, and yet his *baraka* is revitalized at his birth feast, which takes place around the repository of his body.

At these festivals of sheikhs, a common epithet cried out during *zikr* or other solemn occasions when the *baraka* of the sheikh is believed to be abroad, is *madad* ("May you stretch out your grace!"). A sheikh's *baraka* is conceived of as a substance that may be disseminated from its source to devotees through the air, via life-giving foods or through touch, either of his sacred boats or tomb casing. At the same time, to confirm the cyclical

Fig 8.1. The Dematerialized Body: Since his death, the interior of Sheikh Mūsa's cell and sanctuary has been left undefiled. The garments he wore, like the room itself, remain imbued with his spirit and are suspended on the walls, as if to mark his former embodiment. On the floor are heaped the dusty cardboard wrappings of the thousands of biscuits brought to the sheikh by devotees and believed to be similarly permeated with his grace. Photograph by Elizabeth Wickett.

nature of his renewal and power at the "going round," Sīdī Abu'l Ḥajjāj is urged at the beginning of the processional to return:

> They set the time for high noon,
> so the time was set,
> For the return, Abu'l Ḥajjāj
>
> (nasabu ilmiᶜad fiḍḍowī
> nasabu ilmiᶜad
> wi bilᶜawḍa y'abu'l ḥajjāj)

Moreover, at the end, when his sacred boats are placed in their resting place beside the stairs of his shrine, he is urged again:

> For the return, Abu'l Ḥajjāj,
> For the return
>
> (bilʿawḍa y'abu'l ḥajjāj
> bilʿawḍa)

In other words, "May you return [to bestow your grace on us again]." His *baraka* should "return," or materialize, for the specific event of "going round." The sheikh will then become present in his sacred boats, the repositories of his soul, and disperse his *baraka* to the public. After the procession, he will return to his tomb where he and his *baraka* will remain in a latent state of empowerment until his next mūlid feast.

Conclusion

The unique example of Sheikh Mūsa amplifies the analysis of the spiritual power of holy men who attain the status of divinely empowered beings after their death. The divine soul resides near the body for eternity and exudes *baraka.* In the symbiotic relationship between mind and body, the soul's well-being for eternity is contingent on the well-being of the body as well as its revivification at annual birth feasts. Its welfare must be protected by assuring the habitation of the body in a grave or mausoleum. In contrast to the Cartesian notion of separation of mind and body, the Egyptian folk conception of the nature of Luxor sheikhs suggests a continuum that encompasses the etherealization of the body and the substantiation of the spirit.

Notes

1. The eventful history of Luxor, the modern town that once was comprised within the precinct of Luxor temple, may account for the integration and absorption of religious concepts from many diverse epochs into its traditions and cultural identity. Luxor (from Il'uqsor, "the castles," a designation created by the Romans) was relatively isolated during the Middle Ages. Prior to the incursion of Fatimid dynasties, who remained in Upper Egypt for four hundred years, the site was a Roman garrison and then a Coptic

enclave. A Fatimid minaret was imposed onto the first pylon of Luxor temple, probably in the eleventh century, to mark the advent of Islam. Until 1925 the ancient Luxor temple was subsumed and dotted with the tombs of forty-four Islamic sheikhs and four Coptic churches. The site was dominated until 1925 by the domed shrine of its "patron saint," Abu'l Ḥajjāj, at its apex and the descendants of the sheikhs, the Ḥajajjīyya, lived by the shrine, in close proximity to their Coptic neighbors.

The conversion of the town to Islam is believed by Muslims to have been effected by the arrival of Abu'l Ḥajjāj, an ascetic from Iraq, whose domed shrine was fused onto the first pylon of Luxor temple in the fourteenth century, reputedly on top of the ruins of a fabled "church of gold." To this day, however, the Coptic Christian population still predominates in the more ancient sections of Luxor adjacent to the temple. As all the inhabitants of Luxor were moved off the site in 1925, this date marks the beginning of its transformation and the removal of both the Ḥajajīyya and the Coptic populations from the ancient precinct of the Luxor temple and their disassociation from a site continuously occupied for four thousand years, from the dynastic period through the Graeco-Roman (and Coptic) to the Islamic era.

2. A similar epithet was addressed to Abu'l Ḥajjāj in a praise poem: *destur ya mudrikīn ilwādī,* "With your permission [O jinn of the earth], you who have become aware of [or who have reached] the valley" (sÛ)ālihÚ 1971: 161).
3. Again the "valley" is invoked as the image of the boundary between two worlds:

> *Tu parcours la vallée*
> *Tu te diriges vers le ciel*
> *Tu fraternises avec les étoiles*
>
> (Varille 1968: 40)

4. From the tale of ᶜAzīza and Yūnis as told by ᶜAwaḍ Allah ᶜAbdeljelīl in Luxor, 1983, recorded and translated by the author. Yahya conjures in the sand so that the hero, Abu Zayd, may see a vision of the captured Yūnis:

> Abu Zayd said, "My Lord of the state of the two worlds (*ᶜālamēn*),
> Our Lord Master, you who are conscious (*ᶜālim*) . . . of the state of two worlds (*ᶜālamēn*),
> Lead me down to the garden of the Zenātī . . .
> Let my vision go speedily to the three . . .
> The handsome Yūnis, born of Sirhān . . ."

5. Massignon 1908: 85; from Ash-Shaᶜranī, Ṭabaqat IlKubra 1: 156–58.
6. *Tef* in hieroglyphics means "to spit" or "to eject" anything from the body; *teftef* means "to pour out" (Budge 1978, 2: 833).

7. From "The Story of Adam" (qiṣṣit ādam), recorded in Luxor in 1984 by the author. The notion of divine spittle is also embodied in the ancient myth of the Egyptian gods, Isis and Re[c]:

    He let his spittle fall upon the ground.
    He spat it out, casting it upon the ground . . .
    Isis kneaded it with her hand.
    With the earth on which it was, she shaped it as an august snake . . .
    (Piankoff 1984: 56)

8. Oral communication, Jamāl Zakī IlDīn IlḤajājī, 1988.
9. Nicholson, the Orientalist, cites this list of feats as attributable to Islamic sheikhs: "Flying in the air, rain-making, appearing in various places at the same time, healing by the breath, bringing the dead to life, knowledge and prediction of future events, thought-reading, telekinesis, paralysing or beheading an obnoxious person, conversing with animals or plants, turning earth into gold or precious stones and producing food and drink" (1963: 139).
   He was apparently unwilling to examine the cosmological and ideological basis of the system to which these sheikhs belong, as he adds the Orientalist gloss, "To the Moslem who has no sense of natural law, all these 'violations of custom' seem credible" (139).
10. This is also a feature of the posthumous veneration of sheikhs. Offerings are given in the form of bread and dates and left in the tomb as "ex-votos" in return for intercession. As I was told, "One quarter of the sacrificed animal goes to Abu'l Ḥajjāj. This is his due" (oral communication, Luxor). Moreover, the nutritive function of offerings made to Amenhotep, whose cult reputedly continued until Graeco-Roman times in Egypt, was stated in the text, "I savour the food on the occasion of the feasts of Amun in Karnak for the *ka* of the royal scribe, Amenhotep, the justified" (Varille 1968: 3).
11. In Gurna, on the west bank of Luxor, representations of the *hawdaj* to Mecca, which would bear a canopy for the Ka[c]aba of Mecca, are drawn like the canopied litter pulled round in sheikh's processions on the occasion of their *mūlid* are included in the repertoire of pilgrimage paintings traditionally painted on houses. They are similarly referred to as *tābūt* (coffin), plural, *ṭawabīt*.
12. The veneration of the living king Tutankhamun, in Faris in the New Kingdom, is elaborated by Lanny Bell (1985: 31–60).
13. Oral communication, Peter Dorman, Egyptian Department, Metropolitan Museum of Art, New York, 1988.
14. See Richard Parker's study of oracular processions (1962).
15. The earliest representations of Egyptian shrines were of gods situated under domed structures bound by two poles that signified the "poles of heaven." In the representation of the deceased king Ramses IV, in his shrine in his tomb in the Valley of Kings, Luxor

(Field notes, 1984), and in the identically shaped representation in the tomb of Sheikh ITṬayyib, on the West bank of Luxor, the persistence of the dome structure in Egyptian religious shrines can be discerned. In the Delta, sheikhs were also placed under domed vaults (*qubwa*) or stepped mastabas which resemble the most ancient shape of funerary tomb, from the Stepped Pyramid at Saqqara.

16. The four-dimensional polarity of cosmic forces is also manifest in the written representation of spells (*higāb*), where the four corners of the paper are inscribed with the names of four arch saints or celestial "poles" of heaven, in this case, Azra'īl, Jibrīl, Asrafiīl and Mikha'īl, clearly to potentize the spell and anchor it within these forces (Galal 1937: 136).
17. The markings of Egyptian tombs collected by Mohammed Galal in the Egyptian Delta show that the *šāhid* is generally gender-marked. Thus the outward form of the tomb structure would seem to have some prophylactic connection with the occupant of the tomb (Galal 1937: 210).
18. From field research by the author in the village of Kunaiyissit-IḌḌahrīyya in Bahera province—the famous abode of thirty-nine sheikhs—it is clear that sheikhs may also elect to inhabit living trees or trees miraculously able to sustain life while apparently dead: hollowed out tree trunks, devastated by lightening but sprouting leafy green branches such as that of Sīdī Khadr, or mounds such as that of Sīdī Hanasha, which was to be circumambulated seven times as a prophylactic for snake bite.
19. An interesting study of the nomenclature in colloquial Arabic attached to this concept was conducted by Kriss (1960).
20. This ritual of burying the carcass to avoid cot death is described by Atiya (1982: 2–3) and Nelson (1971: 198).
21. As described by Nicholson (1963) but without an attributed source.
22. The *sārī* mast pole of Abu'l Ḥajjāj, which was ceremonially raised at his festival in a ceremony called "The Raising up of the Everlasting" was also believed to be identified with the sheikh and an embodiment of his role as the *qutb dāyir ilaflāk*, "the celestial pole which circuits the heaven" (oral communication, IlḤajj ᶜAbdulla IlḤajājī, Luxor, 1985).
23. Compare, for example, these laments for the father who is described as a migratory bird in fine clothing who has abandoned his children:

    What "plumage," migratory bird—May God be praised—(dark) Moroccan, what clothes you wear . . .
    (ẖalaga wi ya mag̃ rabī subḥān min ẖalagu)
    You in the white cloak, O migratory bird, you in the white cloak,
    From Tunis the green (and fertile) he descended to drink . . .
    (abu ilḥaram abyaḍ yā mag̃ rabī y'abu ilḥaram abyaḏ
    da min tūnis ilẖaḍra nizil yišrub)
    On the fenugreek, the Iraqi goose lighted on the fenugreek
    He abandoned his children and was gone.
    (ᶜalilḥilba ilwizz ilᶜiragī waṭag ᶜalilḥilba

hamal ʿayyālu iṣṣuḡ ayyarīn wi maša)

On the grasspea, the Iraqi goose lighted on the grasspea

He abandoned his small children and left.

(ʿaliljulbān ilwizz ilʿiragī watạg ʿaliljulbān

da hamal ʿayyālu iṣṣugayyarīn wi sār)

(Recorded in 1980 in the Luxor village of IlBayaḍīyya for the author.)

24. Personal communication from a senior member of the family of IlḤajj [c]Abdulla IlḤajājī, Luxor, during research on the mūlid of Sīdī Abu'l Ḥajjāj Il-Uqsorī, May, 1984.

References

[c]Atīya, Nayra. 1982. *Khul-khaal: Five Egyptian women tell their stories.* Syracuse: Syracuse Univ. Press.

[c]Awēs, Sayyid. 1980. *Al-Ibda[c] alThaqafi [c]ala al-Tariqa al-Misriyya* (Cultural Invention, Egyptian Style). Cairo.

Bell, Lanny. 1985. *Aspects of the cult of the deified Tutankhamun. Mélanges Gamal ilDin Mukhtar.* Cairo: Institut Français d'Archéologie Orientale.

Blackman, Winifred. 1926. The "karin" and "karineh." *Journal of the Royal Anthropological Institute of Great Britain and Ireland* 56: 163–69.

Blanchard, R. H. 1917. Note on Egyptian saints. *Harvard African Studies.* Ed. Oric Bates and F. H. Stern, 1: 182–92.

Bleeker, C. J. 1967. *Egyptian festivals: Enactments in religious renewal.* Leiden: Brill.

Budge, E. A. Wallis. 1978. *An Egyptian hieroglyphic dictionary.* New York: Dover.

Creswell, Keppel A. C. 1932–40. *Early Muslim architecture: Umayyids, early [c]Abbasids and Tulunids.* Oxford: Clarendon Press.

Galāl, Mohamed. 1937. Essai d'observations sur les rites funéraires en Égypte actuelle, relevées dans certaines regions compagnardes. *Revue des Études Islamiques,* 2: 131–29.

Hornblower, G. D. [1927] 1960. Traces of a ka-belief in modern Egypt and old Arabia. *Islamic culture,* 426-30.

Kriss, Rudolf, and Hubert Kriss-Heinrich. 1960. *Volksglaube im bereich des Islam.* Wiesbaden: Otto Harrassowitz.

Klunzinger, C. B. 1878. *Upper Egypt: Its people and its products.* New York: Scribner, Armstrong and Co.

Massignon, Louis. 1908. Seconde note sur l'État d'avancement des Études archéologiques arabes en Égypte hors du Caire. *Bulletin de l'Institut Français d'Archeologie Orientale* 9.

McPherson, J. W. 1941. *The moulids of Egypt.* Cairo: Nile Press.

Mercer, Samuel B. 1952. *The pyramid texts* 1-4. New York: Longman's, Green and Co.

Nelson, Cynthia. 1971. Self, spirit possession and world view: An illustration from Egypt. *International Journal of Social Psychiatry* 17: 191–99.

Nicholson, Reynard. 1963. *The mystics of Islam.* Lahore, Pakistan: Sind Sagar Academy, Chowk Minar Anarkali.

Parker, R. 1962. *A Saite oracle papyrus from Thebes.* Providence.

Piankoff, Alexandre. 1984. *The litany of Re.* Bollingen Series: Egyptian Religious Texts and Representations, Princeton, NJ.

Salih, Ahmad Rushdy. 1971. *Al'Ādab ISSha*[c]*bī* (Folklore). Cairo: Maktābit IlNaḥḍa IlMiṣrīyya.

Varille, Alexandre. 1968. Inscriptions concernant l'architecte Amenhotep, fils de Hapou. *Bulletin d'Études* 44. Cairo: Institut Français d'Archéologie Orientale.

Zabkar, L. V. 1968. A study of the *ba* concept in ancient Egyptian texts. *Studies in Ancient Oriental Civilization* 34. Chicago: Oriental Institute, Univ. of Chicago.

Body/Text

The body is written and rewritten in multiple discourses. In medicine, the body is textualized as a physical object. But its humanistic reconstitution as a metaphysical subject is also a textual one. Extruded through Cartesian reasoning, these antithetical inscriptions of the body are pressed together. Texts of the self come to include the body as text.

What is at issue when the body is privileged over its textualizations or the reverse, textualizations privileged over the body? Assumptions about the evidential character of the body, the reality-status we give to its several presentations, and the epistemological weight we grant different modes of apprehension become problematic. The corporeal remains of President Kennedy are transmuted into a textual corpus in which traces of personhood ambiguously inhere.

9. A Body of Texts: The Fiction of Humanization in Medical Discourse

Susan Ritchie

Be All That You Can Be: Locating Humanism in the Body

My internist has a print of Rembrandt's *Anatomy of Dr. Nicolas Tulp* hanging over his desk (fig. 9.1). At first I was uneasy seeing such a graphic depiction of the two aspects of medicine most horrible and mysterious to the layperson (cutting and corpses) decorating the office of a seemingly affable family physician. I have since comforted myself by noting that none of Dr. Tulp's distinguished colleagues observing the dissection are actually looking at the body; instead, their scholarly gaze is focused elsewhere—on the enormous opened book, propped up at the corpse's feet in the right foreground. One of the doctors, assumed by at historians to be Dr. Hartman Hartmansz, holds in his hand yet another text.

But increasingly I am troubled by what seems to be the rather slender difference between the treatment of bodies in medicine and the construction of texts in literary criticism. Indeed, it will be my argument here that it would be a mistake to see the advent of clinical medicine and the birth of the humanities as separate historical moments. To some extent the power of medicine over the corpse issues first from the authority of the text at its feet. Yet the construction is mutual: if the text assists in the construction of the body as an object of knowledge, that body also invents the apparent need for the philosophical text. Dr. Tulp may seem to invent the body himself, yet beyond the frame of the picture are the members of the audience (the dissection took place in a public theater, as

I am indebted to Amy Shuman, Katharine Young, and George Hartley for their careful reading and helpful critical suggestions on various drafts of this paper. I am also grateful to David McArtor for valuable research assistance.

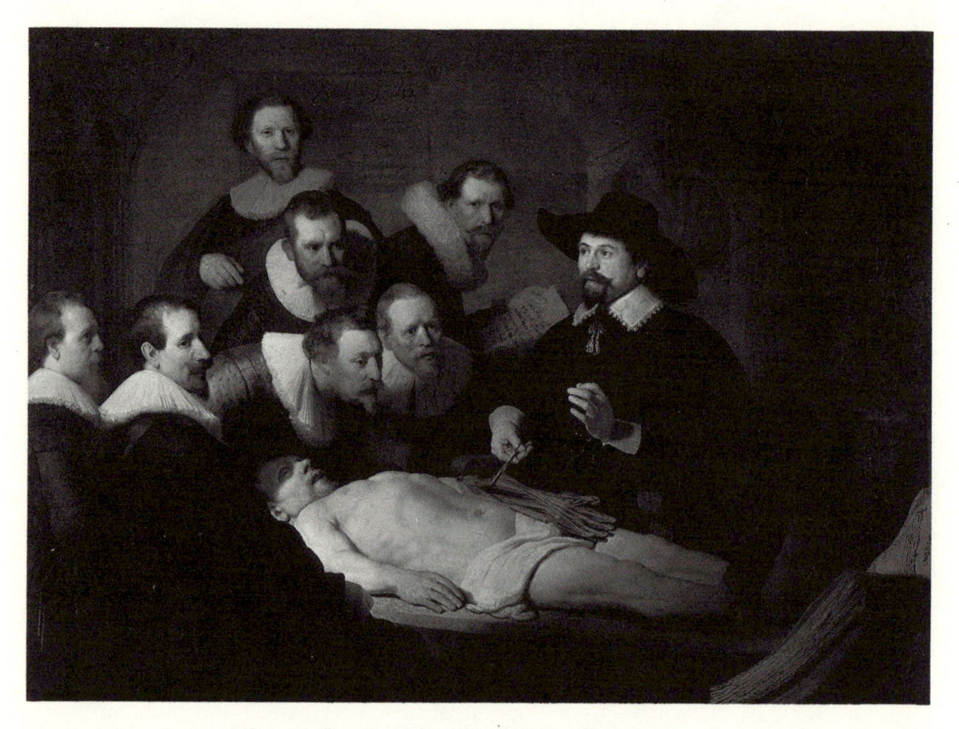

Fig. 9.1. The Body of Knowledge: Rembrandt van Rijn, *The Anatomy Lesson of Dr. Nicolaas Tulp.* Reprinted with permission of Strichting Vrienden Van Het Mauritshuis, the Netherlands.

was the custom) whose spectactorship lends him his authority. And as Francis Barker has suggested, that historical audience might well have included both Descartes and Rembrandt, who legitimized Dr. Tulp's work even as his enterprise informed and legitimized their own pursuits.[1] It is impossible to imagine medicine without Cartesian dualism; Rembrandt's artistic gaze serves above all to extend the spectacular authority of the dissection theater. Nor does the chain of complicity stop with this merely binary exchange of legitimizing practices: Rembrandt, after all, would eventually become Dr. Tulp's patient, having taken to bed for an entire season, convinced his bones were made of wax.

In this textualized negotiation of categories and authorities, medicine and the humanities take on their seemingly disparate disciplinary boundaries precisely because of these complex networks of legitimation and complicity. Disciplinary boundaries are both patrolled and constantly shifting; sometimes they are renegotiated, sometimes even border-raided. The increasing tendency of both medicine and humanism to describe all varieties of bodies, texts, and social phenomena as textualized constructions only seem to indicate the beginnings of true interdisciplinary cooperation. The increasing acceptance within medicine of the textual qualities of the body is hardly a melding of disciplines so much as it is a way reconstituting a humanity (claimed and defined by the humanities) to which medicine, as a discipline, might lay claim.

In *The Glands of Destiny,* Dr. Ivo Geikie-Cobb undertook a study of what he felt was the determinate role of the endocrine system in personality formation. Catherine the Great was entirely motivated by her ovaries, Henry the VIII by his thyroid. That his conclusions seem quaint, improbable, and perhaps even laughable today might be one way of marking the paradigmatic shift in medicine's attitude toward the body from the beginning of this century to its closing years. This shift is usually understood as a moving away from the body-centered essentialisms first developed in the eighteenth century toward a medical practice that appreciates the entire patient as both a social and biological being and has been well documented on the level of both society and of individual medical practice. The once widespread practice of keeping knowledge of fatal illness from patients is now almost universally replaced by the understanding that patients are entitled to know as much as possible about their conditions and, whenever possible, participate in medical decision making.[2] The present-day patient is encouraged to draw on social strengths and family connections to bolster his or her strength—suddenly it is the patient, not the doctor, who is portrayed as having an increasingly active role in the healing process. Nor is this paradigmatic shift from the "physician as hero" to the "patient as hero" apparent only to health-care practitioners (Jones 1988: 1–16). Even television doctor shows and their Marcus Welby–type patriarchs are forever changed: in the fall of 1990 NBC began showing "Lifestories," described as "a many sided look at illness from the viewpoint of the patient."[3]

For the most part, this change has been heralded as a long-awaited humanization of medicine; the dawn of an age in which patients might serve as equal partners with their physician in the health-care process (Barber 1976: 939–43). As reasonable as this description seems, and as difficult it is even seemingly to argue against patient involvement, I am disturbed by the suggestion that the augmentation of the medical model with discourses borrowed from the humanities will automatically dispel any unsavory power imbalance that might previously have marked the physician-patient relationship. A revised medical practice would, after all, not simply turn the physician-patient relationship on its head as much as it would challenge the established relationships of persons and bodies that allow for professionalized power relations. For the relationship of persons and bodies that informs each of the empirical sciences—the assumption that the body has a separate and experimentally determinable existence entirely apart from its inhabitant's humanity—is hardly an assumption that the humanities are in a position to challenge. The humanities participate just as thoroughly in this Cartesian paradigm by proposing to serve the life of the mind.

Hence medical power can hardly erase itself simply by referencing humanism. As William Ray Arney and Bernard J. Bergen (following Foucault) have noted, "We may have to suspend the seemingly self-evident idea that to study power we must focus on exclusionary practices. Instead of asking why medicine tries to keep patients alienated in the medical encounter (as if self-evidently it does so the argument would go), we may have to ask why medicine has started to include patients as partners in medical work" (Arney and Bergen 1984: 6). Instead of accepting medicine's appropriation of humanistic discourse as a token of its breach with its own past, it is important to investigate how its old powers are cloaked by appropriated discourse. In order to enact such an investigation, I understand medical power, just as I understand the humanities, to operate first through the assignment of humanity to bodies, even if it has traditionally bracketed humanity from its own studies. For it would be impossible to accuse medicine of cruelly forgetting the humanity of its patients if that humanity were not already invented and separated out from the body.

So the assignment of individuals to what Howard Brody calls the "sick role" is not the simple result of evil practitioners enjoying a power trip fueled by a perverse sense of personal gratification. Individuals instead find themselves assigned to the "subject-position" of a patient through a more complex set of discursive interactions.[4] The more progressive scholars in the medical humanities have been replacing standard conceptions of the patient as a temporarily compromised, free-willed agent with this Foucauldian understanding of the patient as the marker of a person "interpellated" into a subject-position to great effect (Althusser, 170). By eliminating individual motives or agency from the description of institutional developments, it is possible to develop a sketch of the relationship between fields of knowledge, cultural commodities, and the medical institution. For instance, Edward Shorter, in *Beside Manners: The Troubled History of Doctors and Patients,* is able to suggest that it was the increasing importance of biochemistry and the miracle drug industry in twentieth-century medicine, rather than the behavior or decisions of individual doctors, that originally encouraged the "scientific" rather than personal treatment of the patient. The benefit of this methodological focus on the institution of medicine is its understanding that all cultural or historical variants that occur in the practice of medicine remain social technologies—tools for an institution. In this sense, the basic function of medical discourse's power—the invention of patients as particular kinds of subjects—has not changed much, even if subject-positions shift from requiring the patient to fill a "sick role" (the perfect consumer of miraculous biochemical products) to that of "mutual partner."

Yet the revelation that medicine proceeds from a textual basis as much as from an empirical one is often presented as the final laying bare of scientific power. The fact that even this meta-discourse constructs the body in a certain way, namely as a text, and thus encourages the displacement of that body elsewhere as a body of texts is often overlooked. Thus while Shorter describes the patient of the earlier twentieth century as a consumer of miracle drugs and medicine's increasing biochemical prowess, I suspect this patient now metaphorically consumes the belief that acknowledging the discourses acting on and inventing the patient as a kind of text is a sufficient guarantee of humanization and a kinder, gentler medicine. The disciplinary and institutional conditions that would make such a thought thinkable are my interests here.

David Armstrong (1983: 8) writes that this new, more socially aware medical gaze "identifies disease in the spaces between people, in the interstices of relationships, in the social body itself" and sees its manifestation in the increasing emphasis placed on public health and preventative medicine, which disperses a medical power once concentrated in a specific physical space, the hospital, and relocates a pathology from a particular biological place, the body, to entire social spheres (one thinks of "at-risk" populations). From a traditional viewpoint, it might seem odd to find a science extending its claim beyond the physical world—yet it is this very extension of medical power to the social space that makes it a little easier to see that even modern medicine proceeds in a decidedly unempirical fashion from representation to observation rather than vice-versa. Armstrong, for instance, writes that the medical student is taught to see the anatomical atlas not as a representation of the body, "but the body as a representation of the atlas" (1983: 2). Foucault has termed this dynamic the *medical gaze*—the process by which physicians construct patients by "seeing" some previously represented medical pathology inscribed on their body.[5] Although scholars such as Areny, Bergen, and Armstrong have done a fine job of extending Foucault's landmark analysis and examining the new medical technology as part of the medical gaze, I think that the overextension of the visual metaphor obscures the complicity of the humanities in the construction of power. Understanding the gaze as the sole constructing agent of power runs the risk of once again too neatly aligning bodies with subjects, which leads to a binary model of power—she who is stared at and she who stares. Not only does such a model assume that the physician is an agent in a discourse where it is more appropriate to assume that she simply serves a different subject-position, but it also supposes that the invention of subjectivity unproblematically occurs completely and instantly through a single clinical glance.

Medical discourse is first textualized and often aestheticized before it becomes manifested in practice as a clinical gaze, and thus before corrective remedies may be undertaken. Because the medical student must look up from the "atlas"—the textual discourse of training—before she may set about the practice of medicine on bodies, an examination of medicine's discursive practices, as those moments when medicine is most clearly reliant on notions of textual aestheticism, is most important in rethinking the similar ways in which the sciences and humanities establish power, and the similar ways in which bodies become the stuff and site of that power.[6] I will examine the similarity in two types of texts associated with medicine: the medical training novel and the case history.

The Book Doctors: Medical Training Novels and Textual Therapy

Oddly enough, the medical discursive practice to earn the greatest amount of attention in recent years from both the commercial publishing market and the *New England Journal of Medicine* is the proliferation of fictional and nonfictional accounts of a young doctor's first years in internship or residency. Many older professionals resent these "shrill" complaints that seem to have captured the public's interest over the "sedate and homely writings of country doctors" (Hannaway 1990: 151). Whether one regrets or celebrates the appearance of this genre, it is quite clear that the change is associated with changes in the expression of medical power—and many scholars are tempted to understand the change from memoir to critique as a parallel to the change from a medical paradigm based on doctors' absolute authority to a model of patient participation. This new style of critique, like the shift in medicine itself, is often credited with astounding powers. One physician, writing for one of the country's most respected medical journals, understood the phenomenon in this way:

> [Medicine] has held a mystique rivalled only by that of the Central Intelligence Agency. Unlike the CIA,the inner workings which have only been partly revealed by government reports and former agent's memoirs, medicine's hidden worlds have been progressively unveiled over the past twenty years in a large number of works. There is little that remains behind closed doors. (Borgenicht 1981: 1112)

It is easy to agree with the doctor's understanding that the attraction of these books is based on the intrigue of examining a powerful institution that creates its power and mystique through the delicate and provocative technique of partial disclosure. But what seems most surprising about this characterization of the genre is the implication that these works have already successfully stripped the medical profession entirely bare of its mystique and prestige once and for all.

Even the most optimistic humanities scholar would most likely blanch at the notion that a particular brand of texts could break an entire discipline overnight. Yet within the "new" medicine there is an amazing confidence in the powers of the written word—and ironically, the medical training genre is for many physicians the mark of the humanistic impulse of the discipline. "Ironic" because a genre that usually sees publication in small paperbacks with colorful and dramatic pictures on the front cover is usually not credited (at least not by humanities scholars) with the range of humanization attributed to "higher" literatures. Yet many of the physician-authors of these novels are convinced of the genre's power. In the tenth anniversary edition of his enormously popular *The House of God,* Samuel Shem includes an introduction that lists ten salient points on "How to Remain Human," suggestions ranging from the importance of selecting a pleasant town in which to train to the imperative to "think globally and act locally" if "change" is to be made a priority (1988: 6–7). Many physician-authors have invoked the supposedly character-forming qualities of reading and cite a list of cure-alls available to the general practitioner who embarks upon an appropriate and professionally directed reading program that includes everything from a greater understanding of the snarly ethical dilemmas of genetic engineering to the development of better administrative skills. Courses for medical students in the medical humanities are offered by an increasing variety of medical schools, and even those physicians who object to the idea of such courses do so not on the grounds that the humanities are unimportant but because they are too special to be taught. Although Gerald Weissmann implies that medical humanities courses are too wimpy for medical students ("by the time they arrive in medical school, students ought to be left alone to chew the meat of our tough new science"), it is not because he doesn't think that "culture" is unimportant to the physician, only that "we would be better advised to teach medicine to cultivated students rather than culture to medical students" (1990: 154). Yet the medical training novel, with its handy checklist for humanization, seems to have become an almost parodic—but understandably convenient—version of the impulse of medicine to seek the aid of culture.

Writing for a nonmedical audience has itself come to serve as a testimony to the cultivation and humanity of the doctor-author. The creative act becomes the place to declare that the young medico is successfully resisting dehumanization and, unlike other doctors, still cares about culture. One medical student-poet put it this way: "Every line of poetry I write while in medical school makes me proud of having retained the creative spirit for one more day against great odds."[7] Nor does this commitment to the higher things in life take a lot of time out of the aspiring physician's busy schedule. Melvin Konner writes about reading the plays of Lorca as a medical student: "I had enough time to read only a few pages a day, on the bus, after studying my obstetrics manual. Yet this was enough to keep me in touch with the world of literature and thought. It gave me a sense of transcendence" (Konner 1987: 216).

Yet in its outraged exposure of medical cruelty and in its clear recommendations for a more human medicine, the medical training novel often serves as substitute for actual institutional change. For if some physicians hold great confidence in the power of the "medical expose" to patrol the moral boundaries of the profession, the usual form of the genre itself is quite ill-suited to revolutionary reform. The basic, traditional form of the medical training novel follows almost exactly that of the bildungsroman: the hero invariably transforms initial confusions and incompetence into an enhanced sense of individualism achieved through the performance of remarkable deeds. As such, then, the novels typically detail the process by which physicians purchase their own self-esteem at the cost of understanding their patients as anything other than the objects on which they work their science. In this sense we might be suspicious of the extent to which this genre serves as a radical critique of medicine as a discipline and the extent to which it creates the conditions for its existence. As a humanistic critique of the reductions and cruelties of empirical science, the genre might even be necessary for the protection of those very privileges about which it seemingly complains. Indeed, it is my argument that these books by residents and interns (and increasingly, even medical students) do less to bare the secrets of medicine than to participate in the changing medical discourse that articulates power even while it distracts with alibis—alibis largely borrowed from the humanities, alibis that understand self-reflection and exposure to serve only humanistic ends and that fashion the sanctity of the medical mission. Yet as I plan to demonstrate, these alibis are not simply excuses borrowed from an otherwise innocent humanism—indeed, the image of "borrowing" is inadequate to the extent to which medicine and the humanities represent the same social technology. Although humanism is understood today as an opposition to science, humanism itself was conceived, at least since Kant (along with science), as the rational alternative to religion. In this sense humanism has always borrowed the "grounds" for rationality from the sciences. We should not be surprised, then, to find them working together to invent the most visible ideological creation of our time—the bourgeois individual, perhaps the only historical subject arrogant enough to find in the body's literal singularity a sense of the uniquely human that might transcend all law—natural and historical.

Despite the growing suspicion of humanism's bedfellows (rampant individualism, for instance), most scholars of the medical humanities are prepared to praise works by young medicos on the grounds that stories about the medical profession serve to democratize the power base of medicine simply by providing a complete picture of the exhausted practitioners and poor service that endanger health care consumers. This notion that one might "read more about it" to regain a measure of control over an unexamined situation is, of course, as old as the humanities and as popular as consumer advocacy. Indeed, Stephanie Kiceluk, one of the first scholars to explore these works from the perspective of the humanities, writes, "There might be something subversive about the experience of literature—about telling stories and wanting to know the whole story; and there is something liberating, even therapeutic, in finally getting the whole story" (1984: 249). But it is precisely what Kiceluk astutely notes, that there might be something therapeutic about stories, that alarms me. Often medicine and literature find themselves engaged in similar social technologies, and because of this it is naïve to assume that the humanities might serve to effect a simple rescue of the scientific even as the scientific might enrich the scope of the humanities. Yet this is the model of the medical humanities as it is usually invoked—too often a simple prescription whereby literature provides the ethical component lacking in medicine and medicine provides literary types with an invigorating dose of materialism, as if disciplinary blind spots are minor enough to be corrected by an additive model.[8]

In short, there is no vast gulf between the individual and the institutional body, no distance between aestheticized discourse (literature) and clinical sciences that makes it possible to talk of one without justifying the other. Aesthetics was originally a discourse grounded in the body. It was about, in Terry Eagleton's terms, "the whole of our sensate life together" (1990: 13). The grand struggle of Kant's *Critique of Judgment* provides the model of modern critical theory as a meta-discourse and defines aesthetic judgment as that which serves as a bridge between bodily sensations and abstract notions of beauty or sublimity. Eagleton continues to describe aesthetics' focus on the body:
"The aesthetic concerns this most gross and palpable dimension of the human, which post-Cartesian philosophy, in some curious lapse of attention, has somehow managed to overlook. [The aesthetic represents] the first stirrings of a primitive materialism—of the body's long inarticulate rebellion against the tyranny of the theoretical" (1990: 13).

Aestheticizing representation bridges the gap between bodies and embodiment, and is in this sense the same thing as interpellation. As Katharine Young notes, the status of medical discourse depends on its success in banishing the grotesque or unembodied, uncontainable body from its purview (1993). Medicine thus begins with an abstraction (a disease) that is then lodged, as empiricism requires, in some specific pathology of the body. If literary criticism seeks to extract meaning from the text, thus working in the opposite direction as medicine, both depend on the fantasy of embodiment. There is a certain sense, then, in which bodies and texts are the same things—semiautonomous, bounded entities described and protected by the discourses that invent them. The corpse, the uninhabited body, is much the same threat as a literary work without an author.

Medicine and the humanities, then, have shared this interest in creating bodies through description, medicine inventing the physical body as the object of its clinical discourse while philosophy attempted to describe the body in such a way as to be of service to the bourgeois subject who imagines the human individual to be powerful, unique, and wholly idealistic. These disciplines do not merely create the need for each other but depend on each other's existence. The notion that the human subject transcends the body is unthinkable without attention first being drawn to the body. Hence it is when pathology is located in the body that the category of more-than-body becomes thinkable as a Cartesian soul or residual human essence irreducible to the physical. As this unpenetrable, unanatomical idea of the human subject is invented, medicine claims the body while the humanities claim to safeguard all that is uniquely and unempirically human; even as they continue to lend, borrow and extend these privileges to constitute their own disciplinary authority.

The medical-training genre tends to replay this symbiotic dynamic with interesting variations. In each case, though, the harshness of the clinical gaze creates a category of humanity that comes to reside somewhere just on the edge of the visible. Consider Doctor X, an especially fine student of the Bildungsroman who wrote one of the earliest and most renowned examples of the genre, the 1965 expose *Intern.*[9] At the start of the book, and of his training (the pattern of this genre is usually one of a strict chronology), he is nauseated and overwhelmed by the invasive procedures he is required to perform and is barely able to make himself complete some of the nastier routine "scut work," including the insertion of an IV catheter into a baby's jugular vein. Soon, though, he is acting and talking like a real pro, and by the time he rotates to obstetrics and gynecology he cavalierly refers to patients as "babes" and has adopted a disarming way of rating women's personal worth on their demeanor while undergoing labor and delivery (actually it is still a part of contemporary house office slang to rate some patients as NAT—"Not a Trooper"). He says, clearly disapproving of one women's successful attempt to get through delivery without medication (given the hospital's tendency to prescribe amnesiacs in the place of anesthesia, this seemed like a good choice to me), "She was a good looking girl, too, about twenty three or twenty four years old, good looking girl too, but God! What an unyielding type!" And as he continues his classifications, "Another girl who did well was kind of a goon-girl who acted half-stupefied all through her labor" (1965: 133). It is a little too pat to simply accuse Dr. X of not caring for these brave women. Rather, it is important to understand that if humanity is what is left out when medicine treats patients as mere conditions, it is understandable that this humanity would first manifest itself in the self-esteem of the medical practitioner; if humanity is discovered in the patient, it is from some excess of the physician's: perhaps the doctor has an unexpected luxury of time during rounds, and "discovers" the personality of his patient; perhaps the doctor is feeling especially pleased with his own role, and the result is a kind of transference of personality to the patient.

In *Under the Ether Dome,* Stephen Hoffmann describes his early days as an incredibly enthusiastic intern: "I wanted to be up all night. I wanted to be called to see people who were having chest pain, who were bleeding, or who had arrested" (1986: 26). Part of Dr. Hoffmann's enthusiasm extended to making an extra round in the evening where he "harbored no ulterior intent" except to comfort his patients, and not surprisingly, he represents both his patients and himself as most fully human only in these moments. Only the excess of this young intern's energy for playing doctor in rare combination with a perceived luxury of time could make such "humanity" possible. For the strange paradox of post-Cartesian thought is that, like Dr. Armstrong's anatomical atlas, the possibility of the transcendental individual (who understands a unique human quality that is definable only in opposition to transient bodily qualities) always requires the firm outline of the merely physical body on which to place its complex overlaying transparencies, and from which to deduce that the excess marks a supreme value.

The Bildungsroman formula, in so far as it uses the figure of the physician as extraordinary being as the most basic outline from which to build, then, has obvious limitations as an instrument of health care reform. The genre, however, is changing as rapidly as the medical profession itself. No longer coherent narratives of a young hero's acquisition of knowledge and well-being, the typical expose of medical training today is more apt to resemble books such as Robert Klitzman's *Year-Long Night: Tales of a Medical Internship,* which provides confusing montages of incidents entirely without a narrative unity. The traditional medical Bildungsroman always relied heavily on the unifying presence of the doctor for its narrative coherency, which leant even the most unconnected listings a kind of logic, cohesion and even drama. It is tempting enough to read this as a sign of progress, as an indication that physicians are willing to sacrifice some of their prestige. Yet medical power is more a result of the outline that it inscribes for its patients than for its most privileged practitioners. There is some evidence that the Bildungsroman formula lives on, not in the narratives that physicians make overtly about themselves but in the ones they make overtly about patients—but in which they are nonetheless covertly inscribed as heroes: the case history.

Authorizing Medicine: The Case History

Pathology is not merely found, but inscribed, not only on, but as, the human body. Pathology as a concept has been useful to society in providing both a convincing description of society's others (as mad, as dangerously ill, as contagious) as well as isolating the danger of the pathological state to actual bodies which might in turn be isolated from society.[10] Pathology first exists as a text, as an abstraction that can then be displaced to the physicality of the body. As often as not, in modern medicine, that text is the case history. We are not surprised, then, to realize that the case history is as often about the role of the physician as about the actual patient. In *Under the Ether Dome,* Hoffmann describes starting the day's paperwork, thinking only how the patient's cases would reflect his own role in the drama of their care:

> Each day on call was a novel waiting to be written, a novel in which I would figure as both narrator and participant. Perhaps I could influence the outcome, I would tell myself, author favorable changes in the turn of events. Like as ghostwriter behind the voice of fate, I could try to slant the day's story to advantage. I might initiate a medication on a patient in the hope of modifying his disease or take a seat at his side, hoping to alter his perception of the disease instead. Or maybe I would operate behind the scene. (1986: 40)

It is not hard to read the case history as a summary of this narrative that the young Dr. Hoffman imagines for himself.

The case history is one of the chief medical genres, and perhaps the point at which the relationship between science and the humanities is most clear. The standard form for the case history, the Atchley Form, reminds physicians of their dual service to science and aesthetics: although it directs that the case should be described in so precise and quantitative a fashion that it would be possible to graph, it also instructs the physician to "tell a story" in "graceful" English.[11] Here causality serves to both present an orderly history and tell a story about the efficiency and quality of the medical care provided. The traditional case history, then, is as much a persuasive and often fictional story about the fine quality of medical care being administered as it is a part or record of that care. Nor is this aspect of the case history simply a precaution in case of lawsuit. Consider Dr. Rosalie Slaughter Morton, summarizing the case of an artist-patient in 1937 in the traditional fashion, well before the age of malpractice: "Beatrice: 23 years old; history—pain growing progressively worse, recurring at regular intervals accompanied by three days incompetency, fatigue unduly increased by standing; examination—diagnosed extreme displacement of a pelvic organ; operation restored position to normal; results—symptoms disappeared; prize winner in a national competition; gratitude" (Morton 1937: 193). That Dr. Morton would present her patient's professional accomplishments as an immediate result of surgery in a story where gratitude serves its own necessary narrative place, is indicative of the role of case history in shaping the patient as a subjectivity "freed" by medical intervention. The price of that freedom was first accepting the body as a prison from which deliverance of the higher human qualities was possible, and it is this ontotheological discourse of redemption that medicine secularizes.

Even if the new case history successfully understands the social context of the patient as a complex web that stops neither at the body nor the hospital walls, the character of the case history as the textual place in which both a patient's oppression and redemption are fashioned remains. Consider an example of a "case history" concerned with social context:

> Luis Fontana was triaged to the trauma section of the Emergency Room. A sixteen year old Hispanic, he had tried to kill himself by slashing his stomach in a long slit from one flank to the other. The wound was superficial, never piercing through protective layers of muscle. . . . his girlfriend of five months had left him. His parents separated, and his family poor. His parents, who had been unmarried, had fought incessantly at home. I learned that he had no one to talk to. (Klitzman 1989: 140)

In many ways, this paragraph from Robert Klitzman's pseudo-fictional account of his internship is stylistically indistinguishable from that of a more traditional case history. From its strange implicated causalities ("A sixteen year old Hispanic, he tried to kill himself") to its crisp narrative efficiency, the passage resembles greatly the patient's history as retold by a physician, emphasizing what is of greatest importance. That this case history belongs to a "new" generation more interested in social history hardly matters in the basic construction of the genre. Although Klitzman does not present himself explicitly as the hero of his account, he has nonetheless given a case history that at every step promises the possibility of medical intervention in the chain of already overdetermined causalities, whether that narrative notes the progression of a bacterial infection to meningitis or the disposition of a young Hispanic man to suicide attempts.

Whether the case history includes social details such as make up the fictional history of Luis Fontana, or is a carefully "buffed" document (where all treatments no matter how routine are documented and footnoted) meant to protect the physician from malpractice, the result is still the textual precondition of treatment—the identification of a textualized pathology that must be grafted on the body invented to house it. In Shem's *House of God*,

Roy, the besieged intern, learns his lessons from a savvy resident called the "Fat Man" who teaches him what he didn't learn at BMS (the Best Medical School). The Fat Man's basic principle for medical survival (of the doctor, not the patient—one of his maxims is The Patient is the One with the Disease) is to treat texts, not bodies. The Fat Man conducts rounds by flipping through index cards rather than seeing actual patients, and teaches his "terns" (interns) to avoid treating the older, sicker patients at all. As Roy and his fellow "terns" start to use the patients' medical charts to spin elaborate fictions about nonexistent lab tests ordered, results received, and treatments undergone, their patients do indeed recover, and their faith in the Fat Man is cemented. In a final irony, the *House of God* has been so popular that contemporary house officers often deliberately tailor their own references to medical terms to match the slang in some cases invented by the novel (Konner 314).

Most of the physical sciences have already felt the presence of one or more gadflies, scholars who insist that their models are paradigms (such as described by Thomas Kuhn) rather than real systems.[12] Although the acceptance of this idea is still limited, its dissemination in everything from the current popularity of chaos theory in the popular press to introductory physics textbooks that urge students not to confuse science with actual phenomena indicates the possibility of increasing acceptance.[13] Yet the notion that the connection between medicine and the body is arbitrary, negotiated only by a slippery slope of texts and paradigms, case histories and "scientific" models, works against the understanding of medicine as the practical application of science. If the scandal of medicine is that the patient body is connected to medicine not through a perfect empiricism but through an imperfect representation, then the medical discourse that suggests that the tie to the patient's social sphere be strengthened repairs rather than exposes medical legitimation strategies.[14]

In the vigorous pursuit of the medical humanities, then, we need to remember that it is impossible to read medicine without constructing bodies. The bodies we construct are bodies of texts. As such they are no less coercive than the bodies upon which medicine works, no less a part of institutional sinew. The mark of textuality on the bodies medicine treats is not an indication of the triumph of the descriptive model of the humanities of over that of the empirical sciences. Yet such textualization might be used as a starting place for the study of the social technologies that mark our own complicit participation in the implementation of dominant paradigms we supposed we resisted.

Notes

1. Francis Barker, "Into the Vault," in *The Tremulous Private Body: Essays on Subjection* (New York: Methuen, 1984), 71–112.
2. Other authors note the same shift on a much smaller scale. According to one such study, it was about 1970 that doctors decided patients had the right to know if they were suffering from a fatal disease. See Cassileth et al. 1980: 832–36.
3. "Lifestories," *TV Guide,* Sept. 15, 1990, 28.
4. The term *subject-position* does imply that patients and other subjects are the end result of a network of power relations, yet the term itself evidences the increasing scholarly awareness that bodies are invented as certain kinds of subjects through entire networks of discursive power relations. For *subject-position* is Foucault's apt name for the result of the simultaneous construction of the body and the subject (equally fictitious) by various cultural and political forces. The intersection of these forces at the site of the body make it only seem as if the body were an individual agent—hence Foucault maintains the use of the word *subject.* Yet persons are not so much real subjects as guises that obscure the agency of more subtle forces—hence they occupy *subject-positions.* Foucault spells out his use of *subject-position* Foucault 1972, esp. chap. 4.
5. Foucault 1975. Foucault himself later regretted that the term *gaze* implied too strongly a unifying function of subjects. See Foucault 1972: 54.
6. I understand the "humanities" here to be the institutionalized form of humanism, much as clinical medicine might be understood as the institutional version of empiricism.
7. From *Poetry: A Collection of Poems Written by Medical Students: Selected Works of Finalists in the William Carlos Williams Poetry Competition,* qtd. in Davis 1990: 70.
8. Consider, for example, William Monroe's review of Charles Anderson's book on Richard Selzer—a review that depends very much on the disturbing portrait of a virile male scholar attacking a feminized body of knowledge: "Anderson's writing could make surgeons better doctors, more effective healers. My hope is that Anderson's book will also find its way into the hands of would be writers and teachers and critics. Those of us primarily concerned with the production, distribution and evaluation of culture and cultural artifacts would do well to ground ourselves . . . in the ligaments and tissues of bodies themselves. While the surgeon may commit rape with a scalpel, many poets in their impotence and suspicion have lost the desire to embrace, to touch what is there." Monroe 1990: 32–35, 34–35.
9. Doctor X 1965. Doctor X has since come forth as Dr. Alan Nourse, author of the more recent novel *Practice.*
10. For an extended account see Gilman 1985.
11. The Atchley Form, despite its name, does not provide physicians with a simple series of blanks to fill in like the medical history form that often awaits patients on the first office visit. Rather, as the directions make clear, the doctor is instructed to achieve both an objective standard and subjective finesse. The instructions read: "A good history should

be so precise and quantitative that its essential features could be charted on graph paper with a time coordinate; a good history should be so comprehensive that succeeding physicians need not interrogate further; a good history should 'tell a story'. . . and orderly and interpretive chronicle written in graceful and concise English." The Atchley form is quoted and further discussed in Kiceluk 1984: 255.

12. Two popular examples are Gregory 1988 and Jones 1982; for the original works to explode scientific "objectivity" for the popular press see, of course, Feyerabend 1975 and Kuhn 1982.
13. Interestingly enough, "chaos theory" seems to have found quite a following in the humanities (judging from recent Modern Language Association programs) as way of explaining literary "chaotic" phenomenon such as modernism or postmodernism. That most of these connections make the comparison on the level of "chaos" as a theme is symptomatic of the same impulse that has many scholars understanding relativity as a kind of relativism (although no one was more interested in empirical verification of theory than Einstein). Making a connection between "chaos" theory and the humanities is much better undertaken at the level of noting similarities in the understanding of "construction" used in each lest science once again be used to verify a "finding" in the humanities.
14. Lest I be understood as calling for an end to medicine altogether, I'd like to point out that the arbitrary relationship between medicine and bodies is only a scandal to medicine's legitimization strategies, and not to the idea of health care itself: no one would think to refuse to cash a paycheck, for instance, on the grounds that it represents only an abstract of actual hours worked, or for that matter, refuse money as it is only metaphorical of some imaginary gold standard. Bodies understood without the aid of a true empiricism might still be treated.

References

Althusser, Louis. 1971. *Lenin and Philosophy and Other Essays.* Tr. Ben Bressler. New York: Monthly Review Press..

Armstrong, David. 1983. *Political anatomy of the body: Medical knowledge in Britain in the twentieth century.* Cambridge: Cambridge Univ. Press.

Arney, William J., and Bernard J. Bergen. 1984. *Medicine and the management of living: Taming the last great beast.* Chicago: Univ. of Chicago Press, 1984.

Barber, Bernard. 1976. Compassion in medicine: Towards new definitions and new institutions. *New England Journal of Medicine* 295: 939–43.

Borgenicht, Louis. 1981. American medicine: An annotated bibliography. *New England Journal of Medicine* 304, no. 18 (Apr. 30): 1112–17.

Brody, Howard. 1987. *Stories of sickness.* New Haven, CT: Yale Univ. Press.

Cassileth, Barrie, Robert V. Zupis, Katherine Sutton-Smith, and Vicki March. 1980. Information and participation preferences among cancer patients. *Annals of Internal Medicine* 92: 832–36.

Davis, David. 1990. Even young doctors write poetry. *Medical Humanities Review* 4 (1): 70.

Eagleton, Terry. 1990. *The ideology of the aesthetic.* Cambridge: Basil Blackwell.

Feyerabend, Paul. 1975. *Against method.* London: Verso, 1975.

Foucault, Michel. [1969] 1972. *The archaeology of knowledge.* Translated Alan M. Sheridan Smith. New York: Pantheon Books.

———. [1963] 1975. *The birth of the clinic: An archaeology of medical perception.* Trans. Alan M. Sheridan Smith. New York: Vintage Books.

Geikie-Cobb, Ivo. 1927. *The glands of destiny: A study of the personality.* London: William Heinemann Medical Books.

Gilman, Sandar. 1985. *Difference and pathology: Stereotypes of sexuality, race, and madness.* Ithaca and London: Cornell Univ. Press.

Gregory, Bruce. 1988. *Inventing reality: Physics and language.* New York: Wiley and Sons. 1990.

Hannaway, Caroline, ed. Book notes on Marvin Brown's *House calls: The memoirs of a country doctor. Bulletin of the History of Medicine* 64 (1): 151.

Harrison, Michelle. 1982. *A woman in residence.* New York: Random House.

Hoffman, Stephen. 1986. *Under the ether dome: A physician's apprenticeship at Massachusetts General Hospital.* New York: Charles Scribner.

Jones, Anne Hudson. 1988. Literature and medicine: Illnesses from the patient's perspective. In *Personal choices and public commitments: Perspectives on the medical humanities.* Ed. William J. Winsdale, 1–16. Galveston, Tex.: Institute for the Medical Humanities.

Jones, Roger S. 1982. *Physics as metaphor.* Minneapolis: Univ. of Minnesota Press.

Kiceluk, Stephanie. 1984. Revising the two cultures script: Literary texts in medical education. *Texas Studies in Language and Literature* 26: 242–62.

Klitzman, Robert. 1989. *A year long night: Tales of a medical internship.* New York: Viking, 1989.

Konner, Melvin. 1987. *Becoming a doctor: A journey of initiation in medical school.* New York: Viking.

Kuhn, Thomas S. 1982. *The structure of scientific revolutions.* Chicago: Univ. of Chicago Press.

Lifestories. 1990. *TV Guide,* Sept. 15, 28.

Lydston, Frank G. 1905. *The diseases of society: The vice and crime problem.* Philadelphia: Lippincott.

Monroe, William. 1990. Desperately seeking Selzer. *Medical Humanities Review* 4 (1): 32–35.

Morton, Rosalie Slaughter. 1937. *A woman surgeon: The life and work of Rosalie Slaughter Morton.* New York: Stokes Co.

Nourse, Alan. *See* X, Doctor.

Nye, Robert A. 1984. *Crime, madness, and politics in modern France: The medical concept of national decline.* Princeton, NJ: Princeton Univ. Press, 1984.

Sacks, Oliver. 1978. *Awakenings.* New York: Dutton.

Shem, Samuel. [1978] 1988. *The house of God.* New York: Bantam Books.

Shorter, Edward. 1985. *Beside manners: The troubled history of doctors and patients.* New York: Simon and Schuster.

Sontag, Susan. 1988. *AIDS and its metaphors.* New York: Farrar, Straus and Giroux.

Weissman, Gerald. 1990. A slap in the tail: Reading medical humanities. In *The doctor with two heads and other essays,* 152–67. New York: Alfred Knopf.

X, Doctor [Alan Nourse]. 1965. *Intern.* New York: Harper and Row.

Young, Katharine. 1993. Still life with corpse: The management of the grotesque body in medicine. In *Bodylore.* Ed. Katharine Young. Knoxville: Univ. of Tennessee Press and Publications of the American Folklore Society.

10. From the Body as *Evidence to the Body* of *Evidence*

Barbie Zelizer

Investigations of the body are intensified in instances where its status is contested. The assassination of John F. Kennedy is one such instance. Despite a plethora of documentation attesting to various unidentified assassins, including two official and many semiofficial investigations, closure has not been reached in the assassination story. Indeed, the more one knows, the less one understands.

This chapter considers how the body of John F. Kennedy has been used as a vehicle for retelling the assassination story and for attempting to lend closure to the president's death. Kennedy's body has given retellers of the story a way of sidestepping and rearranging the holes, ambiguities, and falsehoods that have come to characterize the events of November 22, 1963.

The chapter first considers political readings of "the body" in general and applies them to assassination retellings; it then surveys specific techniques of the body that have figured within such retellings; and finally, it explores the implications of such techniques for invoking stories about the body as a term of argumentation. By considering how the body *as* evidence in the story of Kennedy's death has given way to the body *of* evidence, I explore the strategic use of Kennedy's body as a discursive term for retelling the assassination story.

The Body as Evidence

When considering the centrality of the body among premodern Western political thinkers, the proliferation of stories about the body of John F. Kennedy comes as no surprise. Advancing discourse through stories about the body is a mode of cultural argumentation that has taken on particular relevance in political discourse, where the body of the head

---

My thanks to Katharine Young for her tireless efforts at reading earlier versions of this manuscript.

of state has been long co-opted as a reflection of the state itself (Kantorowicz 1957; Turner 1990).

Of particular relevance here are medieval notions about the body of the king. The king was thought to have two bodies—one mortal and potentially destructible, the other a mystical creation reflecting the state of his kingdom (Turner 1990: 13). Recognition of his body as a metaphor for the political domain meant that the safety and safekeeping of the state was embodied in that of the king. This made the body of the king central to discourse about "the body politic," cementing what has been called a linkage between specific human anatomy and the political organization of society (Turner 1982: 258). Underlying ambiguities about the body of the king, therefore, were anxieties about the body of the state. Threat was perceived not only to the person of the head of state but to the politic body he incorporated.

Repercussions of this mode of thought were wide-ranging. In Mary Douglas's words, "Bodily control (became) an expression of social control" (Douglas 1970: 70). The king's body became equated with political power, and harm to that body signified the usurpation or disintegration of such power. All attacks on the body of the king came to be seen as attacks on the body of society. Equally important, the instability caused by harm to the king generated an instability of political process, with a lack of bodily control producing a lack of social and political control. In the most extreme case, this analogy between the body of the king and the body of state extended beyond the king's life to his corpse.

This has offered a curious dimension to the workings of the analogy connecting the body of the king with that of the state, for in persisting beyond the king's personal existence, the analogy underscores the strength of the metaphor with which the human body can be used to shape and recondition political thought and discourse. It suggests a parallel that this chapter will consider directly—namely, that the body can be employed as a discursive term to address more general concerns about political life and discourse.

Using the Body to Retell the Assassination

The centrality of the king's body within political discourse bears particular relevance to retellings of the story of John F. Kennedy's assassination in that one memorable feature about his administration was the regal status he attained for himself and those around him. Over the nearly thirty years since Kennedy died, the locus for authoritatively retelling the story has not stabilized (Zelizer 1990; 1992): public skepticism about official agencies for documentation was originally set in motion by the failure of the Warren Commission and the House Select Committee on Assassinations to provide closure to what happened; it was solidified by other events, such as the Pentagon Papers, the Vietnam War, and Watergate, where the locus for authoritatively retelling events moved from official documentary forums to the memories of nonofficial retellers. In the case of Kennedy's death, such nonofficial retellers of the story—the independent critics, journalists and historians—have gradually become its active and authoritative interpreters, suggesting that much of the authority for retelling has come to rest with the assassination record's folklore. At the heart of many efforts to retell Kennedy's death, therefore, are concerns over the role of laypersons in official political discourse. The precise nature and extent of political involvement one can expect and accomplish has figured into the attempts of many ordinary citizens to involve themselves in retelling the assassination story. This has particularly been the case with director Oliver Stone's movie, *JFK.* It represented yet another move in ongoing efforts by private citizens to tell the assassination tale.

Within this setting, stories about Kennedy's body have proliferated. While addressing concerns over the layperson's role in official discourse, retellers have used the body to retell the assassination story. On the one hand, the body has figured centrally in a wide range of theories about those responsible for Kennedy's death. The accused have included the Mafia, the Soviets, Cubans, the CIA, right-wingers, and Texas oil-men. Retellers, no longer able to obtain access to the original events of the story, have been reduced in many cases to documenting the documents of others. Kennedy's assassination has thus evolved into an event with multiple interpretations that have been documented in various ways. Documents that were sealed have been reopened, testimony has been regiven within different circumstances, and access to secondary sources of information has become as important as access to the original crime. Kennedy's body has remained a vital, if recoded, dimension of nearly every new interpretation that has been set forth.

On the other hand, attempts to reconsider the assassination record have been accompanied by shifts in the means available for interpreting the events of November 1963. This has allowed the body to be reexamined within seemingly new parameters. Shifts in what are considered acceptable categories of documentation have generated different reconstructions of "the facts." For example, when the House Select Committee reviewed autopsy photographs and X-rays in 1978, it used computer-assisted image enhancement techniques that had not been available fifteen years earlier (Kurtz 1982: 162). Similarly, advanced methods for examining acoustic testimony prompted the House Select Committee to overturn the Warren Commission's conclusion of a single assassin and suggest instead an unidentifiable conspiracy. Such shifts in retellings, and the primarily consensual understandings of the assassination on which they are based, thus depend in large part on technology. Changing technologies have not only made certain categories of documentation more accessible than others to retellers over time but also have generated different notions about which technology is better able to authoritatively fix and explicate the "reality" of Kennedy's death. Within this technical discourse, Kennedy's body has been altered, reshaped and reconditioned.

Perhaps one of the first tales about Kennedy's body was published two weeks after his death under the title "Seeds of Doubt: Some Questions About the Assassination" (Minnis and Lynd 1963). The article was divided into sections about the target, the wounds, the weapon, the bullets, and the murderer. The body was seen as the site of the crime, allowing for the establishment of different documentary categories around it. Although this was a far cry from the more sophisticated categories of documentation that began to fill the media following the Warren Commission one year later, it suggested already then that the crime was reconstructed according to the categories of documentation compiled about it. Moreover, it distinctly foreshadowed the technical discourse that advanced often-contradictory theories in later years, when details of the assassination filled the pages of journals such as *Ramparts, The New Republic,* and *Esquire.* Thus within the parameters of technical discourse that facilitated active interpretation of the events of Kennedy's death, the body initially provided background for discussions of the crime.

Yet over time it did not provide background alone. Since Kennedy's death the body has evolved into a discursive term for retellers trying to advance their versions of the assassination record. Because stories of the body remain one of the more tangible and seemingly accessible categories of documenting what happened, they have become a means of generating competitive readings of the same event. They also signal in microcosm more general contestation surrounding the assassination. In many cases nonofficial retellers have forwarded their versions of Kennedy's death by documenting points in the record about his body that were overlooked by official forums. An amateur rock drummer, for example, was responsible for challenging the House Select Committee's assertion that there had been a fourth shot in the assassination. He used a cheap recording of the acoustic evidence that had been distributed with a popular magazine to do so (Belin 1988: 199).

All of this suggests that the shift from the authority of official documentary forums to that of nonofficial retellers is a strategic action that has depended on the evolution of documentary categories that enhance the latter's authority. The body of John F. Kennedy constitutes one such category. It has allowed retellers to attend to the events of Kennedy's death through discourse about a wide range of bodily practices. In many cases, such practices or the site of their employment are familiar and therefore accessible to retellers. Retellers have thereby refashioned discussions of Kennedy's death by focusing on evidence about his body. This has generated a movement in the status of the body as a discursive term.

Techniques of the Body

Marcel Mauss first contended in 1935 that all techniques of the body are socially constructed (Mauss [1935] 1973). Although his own reference was to bodily techniques as culturally coded practices, the notion of social construction is aptly exemplified in assassination retellings. There bodily practices—seen as ways in which one relates to the body in discourse rather than as what one does with one's body—have been differentially codified as acceptable ways of retelling the assassination story. Discourse about different bodily practices can be directly related to ongoing concerns about the role of the layperson in official political discourse.

One evident feature about the body of John F. Kennedy is its centrality to the larger assassination story. It was called the "most important evidence" in the story. Independent critic David Lifton pronounced it "the diagram of the shooting" ("Who Shot President Kennedy?" 1988). Although initially invoked only as background for the crime, the body has been gradually transformed into a more general term for cultural argumentation. As assassination retellings have persisted, the body has provided not only background to the crime but also the site for new readings and analyses of the crime. This has lent credence to the notion that the body constitutes an effective site for the exercise of political power and the locus for control over its political meaning.

Kennedy's body thus offers a double articulation of the events of the assassination: It is a first-order articulation that concretizes the crime itself, yet its second-order articulation as documentation offers a place for nonofficial retellers to locate contested interpretations about the shape of that crime. This was facilitated by public purchase of the Warren Commission Report in 1964, where, for a mere seventy-six dollars, laypersons were readily able to get access to a plethora of medical documentation about Kennedy's body (Welsh and Turner 1969: 62). Laypersons' ability to examine the medical evidence in Kennedy's death has allowed for its eventual and active recoding over time. It is thus no surprise that Kennedy's body has undergone such an array of documentary handlings and mishandlings. As a term in cultural argumentation, it has given nonofficial retellers extensive material with which to advance a variety of interpretations about what happened.

Over time, discourse about the body has displayed a growing degree of complexity. Three main levels of discourse have been invoked. The earliest discussions, which transpired during the sixties, focus on the practices by which Kennedy's body was examined and misread. These have given way to two other kinds of readings. One centers upon mishandlings of Kennedy's body; the other stresses its mis-recordings, focusing on how records detail practices by which it had been mishandled. Each arena—misreading, mishandling and mis-recording—builds on the one that precedes it. Each uses a combination of technical discourse and discourse about the body to generate contesting interpretations of Kennedy's death, and at the same time addresses larger concerns about the ability of the layperson to contest and challenge official political discourse.

Misreading the Body

The first stage of responses to the assassination was shaped around the Warren Commission in 1964. The commission was officially chartered with examining the medical, eyewitness, ballistic, and physical evidence at the scene of the crime and was convened much like an investigation into a murder case, in which observers attempted to delineate exactly what had happened. This was accomplished largely through perspectives provided by official or expert decoders. By the time it had concluded its deliberations in 1964, the commission's documentation contained more than seventeen thousand pages housed in twenty-six volumes (Trillin 1967: 42). It was argued that the crime was committed by a lone assassin—Lee Harvey Oswald.

Although early reception to the report was sympathetic, by 1966 a number of works critical of its views were published. Most raised the possibility of conspiracy. In Decem-

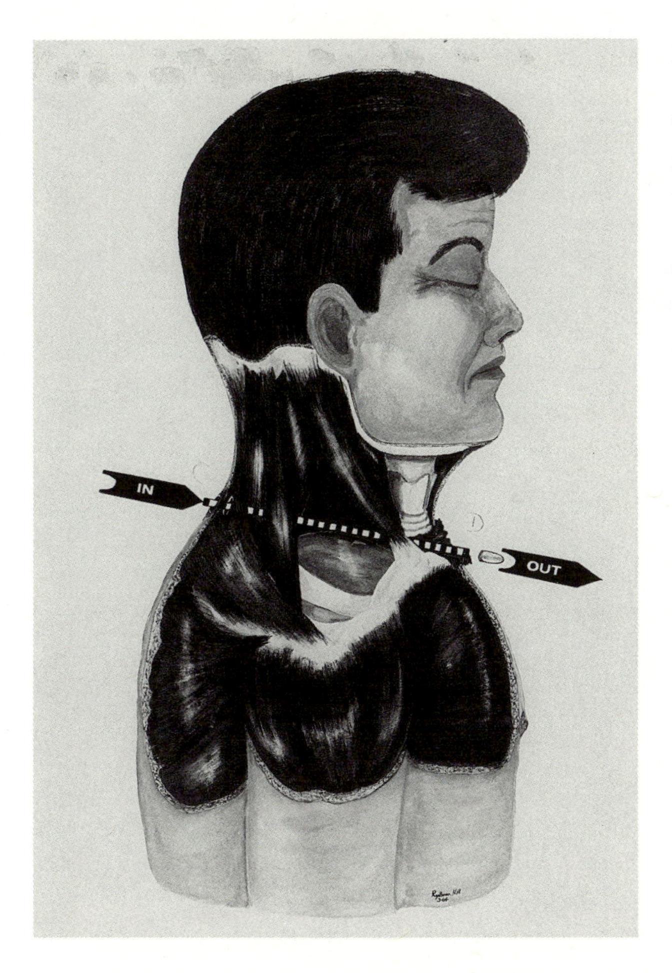

Fig. 10.1. The Corpse as Corpus I: This U.S. Navy drawing represents the bullet's trajectory through Kennedy's neck. Warren Commission Exhibit 385. Courtesy of National Archives.

ber of 1966, *Esquire* published a "Primer of Assassination Theories," which listed thirty alternate versions of Kennedy's death that were at odds with the official documentary record. In 1967 New Orleans district attorney Jim Garrison launched an ill-fated investigation into the assassination that further focused public attention on its particulars. One year later, the Clark Panel reviewed the autopsy photographs and X-rays in the National Archives and revealed "serious discrepancies between the review of the autopsy materials and the autopsy itself" (Kurtz 1982: 87).

Within these parameters, skepticism began to build over the ability of official documentary forums to reliably establish the facts of Kennedy's death. Tales of misreading his body were generated. They centered firstly on the president's head wound. Whether

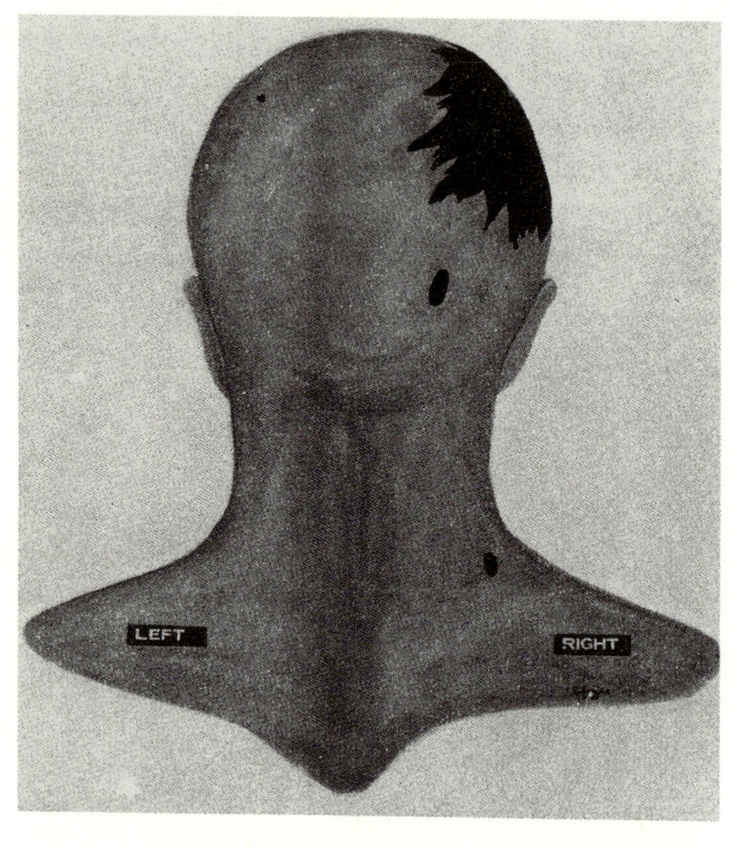

Fig. 10.2. The Corpse as Corpus II: This U.S. Navy drawing represents a rear view of Kennedy's wound. Warren Commission Exhibit 386. Courtesy of National Archives.

Kennedy was hit from behind or the side, from above or below; whether his throat wound was an entry wound or an exit wound; and whether it was possible for one bullet to have wounded both Kennedy and Governor John Connally evolved into one of the most contested arenas of the assassination record. Original depictions of the wound concentrated on its trajectory, nature, and impact. (See figures 10.1, 10.2, and 10.3).

These original appraisals of Kennedy's wound, which include a U.S. Navy drawing of the bullet's trajectory through Kennedy's neck, a navy medical drawing of the rear view of Kennedy's wound, and a navy medical drawing of the trajectory through Kennedy's head all typified clear-cut routes by which the bullet(s) were supposed to have traveled. Yet they failed to generate consensus among retellers, and lengthy discussions challenged the way his body had been examined, and misread.

Readings of the wound differed over its origin. Although consensual medical opinion at Dallas' Parkland Hospital, where Kennedy died, held that the president was hit from

Fig. 10.3. The Corpse as Corpus III: This U.S. Navy drawing represents the trajectory of the bullet through Kennedy's head. Warren Commission Exhibit 388.

the front, this was not the perspective adopted by the Warren Commission, which argued that he was hit from behind. The discrepancy between the two views was never adequately explained, as critic Hugh Trevor-Roper noted: "In the [Warren Commission] hearings, we see the process by which this conclusion was reached: doctor after doctor at first insisting that the shots came from the front, and then gradually, under pressure, with reservations and on conditions—sometimes impossible conditions—yielding to the insistence of the Commission that possibly they might have come from the rear" (Trevor-Roper 1966: 12).

Readings also differed over the nature of the wound. This was exemplified in tales about Kennedy's autopsy, the first official attempt to examine the president's body. Although a number of physicians in Dallas testified that they saw a large exit wound at the back of Kennedy's head, the autopsy described a small entrance wound in the back (Kurtz 1982: 208). The autopsy itself was found to contain irregularities. The doctor who directed the autopsy was not a trained forensic pathologist, as is customary, but a hospital pathologist "who had little experience in doing autopsies on victims of violent death" (Kurtz 1982: 16). Therefore, Kennedy's clothes were not properly examined for traces of exit and entry; the brain did not undergo coronal sectioning, a method that would have helped to trace the path of the bullet; and the fact that there was a bullet wound in Kennedy's throat was missed completely. Moreover, standard points of reference were not used to measure the wounds, so that the location of the back wound was never agreed on ("Who Shot President Kennedy?" 1988).

Tales of misreading Kennedy's body were united in their critique of official documentary forums. Discourse about misreading the body assigned ignorant, sometimes ill, intent to those responsible for reading Kennedy's wound. The implication here was that Kennedy's body had not been adequately read and had, perhaps, been intentionally misread. Such a point made the body into an effective locus for forwarding more general interpretations of conspiracy in the assassination story. It also helped retellers actively consider their own involvement in political discourse in response to questions that these bodily practices raised. All of this suggested that by the late 1960s and early 1970s, response to the assassination remained aligned with classic decodings of a murder case, laced with conspiratorial motivations. Hints of disorder centered on practices of misreading alone.

Mishandling the Body

In the following decade, the relatively nascent thoughts of conspiracy from the 1960s took on more varied and sophisticated forms. Skepticism of things official had extended to a "popular mistrust of official history," with major scandals of the seventies rocking existing trust in public institutions (Morley 1988: 646). Cover-ups in Vietnam, Cambodia, and Watergate prompted *Ramparts* magazine to ask whether it was "equally possible that the assassination of President Kennedy was followed by a cover-up . . . It is clear that a reopening of the investigation is now in order ("A Decade of Unanswered Questions," 1973: 44).

In 1975, the entire Zapruder film was shown on network television for the first time, displaying to millions of American viewers the graphic footage that originally documented Kennedy's fatal head wound ("Good Night America" 1975). In one historian's view, the episode "convinced many that the Warren Commission had erred" (Kurtz 1982: 158). Groups of citizens began gathering signatures for petitions that urged a reopening of the official investigation ("Assassination: Behind Moves to Reopen JFK Case," 1975: 31). Semi-official investigations, such as the Rockefeller commission in 1975 or the Church committee, began reconsidering the murder. Their investigations of links between the assassination and federal intelligence agencies revealed new and deepening twists in the assassination story.

Novels and popular films were produced—such as *Winter Kills, Executive Action,* and *The Parallax View*—that attempted to address the growing public anxiety over the lack of closure lent the assassination story (Condon 1974; Lane and Freed 1973; Singer 1970). In many cases, these efforts revealed unsavory aspects of the Kennedy administration. As one observer later said, "[It was] as if the epistemology of the *New York Times* and the *Washington Post* had been replaced by that of the *National Enquirer* and *People* magazine. Camelot, it seemed, could never again appear to be the pristine place its celebrants had claimed—there were simply too many Mafia dons and party girls dwelling within its precincts" (Brown 1988: 76).

By 1977 such attention produced a second official federal investigation into the assassination, the House Select Committee on Assassinations. Comprised of twelve representatives, the House Committee based its investigation on three categories of information—scientific evidence, government files, and the testimony of witnesses (Kurtz 1982: 161). In reviewing the medical evidence, it used special enhancement techniques to produce what has been called "the most detailed and extensive analysis of the medical evidence in the Kennedy assassination available" (Kurtz 1982: 162). After nearly two years of deliberations, it concluded that there had been a second gunman, but it could not specify his identity.

It was thus no surprise that by the late 1970s, tales of misreading the body no longer constituted a sufficient way of retelling the assassination story. As larger cultural critiques intensified over the ability of official agencies of documentation to reliably retell the story, and the potential presence of laypersons within official discourse about the assassination heightened, tales of Kennedy's body took on new importance within a larger context of questioning official documentary process. Retellers began to emphasize not only the body's misreading, but its mishandling too.

This manifested itself in many forms. The autopsy was again a target. Contrary to medical practice, it was not conducted at Parkland Hospital in Dallas, where Kennedy was pronounced dead. Instead it was delayed until the body was brought back to Washington, where it was conducted under the auspices of the navy at Bethesda Naval Hospital. One doctor testified in the late 1970s that high-ranking officers prevented them from performing it properly.

Moreover, parts of Kennedy's body disappeared. Microscopic slides of brain tissue were nowhere to be found (Kurtz 1982: 100). Later the brain itself, along with the stainless steel container that held it, vanished from the National Archives (Wecht 1972: 28). Theories about mishandling the body particularly began to take hold following the adjournment of the House Select Committee in 1979. The suggestion of conspiracy challenged nonofficial retellers to substantiate the suggestion.

The most renowned of these was a book published by assassination buff David Lifton, under the title *Best Evidence* (1988). Lifton claimed that Kennedy's body had been mishandled for political purposes. According to his scenario, the president's wound was doctored before he ever reached the autopsy table. Lifton based his theory on an FBI report that held that surgery of the head had been performed before the autopsy started. He maintained that wounds were produced to match those of the official assassination record, contending that between the assassination and autopsy, the wounds were altered so as to make it look as if Lee Harvey Oswald were the lone assassin. The "best evidence," in Lifton's view, was that offered by the official autopsy, because it documented ill-intent in handling the president's body. The body became a medical forgery.

Relevant here were the various folk legends that traced the mishandling of Kennedy's body. The body was alternately rumored to have been kept in a vegetablelike state on Onassis's island (De Caro and Oring 1969; Baker 1976), alive at Camp David (Rosenberg 1976), or, as the National Examiner claimed, in the Swiss Alps (Bird 1976). This suggested that the issues condensed in official and popular writings were also diffused through urban legends, a point signifying an overflow of the discourse from its agreed-upon boundaries.

Tales of mishandling the body therefore constitute a second level of bodily discourse implying a heightened degree of manipulative intent by official actors. Retelling the assassination through stories of abuses inflicted on the president's body implies that officials actively and strategically changed official documentation. Implied here were accusations of intentional damage that had been inflicted by official investigatory agencies. Official agencies were criticized for not only misreading Kennedy's body but also mishandling it. This enhanced already rampant conspiracy theories about the assassination.

Such discourse, however, also played into the attempts of nonofficial retellers to challenge the official assassination record. On the one hand, it underscored the need to closely examine documentation and to re-search existing documents. On the other, it signified an increased level of expertise among laypersons intent on deconstructing the record. In order for them to understand how Kennedy's body had been mishandled, they needed more expertise about the bodily practices involved. Attesting to the expert nature of their interpretations, it thereby addressed larger issues about the layperson's role in challenging officialdom.

Mis-recording the Body

By the mid-1980s, theories of earlier decades that implied ill-intent were fairly well-entrenched in public consciousness. There existed a considerable degree of skepticism about official records in Kennedy's death. Yet despite increasingly frequent reports about Kennedy's sexual activity or dubious connections with the underworld, the eighties brought with them few revelations into the assassination record. In one observer's eyes, there was an impatience with the assassination story's ambiguities, and media forums ranging from the *Washington Post* to *Newsweek* were content to admit that the truth would never be known (Morley 1988). This refocused attention on the processes and mis-processes by which the assassination record had been documented.

Thus a third level of discourse signals yet another level of authoritative retelling. This discourse centers on the records by which Kennedy's body has been examined. As discourse about abuses of Kennedy's body has intensified and grown more credible, nonofficial retellers have increasingly held that not only the body but the records about it have been falsified, doctored, and mishandled. Such a difference is particularly important for nonofficial retellers seeking loci from which to forward their claims about Kennedy's death. For even more than stories about mishandling the body, these tales directly justify their own secondary access to existing documentation, the very access on which their authority in retelling is based.

In a sense, the importance of records of Kennedy's body was originally established in absentia, when photographs and X-rays from Kennedy's autopsy were held back from the Warren Commission (Fensterwald 1973: 143). They were found a number of years later, prompting forensic pathologist Cyril Wecht to examine them and publish a rare attempt by a medical practitioner to retell the assassination story. In a much publicized report in *Modern Medicine,* Wecht claimed that the assassination "simply did not happen the way the Warren Commission said it did. I state this because it is clear to me, from a strictly scientific point of view, based on the examination of available records, that the Commission failed to make its case" (Fensterwald 1973: 143). This, too, recalled even earlier claims suggesting that members of the Warren Commission had published an autopsy report different from the original document (Epstein 1966: 47). The official report, for example, was never dated. Two decades later, historian Michael Kurtz supported Wecht's claim, noting that the autopsy protocol published by the Warren Commission was written "months after the assassination." In his view "the original autopsy was destroyed and replaced by one more favorable to the commission's lone-assassin theory" (Kurtz 1982: 145).

There were other vagaries among attempts to record examinations of Kennedy's body. Medical examiners were criticized for providing a death certificate two weeks after the assassination (Kurtz 1982: 69). Pathologist James Humes was criticized for burning his autopsy notes and producing a new version that cast Kennedy's throat wound as an exit wound. Autopsy negatives were said to have been exposed to the light. Photographs of both the brain and the body below the rib cage disappeared from the National Archives (Kurtz 1982: 90, 100). Later interpretations of the medical evidence provided by the Warren Commission constituted one of the most contested areas in the ensuing controversy over the commission's findings (Kurtz 1982: 55).

Public fascination with the records of Kennedy's bodily examinations brought Dallas doctors to the National Archives on a 1988 episode of *Nova,* where they examined the original autopsy photographs. This was an intriguing exercise, for as narrator Walter Cronkite said, the basic question was whether "their recollections of the wounds (would) match the photographs they would be seeing for the first time" ("Who Shot President Kennedy?" 1988). Cronkite's exercise pitted the memories of professionals against the technology which had ostensibly recorded those same memories. Unlike other cases, however, this examination was established on the premise that the record of memories might be different from the memories themselves. The fact that the pictures were found to uphold the recollections of the doctors who first examined Kennedy mattered less than the fact that their memories were held up as alternate documentation to the technologies that recorded them. Had their memories been different, the assumption by this stage of the game would have been that the technology was deficient, by either accident or intention.

This in itself suggests a heightened interest in the authority of memory, and its ability to provide alternate documentation of the assassination record. The performance of such an exercise on *Nova* also provides a significant twist to highly regarded practices of documentation, for it highlights the peculiar fact that the doctors had not been shown the photographs until then. The peculiarity was not lost on Cronkite, who lavished praise on the efforts it took to arrange such a meeting: "The examination was . . . unprecedented. Special permission had to be arranged from the Kennedy family to arrange this. Cameras were barred from the room in which the doctors looked at the pictures. Each took as much time as he felt necessary to examine them" ("Who Shot President Kennedy?" 1988). This suggests the legitimate emergence of nonofficial retellers of the assassination story, and, more important, highlights findings intrinsically connected to the secondary documentation to which they have access. In other words, exercises like that on *Nova* justify the value of examining the record of the record. They legitimate the activities of nonofficial retellers whose mode of documentary exploration consists of the very practices that discourse about mis-recording Kennedy's body undermines. The fact that they can do no better than examine the documents of others is thereby turned into a nonproblematic dimension of their ability to retell the story. Their retelling offers what is seen as a preferred version of the events of the assassination.

Here again popular media underscore the centrality of the body's mis-recording. Prevalent among such efforts is Don DeLillo's 1988 novel *Libra* (1988). It forwards a conspiracy theory via the records that documented and mis-documented Kennedy's death. Television specials begin to fictionalize the events of Kennedy's death. In one observer's view, "Camelot and conspiracy in Dallas were domesticated for prime-time: 'Who shot JFK?' became 'who shot J.R.?'" (Morley 1988: 649). This reached new heights in late 1991, when Oliver Stone used the cinema to address the assassination story—and its contradictory evidence—in his movie *JFK*.

All of this brings us back to one of the original suppositions of this chapter. Why the centrality of the body in retellings of Kennedy's death? In these pages I have argued that tales of the body persist because they have allowed nonofficial retellers to challenge official discourse. The three levels of discourse about bodily practice suggest how the body has provided an effective, accessible, and flexible locus for alternate retellers to forward their theories of conspiracy in Kennedy's death. Practices of misreading, mishandling and mis-recording offer three distinct ways in which to tell their stories; they also constitute three strategic routes of challenging official discourse. The fact that discourse about abuses of the body has given way to abuses of records of the body legitimizes the record of the body as a document in itself. It also, not incidentally, legitimizes the presence of nonofficial retellers in the story. This helps to explain why discussions about misreading the wound have given way to discourse about mishandling the body and mis-recording its records. Tales about Kennedy's body serve to index the energetic and persistent attempts by retellers to maintain their own involvement in reading events of state.

All of this suggests that the physical experience of Kennedy's body has been shaped by the socially constructed categories that mold collective recollections of it. As Mary Douglas maintains, "The human body is always treated as an image of society, and there can be no natural way of considering the body that does not involve at the same time a social dimension" (Douglas 1970: 70). In retelling the assassination, the body functions as a term for cultural argumentation that upholds the active role of retellers in decoding the events of Kennedy's death.

For as discourse about Kennedy's body has persisted, it has implied an increased access on the part of retellers to official documentary records about the body. This implies increased expertise, for examining the bodily record implies a different authority than examining the body itself. Although early attention to the body's wound was provided by physicians and others with medical expertise, contemporary discourse involves laypersons and amateurs who have engaged in extended technical argumentation over records, examinations, charts and files. Such a movement among nonofficial retellers—from reexaminations of the body to reexaminations of the *records* of the body—thereby pivots on its implication that the focus of inquiry is *not* the body as a natural, physical entity, but the *body as a discourse* and fabric of interpretations. For the many nonofficial retellers attempting to tell their versions of the story, the body has legitimated their attempts to place themselves within official discourse. In so doing, the body *as* evidence has become the body *of* evidence.

Thus by subordinating discussions about abuses of the body to abuses of its record, retellers have in effect made a place for themselves within official political discourse. This ultimately brings us full circle to the issue of the king's two bodies, for these pages suggest that within the death of Kennedy's literal body, discourse about the state of his metaphorical body has taken place. This, then, is the ultimate value of the body as a term of cultural argumentation: that it has validated the layperson's attempts to challenge official versions of what happened.

The State of the Body, the Body of the State

This discussion has suggested that the persistence of the body as a term in cultural argumentation aligns itself with fundamental assumptions about the body's importance to the health of society and the state. The persistence of stories about Kennedy's body in retellings of his death suggests the centrality of the analogy between the literal and metaphorical body. Just as bodily control signifies political control, so the lack of bodily control expresses the lack of social control. In the case of Kennedy's death, official inability to exercise control over the president's body matches a larger inability to exercise social control. In such a light, official agencies have lost their right to authoritatively document the story of Kennedy's death, which has been taken over by nonofficial retellers. They, in turn, have effectively used the state of Kennedy's body to address the body of Kennedy's state. Again, discourse about Oliver Stone's movie *JFK* bears this out particularly well.

What does this suggest about the body as a term of argumentation? Denied its literal presence, the body becomes a term in representation, part of the discourse rather than a concrete physical entity which the discourse describes. In other words, the body *as* evidence is reconstituted as the body *of* evidence. Its effectiveness as a term in the territory of discourse is based on two fundamental assumptions about the positioning of observers around it: (1) the body exists as a term to be manipulated by retellers in conjunction with larger sociocultural discursive categories, and (2) bodily manipulation persists as a metaphor for intervention and/or critique of governmental process. By involving themselves in discourse about bodily practice, retellers are better equipped to oppose authoritative and orthodox readings of events of the "real world."

In retelling the assassination, the body emerges as a changeable, but authoritative, token that has allowed nonofficial speakers to make alternative claims about Kennedy's death in credible and persuasive ways. Because the literal, physical body no longer exists, there is an increased focus on its readings and representations that foregrounds the possibility of multiple readings. It is not only that the body cannot be literally reconstituted, but it cannot be conceptually reconstituted either. This appears to permit the simultaneous existence of competitive readings of events around it. In a sense, this is curious, given the fact that "the body" per se has been "gone" for nearly thirty years.

Yet such a twist to the cultural importance of death—which, rather than lend closure to the body, prevents closure—makes Kennedy's death into a permutation of the discourse of the body. His death shifts inquiry from the realm of the literal to the realm of the symbolic.

Thus it is precisely Kennedy's death that underscores the successful invocation of the body as a term of argumentation among retellers of the assassination. By invoking tales about Kennedy's dead body, nonofficial retellers have been able to chronicle the abuses, mishandlings, and transformations of the assassination story in a way that gives it substance. The body as a physical entity has thus given way to the body as a symbolic mode of cultural argumentation.

A second function of invocations of the body is equally important. Invoking the body has allowed retellers to attend to larger concerns about official political discourse and the ability of laypersons to challenge it. Each type of bodily practice retellers discuss suggests a yet more heightened level of bodily expertise on their part. This carries the analogy between body and state one step further, for as retellers have heightened their level of discourse about Kennedy's body, they also have increased their degree of familiarity with bodily practice. Their increased expertise heightens their ability to challenge official discourse.

Retelling the assassination story has been called a "quiet transformation of evidence" (Trevor-Roper 1966: 11). The chronicling of activities of manipulation—doctoring, losing, mishandling, and withholding—has been in step with the attempts of nonofficial speakers to assert or reestablish their control over the story. Using Kennedy's body as a documentary category has given nonofficial retellers a fruitful way to challenge official discourse. Nonofficial retellers are able to claim standing in a discourse dominated by official versions by substituting the symbolic for the literal and turning the body *as* evidence into the body *of* evidence. They invoke the body as a term that not only provides background but also offers a vehicle for advancing variant interpretations of events.

Despite its deliteralization of the body, this discourse rides on the centrality of the body as evidence. Privileging discourse about the body over other perceptions, documents, speculations or recollections does not, however, take place incidentally. For the real implications of this analysis are more broadly grounded in culture: As Bryan Turner has argued, culture produces its own organized responses to the problem of human embodiment and the need for its cultural management (1987: 19). Retelling the story of Kennedy's death through tales about his body offers a body of evidence that constitutes not only an effective mode of cultural argumentation but also a documentary category that is privileged in explicating the terrain of cultural contestation. When seen against larger cultural arguments about the involvement of laypersons in political discourse, this makes sense. For it suggests that the body as a documentary category gives nonofficial retellers a footing in the official discourse that contrives to exclude them.

References

1975. Assassination: Behind moves to reopen JFK case. *U.S. News and World Report,* June 2, 1975, 30–33.

Baker, R. L. 1976. The influence of mass culture on modern legends. *Southern Folklore Quarterly* 40: 367–76.

Belin, David W. 1988. *Final disclosure.* New York: Macmillan.

Bird, S. Elizabeth. 1987. Media and folklore as intertextual communication processes: John F. Kennedy and the supermarket tabloids. In *Communication Yearbook* 10: 758–72.

Brown, Thomas. 1988. *JFK: History of an image.* Bloomington: Indiana Univ. Press.

Condon, Richard. 1974. *Winter kills.* New York: Dial.

De Caro, F. A., and E. Oring. 1969. JFK is alive: A modern legend. *Folklore Forum* 2: 54–55.

1973. A decade of unanswered questions. *Ramparts,* Dec., 12, 42–44.

DeLillo, Don, *Libra* (New York: Viking Press, 1988).

Douglas, Mary. 1970. The two bodies. In *Natural symbols.* New York: Pantheon.

Epstein, Edward J. 1966. *Inquest.* New York: Viking.

Fensterwald, Bernard Jr. 1973. Ten years later: A legacy of suspicion. *Esquire,* Nov., 141–43.

Good night, America. ABC News Division. Mar. 26, 1975.

Kantorowicz, Ernst H. 1957. *The king's two bodies: A study in mediaeval political theology.* Princeton, NJ: Princeton Univ. Press.

Kurtz, Michael L. 1982. *Crime of the century.* Knoxville: Univ. of Tennessee Press.

Lane, Mark, and Donald Freed. 1973. *Executive action.* New York: Dell.

Lifton, David. 1988. *Best evidence.* New York: Carroll and Graf.

Mauss, Marcel. [1935] 1973. Techniques of the body. *Economy and Society* 2: 70–88.

Minnis, Jack, and Staughton Lynd. 1963. Seeds of doubt: Some questions about the assassination. *New Republic,* Dec. 21, 14–20.

Morley, Jefferson. 1988. Camelot and Dallas: The entangling Kennedy myths. *The Nation,* Dec. 12, 646–49.

1966. A primer of assassination theories. *Esquire* (Dec.): 205–10.

Rosenberg, B. A. 1976. Kennedy in Camelot: The Arthurian legend in America. *Western Folklore* 25: 52–59.

Singer, Loren. 1970. *The parallax view.* Garden City, NJ: Doubleday.

Trevor-Roper, Hugh. Introduction. In *Rush to judgment,* by Mark Lane. New York: Holt, Rinehart and Winston.

Trillin, Calvin. 1967. The Buffs. *The New Yorker,* June 10, 41–71.

Turner, Bryan S. 1982. The government of the body: Medical regimens and the rationalization of diet. *British Journal of Sociology* 33: 254–69.

———. 1987. *Medical power and social knowledge.* London: Sage.

———. 1990. The anatomy lesson: A note on the Merton thesis. *Sociological Review* 38: 1–18.

Wecht, Cyril H. 1972. Pathologist's view of the autopsy. *Modern Medicine,* Nov.

Welsh, David, and William Turner. 1969. In the shadow of Dallas. *Ramparts,* Jan. 25, 61–71.

Who shot President Kennedy? *Nova.* PBS. Nov. 15, 1988.

Zelizer, Barbie. 1990. Achieving journalistic authority through narrative. *Critical Studies in Mass Communication* 7: 366–76.

———. 1992. *Covering the body: The Kennedy assassination, the media, and the shaping of collective memory.* Chicago: Univ. of Chicago Press.

Annotated Bibliography

The literature on the body is vast and ramifying, running from body histories to medical procedures, tunneling down into psychoanalysis, angling off toward performance theory, desire in language, and the anthropology of the body, circling communication, traversing the territories of biology, social history, and philosophy of mind. So instead of providing a proliferating but still partial and meager bibliography, we have selected some twenty-five or thirty works, each of which offers a singular, acute, and telling grasp of the body and any of which might provide the underpinnings for inquiry into bodylore. These works cluster in phenomenology, aesthetics, and social theory. No doubt there are others as apt but none more luminous.

Bakhtin, Mikhail. *Rabelais and his world.* Trans. Hélène Iswolsky. Bloomington: Indiana Univ. Press, 1984. The body has been inscribed oppositionally into discourses of the grotesque and the classical or, alternatively, discourses of the grotesque and the classical have been inscribed hierarchically onto the body. The grotesque body is material; not inert matter but fecund, teeming, productive matter. Hence, Bakhtin's preoccupation with the physiological, the sexual, the scatological. The grotesque body is an open body, a body of parts, of apertures and protuberances, an unbounded and therefore transgressive body. In grotesque realism, the body is inscribed as improper: low, coarse, vulgar, and profane. By contrast, the classical body is a closed body, complete, smooth, sealed, and so etherealized. The etherealized discourse inscribes the body as proper: high, pure, aristocratic, and sacred. Because of its pretensions to propriety, the classical body, the etherealized discourse, is threatened by what Bakhtin calls carnivalesque inversions.

Barker, Francis. *The tremulous private body: Essays on subjection.* London: Methuen, 1984. Barker locates the invention of the bourgeois body in its transformation from medieval to modern in the seventeenth century. In the course of this transformation, the body has been, on the one hand, privatized to conceal its grotesque properties and, on the other, etherealized to suppress its grotesque properties. The self, inscribed on the exterior of the spectacular medieval body, has been interiorized in the modern body to create the introspective, reflexive, inner self.

Bateson, Gregory. *Steps to an ecology of mind.* New York: Ballantine, 1972. Bateson redistributes the self in a cybernetic system whose boundaries are not coterminous with the skin. Intelligence, mentality, mind, is not peculiar to the individual but immanent in an ecosystem of which the individual is an aspect. The ground of communication is therefore relationship. An ecology of mind explores the pathways communication and metacommunication (communication about communication) traverse through the system. The body is examined as a primary site for devising and deciphering messages.

Birdwhistell, Ray. *Kinesics and context.* Philadelphia: Univ. of Pennsylvania Press, 1970. Birdwhistell undertakes to formulate a precise technical system for codifying body movement and, at the same time, to put forward a contextual grasp of the production of meaning. He understands the body to be invested in a communication system, part of which is organized internally, part of which is displayed externally, and part of which is elaborated contextually.

Bourdieu, Pierre. *Outline of an theory of practice.* Trans. Richard Nice. Cambridge: Cambridge Univ. Press, 1989. Not only is culture inscribed on the body but also culture is fabricated out of the body. Corporeal properties, of both the literal and symbolic sort, are externalized, materialized, objectified in and as the social body. The body, in turn, takes in aspects of culture in the form of dispositions. Hence, the body as "habitus," a site where theory materializes as practice; practice fabricates theory.

Cixous, Hélène, and Catherine Clément. *The newly born woman.* Trans. Betsy Wing. Minneapolis: Univ. of Minnesota Press, 1986. From the account of a southern Italian ritual, the tarantella, in which women (re)present themselves in public and thereby "cure" themselves of what is perceived as a psychosexual disease, French feminists Cixous and Clément develop a theory of the gendered female body in Western culture. Hysterics and sorceresses are taken to have reinscribed gender on the body. These re-inscriptions are elaborated in *écriture feminine,* women's writings, which display female difference in a way that is dissonant with dominant cultural constructions.

Douglas, Mary. *Natural symbols: Explorations in cosmology.* New York: Vintage, 1973. The body yields "natural symbols," ways of conceiving and arranging phenomena which have their roots in the phenomenology of the body. So the body becomes a source of imagery for conceptions, practices, rituals, institutions, societies, and universes. Specifically, Douglas argues an analogy between the body and the body politic or the physical body and the social body. Tight social boundaries, for instance, are reflected in tight corporeal boundaries. Because of this analogy, the body itself is constituted a symbolic object which takes its coloration from its cultural situatedness.

Eagleton, Terry. *The ideology of the aesthetic.* Cambridge: Basil Blackwell, 1990. Eagleton proposes that aesthetics, as the discourse that describes "the whole of our sensate life together," is the means by which the history of the body can be understood as a history of philosophy. Eagleton surveys the complex relationship between art, bodies, and ideologies beginning with the eighteenth century philosophy of art, in which the singular physical existence of both art and persons begins to give rise to the notions of autonomy and individuality that are so useful to the needs of an increasingly bourgeois ideology.

Elias, Norbert. *The civilizing process.* Vol. 1, *The history of manners.* Trans. Edmund Jephcott. New York: Pantheon, 1978. Manners become a locus of metaphysics. Elias notes that medieval society lacks the repulsions and distastes which separate us bodily from one another, which cause us embarrassment at the sight of other people's bodily functions or the exposure of our own. Modern manners are refinements, rarefications, etherealizations of the body. Their thrust is to raise the "threshold of shame and embarrassment" to its peak in the nineteenth century. The use of the fork, touted as hygienic, is clearly an index of our level of revulsion against the processes of the body. "Disgust is inseparable from refinement."

Foucault, Michel. *The history of sexuality.* 3 vols. New York: Vintage, 1980, 1985, 1988. Foucault's study of the history of sexuality analyzes the shift from Greco-Roman notions of bodily pleasure to the moralizing discourse on sexuality that emerged from the Middle Ages. Disciplining the body focuses the regulation and manipulation directed at the body through the invention of the "experiences of sexuality." The body is located in its "episteme" as an aspect of the ontological assumptions of its history and culture. Foucault concludes that the best way to combat the ideology of sexuality is to speak, not of the constructed experience of sexuality, but instead of "bodies and pleasures."

Goffman, Erving. *The presentation of self in everyday life.* New York: Anchor, 1959. Goffman holds that persons are in the way of presenting themselves, guiding controlled impressions, not necessarily designed to deceive but to sustain a reality. Hence, the theatrical metaphor: life's a stage and we, actors upon it. Two radically different sign activities are involved: (1) the expressions a person *gives,* paradigmatically talk, communication in the narrow conventional sense, and (2) the expressions a person *gives off,* centrally gesture, presumably unintentional communication that is nonetheless symptomatic of the actor. The self is a dramatic effect arising from the scene in which it is presented. The body is regarded as a material site, a sort of front region, for mounting up impressions, "a peg on which something of collaborative manufacture will be hung for a time." Being a self is not a natural condition but a social accomplishment.

Hall, Edward T. *Beyond culture.* New York: Anchor, 1977. Persons find themselves at the center of a roughly concentric series of spatial envelopes, each of which acts as a field of information. Hall distinguishes the characteristics of four such fields at intimate distance, personal distance, social distance, and public distance. The boundaries of the body do not end or begin with the skin. They expand and contract as the person is invested in or invaded by the surround. Proxemics is the study of the social use of space.

Johnson, Mark. *The body in the mind: The bodily basis of meaning, imagination, and reason.* Chicago: Univ. of Chicago Press, 1987. Johnson argues that metaphor appropriates our experience of embodiment to organize abstract understanding. Far from transcending the bodily, rationality is rooted in the body. The Cartesian gap between the cognitive, the conceptual, the formal, the rational, on the one hand, and the bodily, material, and emotional, on the other, is banished. "Image schemata," recurrent patterns of perception, are elaborated metaphorically into abstract thought. Imagination is the gesture by which the bodily informs the conceptual. Johnson embarks on what he calls "a kind of descriptive or empirical phenomenology" with the intention of "putting the body back into the mind."

Kristeva, Julia. *Powers of horror: An essay of abjection.* Trans. Leon S. Roudiez. New York: Columbia Univ. Press, 1982. Kristeva argues that psychoanalytically, maternal authority is responsible for developing a "clean and proper body," a corporeal body image established in opposition to, indeed, through the rejection of, the phallic realm of institutions and laws, symbolic and political. Thus both language and culture establish order and hierarchy only insofar as they succeed in repressing maternal authority, female bodies, and all "corporeal mappings" that might betray the Law of the Father.

Leder, Drew. *The absent body.* Chicago: Univ. of Chicago Press, 1990. Leder provides a critique of what Jacques Derrida calls the "metaphysics of presence." States of awareness attend and disattend aspects of the body. When attention is directed outward, away from itself, the body is what Leder calls *ec-static.* The disattended body falls out of awareness, recedes, disappears. Thus, the absent body. Some aspects of the body, especially its surface, remain marginal to awareness; they can be recalled, thematized in consciousness. Other aspects of the body, especially its interior, cannot be recalled, but they may, in dysfunctional states, announce themselves, what Leder calls *dys-appear.* Hence, absence and presence, the recessive body and the ecstatic body, disappearance (absence) and dys-appearance (forced presence). Recovering a phenomenology of the interior of the body, even as the viscera recede from apprehension, disrupts the dualism which situates the medical body in the realm of objectivity.

Merleau-Ponty, Maurice. *The primacy of perception and other essays on phenomenological psychology, the philosophy of art, history and politics.* Trans. James M. Edie et al. Evanston, IL: Northwestern Univ. Press, 1964. Phenomenology address the split between two traditional philosophical positionings, materialism and idealism. "The perceiving mind is an incarnated mind. I have tried, first of all, to re-establish the roots of the mind in its body and in its world, going against doctrines which treat perception as a simple result of the action of external things on our body as well as against those which insist on the autonomy of consciousness. These philosophies commonly forget—in favor of a pure exteriority or of a pure interiority—the insertion of the mind in corporeality, the ambiguous relation which we entertain with our body and, correlatively, with perceived things . . . And it is equally clear that one does not account for the facts by superimposing a pure, contemplative consciousness on a thinglike body." The primacy of perception in our grasp of ourselves and the world stems from the centrality of embodiment.

Natanson, Maurice. *The journeying self: A study in philosophy and social role.* Reading, MA: Addison-Wesley Publishing, 1970. I am inserted into the world bodily and my experience of the world comes to me through my body. Indeed, Natanson argues, "*I am my body.*" The centrality of the body provides the phenomenological foothold for being in the world. The world holds me bodily as, consciously, I hold it. Consciousness is understood as "the directional force sustaining the entire range of perceptual experience." Consciousness is not a mental act secreted in the cranium but a constitutive act, the creation of a universe. As a consequence of the constitutiveness of consciousness, I become "a self constructing for itself the shape of a world it then finds and acts in." This is the territory the self journeys across.

Scarry, Elaine. *The body in pain: The making and unmaking of a world.* New York: Oxford Univ. Press, 1985. Pain unmakes the world. In the introduction to her phenomenological analysis of the body in pain, Scarry outlines three separate, yet interwoven, projects: "*First,* the difficulty of expressing physical pain; *second,* the political and perceptual complications that arise as a result of that difficulty; and *third,* the nature of both material and verbal expressibility or, more simply, the nature of human creation." By foregrounding the political consequences of the way the body is theorized, she shows how writing about the body can render invisible, dematerialize, the lived experience of human bodies, especially bodies in pain. Her linking of all forms of cultural production to the relief and/or intensification of bodily pain suggests, provocatively, the moral dimension of cultural activity.

Schilder, Paul. *The image and appearance of the human body: Studies in the constructive energies of the psyche.* New York: International Universities Press, 1950. The body image is "the picture of our own body which we form in our mind, that is to say the way in which the body appears to ourselves." The image is formed, broken, and reformed from the perceptual interactions we have with the outside world. Yet a slight discrepancy between the body object and the body image persists. Schilder examines the constitution of the body image, its contractions and expansions, its cloudy or clear boundaries, its labile shape, its shifting mass, its incorporation and dis-corporation of objects and experiences, its crystallizations and dissolutions. How to think the body is the obverse of how to embody thought, the mind/body problem from the other side.

Sommer, Robert. *Personal space.* Englewood Cliffs, NJ: Prentice-Hall, 1969. Sommer takes the notion of personal space from animal ethology and applies it to humans to mean "the emotionally charged zone around each person, sometimes described as a soap bubble or aura, which helps regulate the spacing of individuals" and, by extension, "the processes by which people mark out and personalize spaces they inhabit." The shape of this bodily envelope varies according to aspect of the body, the habit of the individual, and the conventions of the culture. Invasions of the envelope constitute transgressions of the self-boundaries. Extensions of the self can take the form of territorial holds. Indeed, Sommer regards territoriality and dominance behavior as alternative ways of maintaining social order.

Stallybrass, Peter, and Allon White. *The politics and poetics of transgression.* Ithaca, NY: Cornell Univ. Press, 1986. The hierarchical symbolism inscribed on the body reappears at multiple levels of analysis: "The human body, psychic forms, geographical space and the social formation are all constructed within interrelating and dependent hierarchies of high and low." Within these discourses, the low becomes a site of contradiction, commingling categories usually kept separate and opposed: "center and periphery, inside and outside, stranger and local, commerce and festivity, high and low" or again, "high and low, human and animal, domestic and savage, polite and vulgar." The hybridization of these antitheses produces the vitality of the grotesque body whose discursive norms, as Bakhtin makes clear, are "impurity (both in the sense of dirt and mixed categories), heterogeneity, masking, protuberant distension, disproportion, exorbitance, clamor, decentered or eccentric arrangements, a focus upon gaps, orifices and symbolic filth (what Mary Douglas calls 'matter out of place'), physical needs and pleasures of the 'lower bodily stratum,' materiality and parody." Thus the low discourses in general and the lower body in particular are ambivalent, sources of both desire and taboo.

Stewart, Susan. *On longing: Narratives of the miniature, the gigantic, the souvenir, the collection.* Ithaca, NY: Cornell Univ. Press, 1984. Stewart takes the body as our mode of perceiving scale. This is played out in narratives of the miniature, whose aspect is perfection, and narratives of the gigantic, whose aspect is grotesquery. Narratives are seen at once to invent a world and, in the same gesture, to estrange us from it. Hence, they are structures of desire, likewise rooted in the body. The fabrication of worlds for which we long, the fabrication of longing, fabrication itself, all embodied gestures, are her concerns.

Sudnow, David. *Talk's body: A meditation between two keyboards.* Middlesex, England: Penguin, 1980. Sudnow embarks on a course of "embodied description." Casting around among the shifting boundaries of the self, he conveys both the sense that things are internal to the body and that the self is outside the body: "A body incorporates distances and shapes as its own spatial appropriations." Out of this spatial experience, we improvise talk as we improvise music. Sudnow thus orients "toward speech as bodily work."

Wollheim, Richard. *The thread of life.* Cambridge, Mass.: Harvard Univ. Press, 1984. The person exists at the intersection between two dimensions, a temporal dimension, which is its history, and a spatial dimension, which is its corporeality. Wollheim inspects various claims about what it is to be a person with respect to these dimensions, addresses the incommensurability between them, and puts forward a theory of personhood.

Contributors

PHYLLIS GORFAIN is Professor of English at Oberlin College and has written a variety of articles on folklore and Shakespeare with a focus on riddling, several articles on play and *Hamlet,* one essay on narratives and Masada, and two studies of folklore among the Mbeere of Kenya. She is currently at work on a book dealing further with topics of play in *Hamlet.*

DEBORAH KAPCHAN is a Professor of Folklore at the University of Texas at Austin and has been Visiting Professor of Folklore at Indiana University. Her dissertation examines marketplace discourse and performance in Morocco and the semiotic reconstruction of gender, authority, and social identity that is occurring there. Her book, *Gender on the Market: Transitional Economies and Feminine Discursive Domains* (working title), based on this research, is forthcoming from the University of Pennsylvania Press. Other interests include the folklore of North Africa, the body as a nexus of social symbolism and metaphor, and issues relevant to feminism. Her chapter in this volume was awarded the Social Science Research Council's Ibn Khaldoun Prize for 1990.

MAXINE MISKA is a free-lance folklorist who has her doctorate from the University of Pennsylvania. She specializes in Asian folklore, urban folklore, and public sector projects. Her publications include *Tradition and Community in the Urban Neighborhood: Making Brooklyn Home* (New York: Brooklyn Educational and Cultural Alliance, 1983), with I. Sheldon Posen, and "Enduring Images of Ephemeral Objects: Chinese Paper Gods," in *Proceedings of the Symposium on Religion and Folk Art* (New York: Museum of American Folk Art, forthcoming). Her interest in bodylore arose through her investigations of the shape and definition of personhood in Chinese society.

DOROTHY NOYES has recently finished her dissertation in Folklore and Folklife at the University of Pennsylvania on the politics of interpretation in the Patum of Berga. She has been teaching at the University of Pennsylvania, Indiana University, and the University of Barcelona. Her previous work includes the exhibition and catalogue *Uses of Tradition: Arts of Italian Americans in Philadelphia* with the Philadelphia Folklore Project. Bodylore as a field was thrust upon her notice in Berga, where the *patumaires* objected to her camera and little notebook as a means to understanding. Having been walked up mountainsides, thrown into fires, plied with liquor, inundated with water, dragged into the dance, deprived of sleep, and stuffed with local specialties, she was at last obliged to recognize the body's experience as terrain of wonder and source of authority.

JANE PRZYBYSZ is a Ph.D. candidate in the Department of Performance Studies at New York University. The title of her dissertation-in-progress is "Quiltmaking in America: The Political Performance of Pain, Pleasure and Possibility." The materialist feminist/performance studies perspective she brings to the study of revivalist activities has focused on the ways in which dominant cultural ideologies work, not directly on people's consciousness but on their consciousness through the material body. Implicit in this way of understanding how power is articulated in people's everyday lives is the idea that any kind of political "resistance" must, of necessity, address the condition of the material body. To the extent that quilt making functions as a way of (re)writing the body, it is a cultural activity that is potentially politically resistant. She most recently investigated how quilts negotiate experiences of gender, sexuality, class, and ethnicity in two performance quilts presented at "Breaking the Surface: An Interactive Festival/Conference of Women, Theatre and Social Action" at the University of Calgary in November 1991.

SUSAN RITCHIE has completed a dissertation on the development of critical reading as a social technology that invents and maintains the bourgeois cultivation of individual autonomy. Pursuing her interest in the institutional patterns of knowledge, she has published work on the strategic position of Marxism within the humanities and on the development of cultural studies as a meta-critique of the university. The body interests her as the ultimate target and as well as the fabrication of all disciplines. The medical humanities provides her with a socially responsible reason to continue shamelessly to consume Lifetime Medical Television. She currently teaches for the departments of English and Comparative Studies at Ohio State University.

SUSAN SLYOMOVICS is an assistant professor in the Department of Comparative Literature, Brown University. She is the author of *The Merchant of Art: An Egyptian Hilali Oral Epic Poet in Performance* (Berkeley: University of California Press, 1988), a member of the editorial collective of *Women and Performance: A Journal of Feminist Theory*, and specializes in Middle Eastern theater, performance, and film.

ELIZABETH WICKETT has a Ph.D. in folklore from the University of Pennsylvania. An Arabist who has lived and done research in Egypt for many years, she has produced several films on aspects of Egyptian culture, including *For Those Who Sail to Heaven,* which was shown at both the Margaret Mead Festival and the Manchester International Festival of Ethnographic Film in 1990. Her dissertation research investigates the locus of grief in the bodies, texts, and performances of women lamenters in Upper Egypt.

KATHARINE YOUNG is a folklorist who has taught medical humanism at the Center for Science and Culture at the University of Delaware. Her present interest in the phenomenology of the body arises out of a prior interest in the phenomenology of narrative. She has published articles on narrative in *Semiotica, Cahiers de Litterature Orale, Poetics,* and *Western Folklore* and a book called *Taleworlds and Storyrealms: The Phenomenology of Narrative.* She has published an article on the body in *Semiotica* and two articles that bring together narrativity and embodiment in the *Journal of Narrative and Life History* and *Texts of Identity.* She is currently writing a book on the body in medicine, of which the present chapter is a part.

BARBIE ZELIZER is a former journalist who teaches at Temple University's Department of Rhetoric and Communication. She is author of *Covering the Body: The Kennedy Assassination, the Media, and the Shaping of Collective Memory* (Chicago: University of Chicago Press, 1992) and co-author of *Almost Midnight: Reforming the Late Night News* (Beverly Hills: Sage, 1980) and has published in *Critical Studies in Mass Communication, Journal of Communication, Semiotica, Text, Journal of Popular Film and Television,* and elsewhere.

Index